Good W9-CZS-960

Jane Grigson was brought up in the north-east of England, where there is a strong tradition of good eating, but it was not until many years later, when she began to spend three months of each year working in France, that she became really interested in food. *Charcuterie and French Pork Cookery* was the result, exploring the wonderful range of cooked meat products on sale in even the smallest market towns. This book has also been translated into French, a singular honour for an English cookery writer.

After taking an English degree at Cambridge in 1949, Jane Grigson worked in art galleries and publishers' offices, and then as a translator. In 1966 she shared the John Florio prize (with Father Kenelm Foster) for her translation of Beccaria's *Of Crime and Punishment*. From 1968 she wrote cookery articles for the *Observer* Colour Magazine; *Good Things* and *Food With The Famous* are based on these highly successful series. In 1973, *Fish Cookery* was published by the Wine and Food Society, followed by *The Mushroom Feast* (1975), a collection of recipes for cultivated, woodland, field and dried mushrooms. She received both the Glenfiddich Writer of the Year Award and the André Simon Memorial Fund Book Award for her *Vegetable Book* (1978) and for her *Fruit Book* (1982) and was voted Cookery Writer of the Year in 1977 for *English Food*. All of these are published in Penguin.

Jane Grigson died in March 1990. In her obituary for the *Independent*, Alan Davidson wrote that 'Jane Grigson left to the English-speaking world a legacy of fine writing on food and cookery for which no exact parallel exists . . . She won to herself this wide audience because she was above all a friendly writer . . . However much more she knew about this or that than do the rest of us, she never seemed to be talking down to anyone. On the contrary, she is the most companionable presence in the kitchen; often catching the imagination with a deftly chosen fragment of history or poetry, but never failing to explain the "why" as well as the "how" of cookery.'

Jane Grigson was married to the poet and critic the late Geoffrey Grigson.

Jane Grigson

GOOD THINGS

Illustrated by M. J. Mott

Penguin Books

PENGUIN BOOKS

Published by the Penguin Group
Penguin Books Ltd, 27 Wrights Lane, London W8 5TZ, England
Penguin Books USA Inc., 375 Hudson Street, New York, New York 10014, USA
Penguin Books Australia Ltd, Ringwood, Victoria, Australia
Penguin Books Canada Ltd, 10 Alcorn Avenue, Toronto, Ontario, Canada M4V 3B2
Penguin Books (NZ) Ltd, 182–190 Wairau Road, Auckland 10, New Zealand

Penguin Books Ltd, Registered Offices: Harmondsworth, Middlesex, England

First published by Michael Joseph 1971
Published in Penguin Books 1973
Published by Michael Joseph with a new introduction 1990
Published in Penguin Books 1991
10 9 8 7 6 5 4 3 2 1

Copyright © Jane Grigson, 1971
New introduction copyright © Paul Bailey, 1990
All rights reserved

Printed in England by Clays Ltd, St Ives plc
Set in Intertype Lectura

For Geoffrey

Contents

Introduction to the 1990 Edition

by Paul Bailey

I had read, and used, *Good Things* before I met Jane Grigson in the summer of 1975. There was one good thing, in particular, I had already come to love – the curried parsnip soup described on pp. 223–4. I did not know for years that this beguiling recipe is Jane's own invention. I had assumed it was a classic.

'I think food, its quality, its origins, its preparation, is something to be studied and thought about in the same way as any other aspect of human existence,' she declares in her Introduction. The sentence explains Jane's purpose as a writer. To be indifferent to the quality of food is almost to be indifferent to the quality of life itself, she believed. In *English Food*, that pioneering work of great, but lightly worn, scholarship, she takes the British to task for being such constant masochists at the dining table. We have a culinary inheritance which we have abused and debased, she reminds us. We do not have to make do with the stodgy and the soggy. Eating is a pleasurable necessity, and cooking – as she says in *Good Things* – an art to which many people, not just a chosen few, can aspire.

Jane was drawn to the good things in life – to poetry, painting and music; to a proper appreciation of the natural world and the varied wonders it contains. These enthusiasms she shared with her adored, and adoring, husband Geoffrey, who was her teacher and mentor as well as lover. We became friends after I had written a review of one of Geoffrey's books, in which I expressed the still unfashionable opinion that Geoffrey was, essentially, a celebrator. I felt then, and I feel now, that the artists and writers he savaged merited savaging. His reputation as a rescuer of the genuine has yet to exceed his reputation as a basher of the phoney. When I wrote the piece, I did not – could not – imagine what happy consequences would come in its wake. Those happy consequences have turned into cherished memories – of long, leisurely meals in the garden at Broad Town, the food lovingly prepared by Jane for Geoffrey and their guests; of talk, changing in an instant from the reverential to the gleefully irreverent.

Jane herself was a good thing. She was a thoroughly good thing. She possessed that rarest of attributes, a capacity for loving kindness. It extended beyond her family, who all benefited from it, to those she honoured with her friendship. She was a walking reminder that to be good is not to be dreary. One of her favourite words was 'daft', which she spoke with a flat Sunderland 'a'. She had a keen appreciation of what was 'daft' and the thought of it inspired her to laughter. Her laugh was like a hoot, rising and rising in volume, and there were times when I thought it would never stop. It was a wonderful noise she made – warm, generous, unconstrained.

In the spring of 1989 I went with Jane on an eating tour of the Highlands of Scotland. One day we came across something memorably daft – a notice outside a hotel which read 'ROOMS. LESS GOOD – £12. SLIGHTLY BETTER – £16. BEST – £30'. I waited for Jane's hooting to cease, as curious passers-by stared in amazement. In that same small town we went in search of a cotton shirt which I wanted to buy. The assistant in the men's clothing shop told us, 'Ye'll nae get a cotton shirt here. Try the tobacconist across the street.' The tobacconist indeed sold shirts, but not cotton ones – 'There's no call.' It was typical of Jane that she kept her laughter in check until we were outside. '"There's no call,"' she repeated, and we both had hysterics for the second time.

I remember, too, that we stopped to have a picnic by Loch Ness. The monster was otherwise engaged, but an unidentifiable seabird compensated for his, or her, absence. It ate bread, cheese and salami on the bonnet of the car. Jane smiled, and said of the husband whose death had left her desolate, 'Geoffrey would have recognized the bird in an instant.' She opened a bottle of alcohol-free white wine someone had given her. 'What do you think?' she asked after we had taken a sip. Before I could reply, she said, 'It's disgusting, isn't it? Let's have the real thing.' So we did.

Jane's writing will outlive her, as careful, considered, lively writing always outlives those who write it. She is *there* in her books, a benign and occasionally bossy – bossy in the nicest way – presence. Reading her, you encounter a person who wants to convey her enthusiasm for, and delight in, one of the world's greatest and enduring pleasures, and with no snobbish nonsense about *haute cuisine*. I cannot imagine that her *Vegetable Book* and *Fruit Book* will ever be superseded. They belong with the masterpieces of Eliza Acton and Elizabeth David – books to live with and learn from; to keep among the pots and pans, for ever.

'Oh, sod it all' was the phrase Jane found to express her feelings about the terrible cancer that eventually killed her. She employed it to suggest anger, frustration, helplessness. It was the cry of a true stoic. The indignities she had to endure and the cruel pain that was their cause and accompaniment were dismissed with that 'Oh, sod it all'. To her friends, she has left a lasting beneficence; to her readers, innumerable receipes for living well. Her goodness won't go away.

Paul Bailey
May 1990

This is not a manual of cookery, but a book about enjoying food. Few of the recipes in it will contribute much to the repertoire of those who like to produce dinner for 6 in 30 minutes flat. I think food, its quality, its origins, its preparation, is something to be studied and thought about in the same way as any other aspect of existence.

Anyone who likes to eat, can soon learn to cook well. Such a range of cookery books can now be bought for a few shillings in paperback, from the basic *Penguin Cookery Book* by Bee Nilson, to the best and most stimulating of them all, *French Provincial Cooking* by Elizabeth David, that there's no reason for not eating deliciously – and simply – all the time. So why don't we? After all, in the eighteenth century our food was the envy of Europe. Why isn't it now?

There are many reasons for this, social and historical as well as agricultural and psychological. For a start we're so used to eating, why take trouble? There are enough frozen and packaged foods about for even the worst cook to keep her family alive without them noticing how little skill she really has. Intelligent housewives feel they've a duty to be bored by domesticity. A fair reaction to dusting and bedmaking perhaps, but not, I think, to cooking. The great chef Carême had the right idea when he wrote, 'From behind my ovens I regard the cooking of India, China, of Germany and Switzerland, I feel the ugly edifice of routine crumbling beneath my hands.'

This is not to say that I resist deep frozen and canned and packaged food. I think we should be thankful for being relieved of the famines and inconvenience that the seasons used to bring to many communities. I have no patience with food puritanism of that kind (though I do wonder why the run of frozen food is not better – why so many tasteless sliced beans, when one could have *haricots verts?*).

Having said this, and being always grateful for the background of an unfailing larder, I feel that delight lies in the seasons and what they bring us. One does not remember the grilled hamburgers and frozen peas, but the strawberries that come in May and June straight from the fields, the asparagus of a special occasion, kippers from Craster in July and August, the first lamb of the year from Wales, in October the fresh walnuts from France where they are eaten with new cloudy wine. This is good food. The sad thing is that, unless we fight, and demand, and complain, and reject, and generally make ourselves thoroughly unpopular, these delights may be unknown to our great-grandchildren. Perhaps even to our grandchildren. It is certainly more convenient with growing populations to freeze the asparagus and strawberries straight from the ground, to dye and wrap the kippers in plastic, to import hard, red frozen lamb from New Zealand, and to push the walnuts straight into drying kilns. It is easier to put no seasoning to speak of into a sausage – it offends nobody, everybody buys it. This is the theory. We're back to the primitive idea of eating to keep alive.

When one thinks of the civilization implied in the development of peaches from the wild fruit, or of apricots, grapes, pears, plums, when one thinks of those millions of gardeners from ancient China right across Asia and the Middle East to Rome, then across the Alps north to France, Holland and England of the eighteenth and nineteenth centuries, how can we so crassly, so brutishly, reduce the exquisite results of their labour to cans full of syrup and cardboard-wrapped blocks of ice? These gardeners were concerned to grow a better-tasting fruit or vegetable, a larger and more beautiful one too, but mainly a better-tasting one. Would they believe us if we told them that now tomatoes are produced to regular size and regular shape, that only two or three kinds of potato are regularly on sale, that peas taste like mealy bullets? It's odd that we should have clung on to traditions that hardly matter – beefeaters, Swiss guards, monarchies, the paraphernalia of the past – and forgotten the true worth of the past, the long labouring struggle to learn to survive as well and as gracefully as possible.

I do get the impression, though, that people begin to see the

problem. The encouragement of fine food is not greed or gourmandise; it can be seen as an aspect of the anti-pollution movement in that it indicates concern for the quality of environment.
This is not the limited concern of a few cranks. Small and
medium-sized firms, feeling unable to compete with the cheap
products of the giants, turn to producing better food. A cour-
ageous pig-breeder in Suffolk starts a cooked pork shop in the
high *charcuterie* style. People in many parts of the country run
restaurants specializing in locally produced food, salmon from
the Tamar, laver and sewin from the Welsh sea, snails from the
Mendips, venison from the moors of Inverness. I notice in the
grocers' shops in our small town the increasing appearance of
bags of strong flour, wholemeal and scofa meal, and the pro-
minence given to eggs direct from the farm.

Many families, not just the housewife, now do the cooking between them, and enjoy a protracted sociable meal as an
opportunity for talking and discussing with an enthusiasm that
was not encouraged at dinner parties thirty years ago. Cooking
something delicious is really much more satisfactory than painting pictures or throwing pots. At least for most of us. Food has the
tact to disappear, leaving room and opportunity for masterpieces
to come. The mistakes don't hang on the walls or stand on the
shelves to reproach you for ever. It follows from this that kitchens
should be thought of as the centre of the house. They need above
all space for talking, playing, bringing up children, sewing, having
a meal, reading, sitting and thinking. One may have to walk about
a bit, but where's the harm in that? Everything will not be ship-
shape, galley-fashion, but it's in this kind of place that good food
has flourished. It's from this secret retreat that the exploration of
man's curious and close relationship with food, beyond the point
of nourishment can start.

I should like to thank Elizabeth David, and John Thompson,
until recently editor of the *Observer Colour Magazine*: they first
gave me the opportunity of writing the chapters which follow.
Then I should like to thank the many friends and readers who
have sent me recipes and information, in particular Mrs Farida
Abu-Haidar of Highgate; Mrs Bobby Freeman who ran the Compton House Hotel at Fishguard; Mr Paul Leyton who runs the
Miner's Arms at Priddy in Somerset; Mrs Mary Norwak of the
Farmer's Weekly; Mrs B. M. Round of Lardy in the Essonne; Mrs

Charlotte Sawyer of Woodsville, New Hampshire; Mrs Ann Irving of Littleton, Massachusetts; Mrs Tao Tao Sanders of Oxford who has given me the Chinese recipes in this book. Signor Adragna of the Italian Institute for Foreign Trade; Mr Jack of Preston-next-Wingham in Kent; Mr Paske of Kentford in Suffolk; Mr D. Ritchie of Rothesay, Bute; and Mr K. L. Robson of Craster in Northumberland, have all replied patiently to my requests for information.

My thanks are also due to the following publishers and authors who have allowed me to quote from their works: Thomas Nelson & Sons, for a quotation from *A Book of Middle Eastern Food* by Claudia Roden; Hamish Hamilton, for a quotation from *Gourmet's Basic French Cook Book* by Louis Diat; Martin Secker & Warburg, for a quotation from *Earthly Paradise* by Colette; Oxford University Press, for a quotation from *The Pillow Book of Sei Shonagon* translated and edited by Ivan Morris, and to the author's Literary Estate and Chatto & Windus, for a quotation from *Anatomy of Dessert* by Edward Bunyard.

Last and most important of all, I should like to say thank you to my family and friends. They have endured carrots and sweetbreads or whatever it might be, for twelve and fifteen meals at a stretch; they have sometimes been confronted with three or four versions of a dish at one meal. Their comments have always been interested, and usually polite. Of my friends, I owe most to Mrs Marjorie White; without her help, adaptability and kindness I should never have had the time to write a word of this book.

Broad Town, 1970   JANE GRIGSON

Fish

Kippers and other Cured Fish

Over the centuries we have developed various ways of curing and
keeping the herring, that splendid northern fish which Shakespeare's contemporary Thomas Nashe – loyal to his East Anglia –
grandly and comically called the 'Semper Augustus of the sea's
finny freholders'. Our best and longest known forms are the red
herring, the bloater, and the kipper – in that order of seniority.

Yarmouth, the great herring centre since the Middle Ages, foun-
ded its wealth first of all on the long-keeping, long-cured red
herring. Smoked after days in brine, until very red and fairly dry,
this was the ultra-strong-flavoured herring which we used to eat
especially in Lent. Red herring is worth trying as an hors d'œuvre.
The trouble is to get hold of one – even in Yarmouth, which has
produced red herrings for centuries, but now sends all or most of
them abroad to the Mediterranean, Africa, the West Indies and
South America.

I've tried to get red herrings from leading food departments of
London stores. They thought I was being funny, but you may be

lucky in finding red herrings in a Cypriot delicatessen, or in a district where West Indians do their shopping. In the end you will probably have to write to the fountain head of supply, Henry Sutton's of Great Yarmouth. The red herrings they export to the eastern Mediterranean are soaked and cut into strips and eaten as hors d'œuvre or appetizer. Sometimes they're served on dry bread, as an accompaniment to Greek bean soup. Sutton's still cure a black herring, the ultimate in hardness, almost brittle. It's much in demand in very hot difficult climates such as the West Indies, Africa and South America, because it will keep almost indefinitely without refrigeration. Black and red herrings used to be slave fodder, they still tend to go to the poorer populations of these countries.

The bloater, unsplit, soft and plump (i.e. 'bloated' – it used to be called the 'bloat herring') we seem to have been eating for some 400–500 years. It is lightly salted and lightly smoked for flavour rather than long keeping. This light style of curing has been developed in Holland; and in France, where one buys the most succulent *harengs saurs* or *bouffis*, which means precisely 'bloaters'.

Then comes the kipper, first produced – or so it is said – on the Northumbrian coast early in the nineteenth century, split, soaked in brine, and smoked on tenterhooks for 10–20 hours.

Some ordinary kippers are passable, I would agree. But if you really want to know what a kipper should taste like, luscious and bland, the surest way is to order them from kipperers at Craster (L. Robson & Sons, Craster, Alnwick, Northumberland); on Loch Fyne (Ritchie Bros, 37 Watergate, Rothesay, Bute); or on the Isle of Man (T. Moore & Sons, Mill Road, Peel). Such small kippering establishments choose the best and fattest herring at their peak (from June to October), they smoke them properly over oak fires, and they do not colour them by adding dye to the brine. One kipperer of the splendid Loch Fyne herrings told me sadly and sarcastically that the big firms are 'turning kippers all into painted ladies'.

A good kipper won't be thin and skimpy or dyed (to the colour of an old mahogany commode). It will be silvery brown. It will still be in possession of its head, tail and backbone. And, full of its own fat, it won't need to be sold with pats of butter.

The good kipper is one of this country's worthy contributions to fine food. That indifferent kippers should now dominate the fish counter strikes me as a minor national disgrace. But then we so often lack piety towards our best things.

Kippers for breakfast

Everyone has a favourite way of cooking kippers, but it's worth trying a new method sometimes, even if breakfast does not seem the right meal for experiments. There are only two rules to observe: don't overcook them, and don't add butter until they are served, as good kippers cook in their own juice.

Jugged kippers are my favourite for breakfast. Put them, head down, into a 2–3 pint stoneware jug. Pour boiling water onto them straight from the kettle (as if you were making tea), right up to their tails. Leave in a warm place for 5–10 minutes, drain well and serve. They can be laid in a roasting tin, instead of a jug, but this is dangerous as the boiling water slops about if one makes a careless, half-awake movement.

Baked kippers. Wrap them loosely in kitchen foil. Bake for 10–15 minutes in a moderately hot oven. This saves washing up.

Grilled kippers. (1) Place the kippers *skin side up* on a piece of foil on the grill rack. Grill gently for 5 minutes until the skin is deliciously crisp, not charred. (2) Jug the kippers for 2 minutes, then grill for 2 minutes on each side.

Fried kippers. Grease the frying pan lightly with butter, just enough to prevent the kippers sticking and no more (unnecessary with a non-stick pan). Fry gently for 2–3 minutes on each side.

Whether grilled, fried, baked or jugged, eat the kippers with plenty of bread and butter. Lemon quarters, pats of butter or parsley butter can be served as well.

Kippers with scrambled egg (for 4)

A good dish for late Sunday breakfasts that merge into lunch. Try it too as an hors d'œuvre, or in sandwiches. The kippers can be cooked or not, as you please. The main thing to notice is the use of garlic – Escoffier's idea – which enhances the flavour of the eggs without stridency.

The best garlic to use is the fat, white, juicy kind imported from France.

> 2 kippers
> 6 eggs
> 3 oz. butter
> large clove garlic
> salt, pepper
> buttered toast

Divide the cooked or uncooked kippers into large flakes, or strips. Beat the eggs for five minutes with a fork stuck firmly into the clove of garlic. Season with salt and pepper. Melt the butter in a thick pan over a low heat, pour in the eggs through a strainer and cook as slowly as possible, stirring from time to time. When the eggs are beginning to solidify, but are still fairly liquid, add the kipper pieces. Don't overcook. Serve on buttered toast.

If this dish is to be served as a cold hors d'œuvre, it's best to scramble the eggs on their own, and lay strips of kipper across them just before serving.

Craster Kippers (for 4)

Craster is a grey stone fishing village tucked down on the Northumbrian coast, half a mile below its handsome entry arch. In the small harbour are cobles used for lobster, crab and salmon fishing, brightly painted in stripes. To the north the ruins of Dunstanburgh Castle squat dramatically on a cliff; to the south lies the quiet beach of Howick with ochre rocks and grey sea buckthorn. In sheds above the harbour the Robson family cure some of

the finest kippers in Great Britain. These plump, silvery brown.
almost translucent fish are best eaten ungrilled, unbaked, un-
jugged, unfried – in other words, just as they are, like smoked
salmon.

>   2–3 kippers
>   4 lemon quarters
>   granary or rye bread
>   unsalted butter

Slice the kippers horizontally and thinly, after removing the bones.
Serve with lemon quarters, and thin slices of bread and butter.

>   2–3 kippers
>   4 egg yolks
>   4 slices granary or rye bread
>   unsalted butter
>   lemon slices and juice

Skin and bone the kippers. Cut them with scissors into strips.
Butter the bread generously, right to the edges, and trim into a
neat shape. Arrange the kipper pieces on each slice to build up a
nest-like circle. Using a spoon, slip an egg yolk into the centre,
sprinkle with a few drops of lemon juice and serve with half a slice
of lemon arranged on each side of the kipper.

To eat, break the yolk with a fork and mix into the kipper
pieces. Use the lemon slices for extra seasoning. This is delicious,
providing the kippers are good and the eggs really fresh.

Kippers or bloaters with potato salad (for 4)

This favourite European dish is deceptively simple to prepare. Its
success depends on using ingredients of the highest quality – the
finest olive oil, the best-flavoured smoked herring (classy kippers,
bloaters, *harengs saurs*, matjes herring), waxy potatoes, wine vinegar and a firm seasoning of an onion flavour.

>   6–8 fillets of kippers, soaked in olive oil for
>   two hours
>   1 lb. waxy potatoes

dressing:

4 tablespoons olive oil
1 tablespoon red wine vinegar
good teaspoon French or German mustard
salt, black pepper
½ teaspoon sugar
heaped tablespoon chopped chives, shallot,
    mild onion, or spring onion

If salty herrings are used, soak them for several hours in milk and water, before drying and putting into olive oil. As oil acts as a preservative, the fillets can be submerged in it a day or two before they are eaten; it's advisable to cover them over and store in a refrigerator.

Scrub and boil the potatoes. Mix oil, vinegar, mustard, and seasonings in a bowl. Peel and cube the cooked potatoes, adding them to the dressing while still warm. When cold add the chopped chives. Chill. Arrange on a serving dish with the kippers, which should be drained of all but a teaspoonful or so of their oil.

To fillet bloaters: Remove the skin, which peels off quite easily. Slit open along the belly, open out a little and put cut side down onto a board. Press firmly and steadily along the back of the fish. Turn it over and you will be able to remove the backbone quite easily, and small stray bones too. Separate the two fillets. See illustrations (opposite).

Kippers or salt herring fillets with dill salad (for 4)

Dill is an under-used herb in this country – which is a pity. It is easy to grow, and its subtle flavour of caraway goes well with fish, and all kinds of vegetable dishes. Dill weed, i.e. the leaves as opposed to the seeds, which are also used as flavouring, can be bought in the McCormick range of herbs and spices. An alternative is the stronger, slightly liquorice-flavoured fennel, which is grown as a garden herb and can also be found wild on many cliffs of England and Wales.

1. Slit along the belly

2. Lean on backbone to flatten the fish

3. Pull out the backbone

FILLETING FISH

6–8 kipper fillets, or soaked salt herring fillets
½ lb. eating apples, diced
6 oz. beetroot boiled and diced
1 small mild onion, chopped

dressing:

6 tablespoons olive oil
1½ tablespoons wine vinegar
good teaspoon French or German mustard
scant teaspoon sugar
salt, black pepper
heaped tablespoon chopped dill weed

Cut the fish fillets into strips. Two or three hours before the meal prepare the dressing and mix it into each of the main ingredients, in separate bowls. Before serving, arrange the drained ingredients on a serving dish (or on pieces of bread and butter as open sandwiches), and chill.

Alternative dressings are sour cream beaten with a little lemon juice to taste, or mayonnaise. Plus dill.

Kipper paste

Some people object to the restaurateur's habit of describing our native potted fish pastes as 'pâtés'. I agree. We lack a proper pride in the good food we can produce in this country. It would be better if dishes like this one were given their proper names and starred as specialities. We might even begin to acquire a gastronomic reputation.

The interesting thing about potted fish – and meat – pastes is that they are becoming popular again, after half a century of neglect. When elbow-power in the kitchen was cheap, they were easy to produce. Now liquidizers can replace the poor slaves of the past.

> 1 fat kipper
> 8 oz. unsalted butter
> salt, Cayenne pepper, lemon juice

Jug the kipper for 5 minutes. Drain and remove skin and bones. Melt the butter, cut in pieces, over a low heat. Put kipper pieces and butter into the liquidizer goblet. Whirl at top speed until they are smooth and perfectly blended. Season and put into two or three small pots. When cold and set, cover with a layer of clarified butter (butter boiled for a few seconds, then strained carefully through muslin). This will keep in the refrigerator for a few weeks, if covered well with kitchen foil so that the clarified butter does not dry away from the sides of the pot.

Bloaters can be used for this paste too. About 8–9 oz. of filleted fish is required.

Kipper flan (for 6–8)

This useful dish can be served as a first course at dinner, or as a main course at midday or for a picnic. Eat it warm for the best flavour, but it is still good when cold. When I first made the flan, I did not expect the smoky flavour of kipper to blend well with the cream and egg custard. I thought it would taste oily, particularly when cold. In fact, it's delicious.

> short pastry, made with 6 oz. flour
> 1 fat kipper (9 oz.)
> 8 oz. double cream, or 4 oz. each double and
>   single
> 3 eggs
> good tablespoon French or German mustard
> lemon juice
> salt and pepper

Line an 8½ inch tart tin with a removable base with the pastry. Prick all over and bake blind for 5 minutes, until set but not browned. Meanwhile jug the kipper (p. 19). Remove bones and skin and arrange pieces on the pastry case. Beat together the cream and eggs, add the mustard gradually to your taste. Season. Pour over the kippers and bake at Mark 4, 350°F, for 30–40 minutes, until the filling is golden brown and puffed up. Now quickly squeeze half a lemon over the flan.

Red herrings

Need soaking, indubitably. The best way to do this is to bring some pale ale, or water, to the boil and pour it immediately over the fish. You will discover by tasting, and by experience, how long the fish need to be soaked. Start by soaking them overnight.

To cook red herrings, drain them and dry them well. Brush them over with melted butter, and grill lightly at a gentle heat (they need to be warmed through, rather than cooked).

Serve them with hot boiled potatoes and butter. Or with melted butter flavoured with mustard. Or with plenty of bread and butter. In the eighteenth and nineteenth centuries, buttery scrambled eggs and mashed potatoes were sent up with the red herrings.

Once soaked, the herrings need not be cooked. Dry them and store in olive oil in the refrigerator, as they do in Italy. Serve them as part of an hors d'œuvre, with the fillets cut into small slices.

Try them, too, with Napoleon's haricot bean salad (p. 182) instead of the usual potato salad.

Salted and spiced herrings

Preserving herrings is not at all difficult. Gut and scale them, but leave the heads on. Soak them in vinegar overnight, then drain them well. Pack tightly together in a large pot, between layers of salt and spices. For 50 herrings:

> 1 lb. sea salt
> ½ lb. sugar
> handful bay leaves
> ½ oz. each black peppercorns and allspice,
>   slightly crushed

Cover and weight the herrings, until the salt turns to brine. Make sure that the herrings are always submerged. Store in a cool, dry place.

Before using salted herrings, they need to be soaked. Length of time depends on the length of time they've been in salt. It's a good idea to fillet the herrings before soaking them (see p. 23).

Danish sweet-sour herrings: soak fillets in milk-and-water, half and half. Meanwhile bring to the boil 8 oz. granulated sugar, 5 oz. wine vinegar, 6 peppercorns and 1 teaspoon pickling spice. Remove from the heat after 3 minutes boiling. Cool. Cut the fillets into inch strips and arrange in a plastic box or screw-top jar in layers with slices of raw onion. Pour over the marinade, cover and leave for 5 days in the refrigerator before eating.

Scottish tatties an' herrin': put a layer of evenly-sized potatoes in a large pot. Lay some salt herrings, which have been soaked, on top. Put enough water in to come ¾ of the way up the potatoes. Cover and simmer for an hour. A homely dish, requiring butter (drain off the cooking liquid before serving).

Scandinavian pickled salmon (or mackerel or trout)

Cheaper Canadian salmon may be used for this delicious preparation. It's easy, and it makes a much cheaper start to a meal than smoked salmon. Everyone enjoys its fresh, unfamiliar flavour:

> 1½–2 lb. tailpiece salmon
> 1 large tablespoon sea salt
> 1 rounded tablespoon sugar
> 1 teaspoon coarsely ground black pepper
> plenty of dill weed
> 1 tablespoon brandy (optional)

Slice the piece of salmon in half, carefully, and remove the backbone and any little bones, but leave the skin. Rinse very quickly, dry well and put the first piece, skin side up, in a dish. Mix salt, sugar, pepper and brandy together. Rub about a quarter of this into the skin of the first piece, turn it filleted side up and rub in half the mixture; sprinkle liberally with dill weed (sold in the McCormick range of herbs) and put the second piece on top, filleted side down. Rub the rest of the mixture into the skin, and sprinkle with more dill weed. Put a piece of foil on top, then a couple of tins as weights. Leave for at least 12 hours, and at most 4 days, in the refrigerator or in a very cool place.

To serve, drain the pieces and slice them diagonally or horizontally starting at the thick end. Serve with thinly cut wholemeal or rye bread, and butter, with lemon quarters. In Scandinavia this mustard sauce usually accompanies pickled salmon – and very good it is:

> 1 heaped tablespoon French or German mustard
> ½ tablespoon sugar
> 1 tablespoon wine vinegar
> 4 tablespoons olive or salad oil
> dill weed to taste

Mix all the ingredients together to a thick, smooth yellow sauce. A crushed clove of garlic, a small one, may also be used.

Mackerel (or herrings) in white wine

This popular French hors d'œuvre tastes even better one or two days after its preparation. Muscadet is the traditional wine to use, but an ordinary dry white wine is quite satisfactory. Clean four fat mackerel (or herring) removing the soft roes for another dish. Simmer together for 30 minutes:

> ¾ pint dry white wine
> ¼ pint water
> medium sized carrot and onion, sliced
> 8 peppercorns, slightly crushed
> 1 teaspoon pickling spices, including red chilli
> ½ teaspoon salt

Leave this *court-bouillon* to cool, then strain the liquid over the fish which should be placed in a single layer in a saucepan or casserole. Pick the chilli and 3 slices of the carrot out of the debris from the *court-bouillon*, throwing the rest away. Bring the pan of fish slowly to the boil, bubble for 1 minute, then cover and leave to cool.

Divide the fish into fillets, by removing skin, heads and bones. Lay them in an oval serving dish, and put the chilli and carrot slices on top, plus 2 or 3 small sliced gherkins and a sliver of lemon peel. Reduce the *court-bouillon* by boiling hard, until it has a good concentrated flavour. Pour a little of it over the fish as a dressing, and keep the rest as a basis for fish soup or a sauce to go with fish.

To store for a few days, put the fish with its garnish into a jar or refrigerator box. Reduce the *bouillon* and pour over the fish to cover it. Put the lid on the jar or box and keep in the refrigerator.

Note: there are many British recipes of a similar kind for herrings. They make use of vinegar, malt vinegar at that, instead of wine. The result can be very aggressive.

Lobster

The lobster has never, it seems, been a democratic food. I mean in the way that salmon was, before our rivers were polluted. Before the industrial revolution people used to grow tired of eating salmon. I've never heard of anyone being tired of eating lobster.

Nowadays it's become almost exclusively a speciality of grand restaurants, an expensive dish on any menu, lobster Newberg, lobster *américaine* or *armoricaine* according to your fancy, *bisque de homard*.

This is not surprising, for, as the authors of one sea shore guide remark, it's not so common as many would wish in spite of its wide distribution. Then there's its marvellous, daunting appearance. The blue carapace that turns fiery red when cooked. The tail fiercely flexible like fine armour (for this reason, soldiers used to be called lobsters: when armour went out, the name still did for red coats). The rapid movement of the creature, the vicious nip of its great claws. Its ability to lose a limb or joint and survive. 'All the ingenious men,' wrote Kingsley, in *The Water Babies*, 'and all the scientific men, and all the imaginative men in the world could never invent, if all their wits were boiled into one, anything so curious and so ridiculous as a lobster.'

Don't let price and shape put you off trying a lobster occasionally. It's worth asking for. Of all the things one can eat, it's difficult to think of anything more delicious, anything so sweet, firm and succulent. It you live at all near the sea (nowhere in Great Britain is farther than 60 miles away from it), try and discover a direct supply of lobsters. An expedition to Weymouth, say, or the western coast of Scotland, for those who have no more than 30 or 40 miles to go, can be most rewarding.

The actual cooking and preparation of lobster is not difficult. Like most expensive food – steak, caviare, smoked salmon – its presentation, particularly if you are buying a ready-boiled lobster, is within the competence of a child. It's a reasonable argument that the best way of eating such a delicious substance is the simplest; that hot, lobster needs no more than melted butter and lemon juice: that cold, it needs no more than mayonnaise or vinaigrette. The raw eggs of the hen lobster are said to have a strange and delicate flavour: to the cook they are the 'coral', because when the lobster is boiled they, too, turn red. When they are cooked, the flavour has gone but they can be used to colour the sauce.

Lobster can be bought all the year round (many fishmongers store them ready-boiled in their deep-freeze), but the high season runs from May to October when off-shore fishing is at its peak. A fisherman who has the luck to find one in his net or lobster-pots will store it a while, perhaps in a crate submerged in the sea water, and send a batch of lobsters off to market every so often. In France there is a scheme for sinking used cars off the shore, to provide a lobster-paradise which can easily be tapped by the fishermen. Perhaps with such encouragement lobsters will increase and we may adopt the scheme in this country. I hope so.

If you want your lobster alive, it's best to order it several days in advance. It may seem unwise to buy lobster after it's been boiled, but a good fishmonger can be relied upon to see that you get value for your money. He would like you to come back. As with all fish, freshness is the desirable quality. 1½–2 lb. is the desirable weight. Canned lobster meat is not, in my experience, worth buying: it's expensive and has a minimal flavour.

To boil a lobster

The method of doing this in the past, and today in most professional kitchens, is to plunge the lobster into a pan of boiling, salted water. However the R.S.P.C.A. recommend that it should be put into a pan of cold or tepid water, which should then be brought slowly to the boil. Put a weight on the lid, whichever method you use. Lobster boiled in the first way will take 20–30 minutes to cook, according to size: it will require 10–20 minutes in the second way, once the water has come to the boil.

Hot boiled lobster can be served with melted butter, with hollandaise or cream sauce. Cut it in half lengthways, and crack the claws before serving it.

For serving cold, lobster is usually left to cool in the cooking liquid. Mayonnaise is the most popular sauce (the coral should be pounded and beaten with the egg yolks before the oil is added). The lobster meat should be removed from the shells and mixed with the mayonnaise: use the head and the better bits of the shell as decoration, plus lettuce leaves, stuffed eggs, tomato quarters and so on.

Instead of water, a *court-bouillon* is often used to give the lobster the benefit of herbs, spices and wine. Boil the following ingredients for 1 hour:

> 2 sliced onions
> 2 sliced carrots
> bouquet garni (3 parsley stalks, 2 thyme sprigs, 1
>   bay leaf)
> ¼ pint wine vinegar
> ½ pint dry white wine
> salt, pepper

Put the lobster into this boiling stock: or let it cool and follow the R.S.P.C.A. method.

As a change from mayonnaise, try this way of dressing cold lobster. I've taken it from Alexandre Dumas's *Grand dictionnaire de cuisine*. Put the cooked lobster meat into a basin. Mix it with about 5 tablespoons of olive oil, up to a tablespoon of Dijon mustard, a handful of parsley, tarragon and chives, all chopped, 1

heaped tablespoon finely chopped shallot or mild onion, 12 drops
of Chinese soya sauce, and some freshly ground white pepper. The
final flavouring is a glass of anisette (e.g., Marie Brizard) and
lemon juice to taste.

Homard à l'américaine (for 4)

The trouble about many famous lobster dishes, including this one,
is that the cook is expected to cut the creature up while it's still
alive. Although the first cut between tail and head kills the lobster, it's not an idea that appeals to most people. One solution is
to plunge it into a pan of boiling water for exactly 2 minutes: this
kills it without spoiling the flavour, which is the point of using
lobster this way.

When cutting a lobster into pieces, start with the claws and
crack the large ones after they're removed from the body. Cut the
tail from the head. Divide the tail into sections across the joints;
split the head down the middle. Discard the intestinal canal and
the little sack of grit from the head. Take out the coral and keep
to one side (the 'coral' will not be coral, but a collection of black
eggs).

Now you are ready to start on Lobster *américaine*, one of the
most discussed recipes in the European repertoire. The delicious
flavour is not in question, it's the title that worries people. Un-
questionably this is a French dish, with affinities with provençal
cooking – tomatoes, garlic and olive oil. There are early recipes of
a similar kind, using a different kind of lobster, the crawfish,
which is more common in the Mediterranean, before the great
popularity of the dish in the late nineteeth century. It's also been
suggested that the recipe has a Breton origin, that it should be
called Lobster *armoricaine*: but the ingredients and method of the
recipe don't belong to the rather humble style of Breton cooking,
Brittany having been until recently one of the poorest and most
neglected parts of France. One has only to read shocked English
nineteenth-century accounts of the low standards of life in those
parts – and remember that our middle-class travellers were used
to low standards of life for the lower orders – to see that a

fine recipe of this type is unlikely to have been invented in such an area at that time.

> 4 tablespoons olive oil
> 1 lobster, cut up as above
> 2 tablespoons chopped onion
> ¾ lb. tomatoes
> 1 large clove garlic
> 1 teaspoon tomato concentrate
> 2 teaspoons sugar
> parsley, tarragon
> ¼ pint dry white wine
> ¼ pint beef or fish stock
> 1 glass brandy
> 1 oz. butter
> 1 teaspoon flour
> salt, pepper

Heat the oil in a large pan, and cook the lobster for about 5 minutes (it will turn bright red). Remove and add the onion, and cook it gently until it's melted and golden. Add the peeled and quartered tomatoes, the crushed garlic and herbs; then when they begin to boil, pour in wine, stock and brandy. (Other versions of Lobster *américaine* use the brandy, warm, to flambé the lobster when it has been fried in oil with the onion at the beginning of the recipe.) Season with salt, pepper, a teaspoon or more of tomato concentrate depending on the flavour of the tomatoes, and the sugar. Put the lobster back in the pan to complete the cooking (10–15 minutes). Meanwhile mash the coral with the butter and flour.

When the lobster is cooked, arrange it on a hot serving dish. Boil the sauce hard until it's reduced to a good flavour and consistency. Stir in the coral butter, bit by bit, and let the sauce simmer for a few moments. Sieve it over the lobster. Serve with a pilaff of rice.

Note: the lobster meat may be removed from the shell for serving, but it's usually left to the eaters to do this for themselves.

Lobster Thermidor (for 4)

There's a story that one of Napoleon's chefs invented this dish, and that his master suggested the name Thermidor, which he'd given to the hottest month of the newly divided year. Presumably as an acknowledgement of the essential ingredient – mustard? Or of the bubbling heat of the lobster itself? But as food appreciated by Napoleon went quickly into the recipe books, and Lobster Thermidor does not make much of an appearance before this century, I feel more inclined to believe a less romantic tale – that the dish was invented at the restaurant Thermidor in Paris towards the end of the nineteenth century.

There are many versions of the sauce. The simplest one is a béchamel, enriched by cream and spiced with mustard. I prefer this sharper sauce:

> 2 lobsters, about 2 lb. each
>
> *sauce:*
>
> 2 tablespoons chopped onion or shallot
> 12 peppercorns, slightly crushed
> 1 dessertspoon tarragon vinegar
> large glass white wine (5–6 oz.)
> 1 oz. butter
> 2 rounded tablespoons flour
> ¾ pint hot milk
> 4 tablespoons cream
> mustard powder (or French mustard)
> salt, pepper
>
> *to finish:*
>
> 2 oz. grated cheese, preferably Gruyère
> 1 heaped tablespoon breadcrumbs
> 1 oz. melted butter
> lemon quarters

Boil lobsters in the usual way. Remove claws, crack them and extract the meat. Split the body in half lengthways and clean; add the edible parts to the claw meat and dice it all as evenly as possible. Put the coral aside.

To make the sauce, put onion, wine, vinegar and peppercorns into a heavy pan. Boil hard until the liquid is reduced by half. Add the butter: when it's melted, stir in the flour, and, gradually, the hot milk. Let the sauce simmer until it's reduced to a thick smoothness, giving it an occasional stir. Sieve it into a clean pan, add the cream, mustard to taste, salt and pepper. Start with just a little mustard, then add more; remember that English mustard powder is very fierce in flavour compared with French-made mustard of the Dijon type. You might think that this sort of flavour is too strong for the sweetness of lobster, but it isn't, it seems to emphasize it by contrast.

Pour a little of this sauce into the empty lobster shells, put the lobster dice on top, and cover with the rest of the sauce. Arrange the lobsters on a baking tray, using crumpled lengths of silver foil to steady them. Mix breadcrumbs and cheese and sprinkle them over the top; dribble the melted butter over them as evenly as possible.

Put under a medium hot grill to reheat and to brown. They should be served, sizzling hot, garnished with lemon quarters.

This dish may conveniently be assembled several hours before it's to be eaten. In this case it's a good idea to heat the lobster through in the oven first (Mark 6, 400°F) before finishing it under the grill.

Note: this is a good way of serving cooked salmon and crab. The sauce can also be used with scallops in a similar way: fry them first in a little butter, until they are opaque – about 3 minutes on each side.

Bisque de homard (for 6–8)

I can say without qualification of any kind that bisque de homard is the best of all soups. If you've only made its acquaintance through tins or dehydrated packets, go out and buy a small lobster and make some. You can also use the shells and debris of lobster from yesterday's feast; if you intend to do this, have the forethought to hide away one or two nice pieces of lobster meat.

A consolation – if the soup is made with a whole lobster, it's a particularly filling dish. Follow it with fruit, perhaps some cheese, and most people will be well satisfied.

1 small lobster
1 large carrot, diced
2 heaped tablespoons chopped onion
4 oz. butter
bouquet garni
¼ pint white wine
glass of brandy
3 pints fish or chicken stock
2–4 oz. rice (see recipe)
4 oz. cream
salt, pepper, Cayenne pepper, parsley

If the lobster is alive, cut it into pieces reserving the coral (see p. 32). Simmer the vegetables in 2 oz. of butter in a frying pan, until they begin to look golden. Add the lobster and cook until it turns bright red – about 5 minutes. Pour on the wine and boil hard until the liquid is reduced by half. Add enough stock to cover the lobster; simmer until it's cooked – about 5 more minutes. Take the pieces out of the pan, set the meat aside and put the shells into a clean pan. Pour in the vegetable and wine mixture, add the rest of the stock, the bouquet garni and 2 oz. of rice. If you have time and patience, it's a good idea to pound the less tough pieces of shell before putting them into the saucepan.

In about 20 minutes when the rice is cooked, take out the lobster shells and bouquet. Put the rest of the butter, the coral and the contents of the saucepan into the liquidizer, or through the *mouli-légumes*, plus the lobster meat, except a nice piece or two to make a garnish. Pour through a strainer (to make quite sure no tiny pieces of shell remain in the soup) into the washed-out pan. Reheat.

Correct the seasoning with salt, pepper, Cayenne pepper. Stir in the cream and brandy, the lobster pieces cut into neat slices, and serve very hot.

If the lobster is already cooked, remove the meat from the shell and set it aside. Simmer the vegetables in butter in a large saucepan, add stock, shell, bouquet and 2 oz. rice (use 4 oz. if you're short on lobster meat). Finish as above. This is an excellent soup, which can be adapted to crab, shrimps and prawns. Sometimes a little tomato is added to improve the flavour, when one is relying mainly on shells.

Aragosta Luculliana (for 4)

This grand recipe has been sent to me from Italy. At least I think it's grand, but I've a suspicion Lucullus would have thought it sadly simple. This Roman gourmet had a series of dining-rooms, of increasing splendour. If he ordered dinner for ten friends in, say, the blue room, his slaves knew without further instruction that the meal was to cost £100. Other rooms meant far more. One day Lucullus was, exceptionally, dining at home without guests. The slave asked which room he would like the meal to be served in, expecting a £10 answer. Lucullus named the most expensive room of all.

After that, it may come as a surprise to you that the only ingredients demanded by this recipe are:

> 2 lobsters
> 1–2 dozen oysters
> 4 oz. butter
> 12 tablespoons breadcrumbs
> milk
> 8 tinned anchovy fillets
> mustard powder, Cayenne pepper, salt

Split the boiled lobsters in half down the middle. Now ease the flesh, without removing it from the shells, as if you were cutting a grapefruit. (If the lobsters are alive, split them down the middle, dot them with butter and bake in a hot oven, Mark 6, 400°F.)

Arrange the raw oysters, removed from their shells, along the cut sides of the lobsters; pour in the oyster juice. Moisten the breadcrumbs slightly with a little milk, squeezing out the surplus. Chop the anchovy fillets finely, mix into the bread and put this mixture over the oysters. Melt the butter, season it with mustard, Cayenne pepper and salt. Brush this evenly over the breadcrumbs. Heat for 10 minutes under the grill, or in a very hot oven, to brown the crumbs and heat the lobster.

Note: I suspect this recipe was intended for crawfish, which lack the large claws of the lobster. For this reason, I usually remove all the lobster meat from claws and body and throw away the inedible bits. This leaves room in the shells for all or most of the lobster meat; if there is too much keep it for another dish.

Lobster Newberg (for 4)

This is one of the best of all lobster dishes, expensive, easy to prepare and easy to eat. It's credited to America, and it was first served at Delmonico's restaurant in New York in the early 1890s. But, like *crème vichyssoise glacée*, it was the invention of a French chef, and it's in the purest French tradition. The proprietor first called the dish after one of his wealthy clients, Mr Ben Wenberg, in particular because he'd popularized the use of the chafing dish, i.e. cooking done at the table instead of in the kitchen, as in this recipe. Either Mr Wenberg did not appreciate the delectable compliment, or he fell out with the proprietor for some other reason, because the name was soon altered simply but unrecognizably from Lobster Wenberg to Lobster Newberg or Newburg.

Original style

> ¾–1 pint cooked lobster meat, diced
> ¼ pint Madeira or sherry
> ¼ pint double cream
> ¼ pint single cream
> 3 egg yolks
> salt, pepper

Using a shallow pan on a table cooker, heat the double cream to just under boiling point. Add the single cream beaten up with the egg yolks. When the sauce is thick (*it must on no account boil once the egg yolks are added*), pour in the Madeira, and stir in the lobster to reheat. Serve with rice.

With boiled lobster

ingredients as on p. 38, plus 4 oz. butter

Heat lobster with 2 oz. of butter in a large pan. Pour in the wine and rapidly boil it down to half; draw the lobster to the side so that it doesn't overcook. Stir in the double, then the single cream beaten with the egg yolks. Thicken over a low heat. Just before serving add the extra 2 oz. of butter cut into little pieces: they should melt into the sauce without cooking, to give it a glaze and extra flavour.

This makes a finer flavoured dish than the original chafing-dish recipe.

With live lobster

ingredients as on p. 38, plus glass brandy

Pound the coral with 2 oz. of butter, and set it aside. Cook the lobster, cut in pieces, in 2 oz. of butter until it turns red. Warm brandy, set it alight and pour over lobster in the pan. When flames have died away, add the Madeira. Finish the sauce as above, adding the coral butter at the end.

Best version of all. Brandy seems to have a special affinity with lobster. This recipe can be used for scallops.

Mussels and Scallops

Scallops and mussels offer the best chance these days, the only chance for many of us, of enjoying the true shellfish quality of sweet succulence perfectly combined with salty freshness. A quality, I might say, that vinegar in the British style does nothing to improve.

Mussels, particularly, are a bargain (only the herring gives greater value for money). Scallops cost more – especially the huge ones from the Isle of Man – but they're worth the money, and can be more reliable than shop-boiled crab, or shop-boiled lobster, for a special occasion.

Best of all for freshness and sweetness are the tiny mussels one eats in Normandy, often gathered straight from the rocks below the restaurant. Mussels can also be gathered from rocks and wooden posts at the seaside in Britain, but the greatest care is needed to make sure they are far from any source of pollution such as sewage outfalls. This is so difficult nowadays that one is wise to stick to fishmonger's mussels, which have spent a few days in cleansing beds before being sold.

Scallops are not so gratifyingly supine to the holidaymaker's hand. They live out in deep waters, eluding their main enemy, the starfish, with strange flying leaps. Such waterjet-propelled motion must have given Venus a rough ride ashore on *her* scallop shell.

The scallop has another patron as well as Venus, the Apostle St James the Greater. The shrine at Compostela in north-western Spain, built over what is claimed to be his body, brought the Holy Land into Europe most conveniently. Medieval pilgrims came in numbers like stars in the Milky Way (which is said to touch the earth at Compostela), wearing St James's shell on their wide-brimmed hats. No one knows why the scallop became the badge of St James's pilgrimage, but we've decorated our lives with its elegant shape ever since. We see it everywhere – on doorlights, fountains, silver, furniture – and petrol stations. I hope that a meal of skewered scallops, if not curried scallops, was thrown in with the price those pilgrims paid for their badges, their *coquilles St Jacques*.

Preparation

Although mussels are best used the day they're bought, they can be kept for a couple of days in a bucket of water with a small handful of salt – sea salt – added. For use later on the same day, persuade your fishmonger to put them straight into a plastic bag and leave them there until required for cleaning. Scrub them under a cold tap, with a nailbrush. Beards and barnacles should be scraped off with a sharp knife. *Any broken mussels, or any that stay open when tapped lightly, should be thrown away.*

To open mussels, put them into a large heavy pan over a moderately hot gas or electric plate. A quarter of a pint of water or wine may be added if demanded by the recipe, but it's not necessary. Put the lid on the pan and leave for 5 minutes, shaking gently once or twice. Remove the opened mussels with a pair of kitchen tongs to a colander, set over a bowl to drain. *Discard any mussels which obstinately refuse to open.* If the mussel liquor is not required in the recipe, keep it in the refrigerator and use next day for fish soup or a sauce.

Note: 2 lb. of mussels are more or less equal to a quart. This is only a rough guide as the size of mussels makes a difference to the measurement of capacity.

Scallops are usually opened by the fishmonger. If you have to do it, the shells can be prised apart with an oyster knife, but it's safer to put them on a baking tray and leave in a very hot oven for a few minutes. Use a knife to lever the shells apart once they've begun to open. Detach the scallops carefully from their shells, discard the black part, rinse the white part and the coral, and pat dry.

Coquilles St Jacques à la provençale (for 4)

The point of this dish is the crisp contrast of fried breadcrumbs with garlic and moist sweet scallops. Very appetizing. Don't try to do the cooking all in one pan, as the crumbs will soak up juice from the mushrooms and scallops and become soggy.

> 10–12 scallops, sliced across
> ¼ lb. mushrooms, sliced downwards
> 4 large cloves garlic, chopped
> 2 tablespoons butter
> 4 oz. white breadcrumbs
> 5 tablespoons olive oil
> plenty chopped parsley
> 4 lemon quarters

Fry the white parts of the scallops, the mushrooms and the garlic, in butter and 2 tablespoons of olive oil, for 4 or 5 minutes. Add coral and cook a further 3 minutes. Drain off any liquid. At the same time, fry the breadcrumbs in another pan in 3 tablespoons olive oil. Stir them around so that they brown evenly. Combine the contents of the two pans just before serving. Stir in chopped parsley. Divide between four small, heated bowls, and put a lemon quarter on top of each one.

Mussel and tomato soup (for 4)

A soup of provençal type, which depends for its success on well-flavoured olive oil, enough garlic, and tomatoes of quality. As far as the last ingredient is concerned, better results are obtained from tinned tomatoes and a good seasoning of sugar and tomato concentrate, than from the fresh tomatoes normally on sale.

> 2 lbs. mussels
> 2 tablespoons olive oil
> 2 large cloves garlic, crushed
> ¾ lb. peeled tomatoes, or drained tinned tomatoes
> sugar and tomato concentrate
> salt, pepper
> water
> croûtons of bread fried in olive oil

Put ¼ inch of water in a large pan and open the mussels in it. Remove them from their shells (which should be thrown away). Strain the mussel liquor into a measuring jug, and add water to bring it up to 2 pints.

Meanwhile put the oil into another pan, add the garlic and tomatoes. Cook for 5 to 10 minutes, pressing them into a rough purée without too many large lumps. Add the 2 pints of mussel liquor and season with salt and pepper. Simmer for 15 minutes, then adjust the seasoning with sugar and tomato concentrate. Add the mussels to reheat for a few seconds (not for long, or they will turn rubbery), and pour into the soup tureen. Serve with the croûtons, added at the last moment and sizzling on top of the soup.

Mussel or scallop chowder (for 4)

Chowder sounds uncompromisingly North American to us – Newfoundland chowder, Manhattan chowder, New England chowder. In fact this old one-pot meal of fish, potato, onion and salt pork was taken across the Atlantic by Breton sailors searching for cod.

Like their wives at home they made it in a huge iron *chaudière* (in other words, a hotpot or cauldron, anglicized in the eighteenth century to 'chowder'). Circumstances demanded the substitution of ship's biscuit for potatoes, but once the dish settled down on the eastern seaboard of Nova Scotia and New England, potatoes went back into the pot. In time a new local ingredient, milk, was added to enhance the stew, where a Breton cook would have used, and still uses, cider or wine.

I like these satisfying dishes of the pre-oven age. Like Lancashire hotpot or Irish stew or Welsh cawl, fish chowders are easy to prepare and very easy on cost (what could be cheaper than this recipe?), yet they make the most of the simple ingredients. They have a basic goodness which pleases everyone.

> 2 lb. fish bones and trimmings
> 1¼ pints water
> 4 oz. salt pork, or green streaky bacon, diced
> 8 oz. chopped onion
> 1 tablespoon flour
> 1 pint scalded milk
> teaspoon sugar
> 1 lb. potatoes, cubed
> 2 lb. mussels or 4–6 scallops
> salt, Cayenne pepper
> chopped parsley
> 4 dessertspoons double cream, or 3 oz.
>   single cream

Most fishmongers will give you a free handful of fish bones and trimmings, or will charge you at most a few pence for them. Put them into a heavy large pan with a pint of water and simmer for 40 minutes without seasoning, while preparing the vegetables. Put salt pork or bacon pieces into a heavy pan on a low heat. When the fat begins to run, put in the onion and brown lightly. Stir in the flour, then, bit by bit, the strained fish stock and hot milk. Add seasoning, sugar and potato. Cook until potato is just done, but not in the least mushy.

Meanwhile open the mussels in ¼ pint water, remove from their shells and keep warm. Strain the mussel liquor into the chowder, correct the seasoning with salt and Cayenne pepper, and simmer for a moment or two. Just before serving add the chopped parsley, mussels and cream.

If scallops are used, remove the coral. Slice the white part and add to the chowder when the potatoes are almost done. Simmer five minutes, correct seasoning and add coral. Simmer for another three minutes, then add parsley and cream and serve.

Toast and hot water biscuits are usually served with fish chowders.

Mussels on skewers

Here's quite a different combination of mussels and bacon, this time piquant and savoury. It's a good way of using the large mussels on sale in this country. For each person:

> 12 large mussels (about 1 lb.)
> ¼ pint water
> 3 rashers fat bacon
> dessertspoon cream
> teaspoon chopped parsley
>
> *serve with* plainly boiled rice

Cut the rind off the bacon and divide it into 14 pieces. Open the mussels with ¼ pint of water in a heavy pan in the usual way. Discard the shells. Beginning and ending with bacon, thread mussels and bacon on two skewers. Grill quickly, turning twice, for 5 minutes. As the bacon browns and crisps at the edges, its fat keeps the mussels basted.

Put the skewers on a bed of rice in a warm oven, while making the sauce. Pour the mussel liquor into the juices in the grill pan. Boil hard to reduce the liquid to a good flavour, and scrape in all the little brown bits and pieces. Add the cream to bind, then season to taste, and add the parsley. Serve separately in a sauce boat.

Alternatively the skewers can be rolled in beaten egg, then in breadcrumbs, and deep-fried. The sauce will then depend solely on the mussel liquor and cream.

This dish is very good when scallops are used instead of mussels. Slice the white part across into two pieces, and grill at a slightly lower temperature to cook the thicker scallops.

Mussel omelette (for 4)

A simple, cheap, delicious recipe.

> 2 pints mussels
> 6 eggs, beaten
> 3 oz. butter
> 3 level tablespoons chopped shallot, or mild
>   onion
> 2 level tablespoons chopped parsley
> salt, pepper

Put the mussels into a large pan with just enough water to cover the base. Stand over a good heat, with a lid on the pan, until they open. Remove the mussels from their shells, and keep the liquor for fish soup. Meanwhile melt the shallot or onion in the butter. When it's soft, add the mussels and cook for a few moments until the edges just begin to curl up. Mix into the beaten eggs and make 1 large or 2 small omelettes in the usual way. Taste the mixture and season, before cooking the omelettes.

Mussels at Mesnil-Val (for 4 or 5)

One of the first things we do on arriving in France (and, sadly, one of the last before leaving) is to eat a dish of tiny Normandy mussels. The slow progress through scores of these particularly delectable molluscs is soothing after a long day's drive. Their freshness can be guaranteed as far inland as Evreux, but best of all are the mussels served in small villages on the coast, where they go from beach to table in three or four hours. At Mesnil-Val the handsome navy-blue appearance of the mussels is set off by a yellow sauce:

> 1 tablespoon sliced onion
> ¼ pint white wine
> ½ small bay leaf
> 4 lb. mussels (about 2 quarts)
> 3 egg yolks
> 4 oz. unsalted butter

¼ pint cream
salt, pepper, lemon juice, parsley

Simmer onion and bay leaf in the wine for 5 minutes. Add the mussels to the pan, and open them. Remove one half-shell from each, if they're large. Reduce the liquor to about half a pint, or a little less.

Beat egg yolks and cream together in a large pudding basin. Pour in the strained mussel liquor, set the pudding basin over a pan of simmering water, and stir gently but steadily. Add the butter in small knobs one by one. Don't hurry this part of the cooking, or the sauce will turn lumpy. Don't overheat the sauce either, or it will curdle. This may sound difficult, but it's not; it's only a question of patience. Season when it's the consistency of thickish custard, with lemon juice, salt and pepper. Quickly transfer the mussels to a hot serving bowl from their colander, and pour the sauce over them. Sprinkle well with chopped parsley. Serve with plenty of good bread.

Mouclade d'Esnandes (for 4)

This recipe shows how mussels are cooked on the Atlantic coast of France around La Rochelle. Many people there (including the inhabitants of Esnandes) work in the mussel fisheries. Miles and miles of wooden stakes, or *bouchots* are driven into the seabed where the water is shallow, and on these stakes mussels increase and grow fat. At low tide men come out in flat-bottomed boats to remove them for market, and for their own *mouclade*, a version of *moules marinières* which usually includes white wine and cream. Don't omit the aniseed flavouring, which goes so well with fish.

> 4 pints mussels
> ½ pint dry white wine
> 2 large cloves garlic
> 6 oz. finely chopped shallot or mild onion
> 1 tablespoon flour
> 1½ oz. butter
> ¾ pint milk
> generous tablespoon double cream
> 2 egg yolks
> aniseed to taste

Use the wine to open the mussels. Remove and discard one shell, and keep warm. Melt shallot and garlic in the butter meanwhile, very gently, for 20 minutes to half an hour. Stir in the flour, strained mussel liquor, milk and aniseed to taste (start with a little, then add more to your liking). Season and boil down a little. Beat egg yolk with double cream, and add to the sauce. Cook without boiling, until the sauce thickens. Correct the seasoning. Put the mussels into a soup bowl, and pour the very hot sauce over them.

Curried scallops (for 4)

This delicious dish has no connection at all with Indian cooking. Curry powder is used as a convenient spice blend, to flavour a cream sauce in the best French tradition. Denmark is another country where curry powder is used in this way, and not to imitate Indian cooking. Sometimes, in fact very often, it's used to flavour mayonnaise – an idea to be adopted for shellfish salads.

12 scallops
¼ pint dry white wine
bouquet garni
2 oz. butter
¼ teaspoon curry powder
½ pint double cream, or whipping cream
2 tablespoons top of the milk
2 egg yolks
salt, pepper

Simmer the white parts of the scallops, sliced across into two circles, in the wine, flavoured with the bouquet garni. Remove and drain after 4 or 5 minutes then sauté gently in the butter and curry powder for 4 minutes. Remove the scallops to a warm dish, and pour the wine into the butter, and boil hard to reduce. Stir in the double or whipping cream, and season well. Boil hard again for about 2 minutes. Beat up the egg yolks with the top of the milk, and amalgamate carefully with the sauce. Cook gently for a further 2 minutes, having added the scallops to reheat, *but without boiling* or the egg yolks will curdle.

Serve with plainly boiled rice.

Trout

A good trout, rainbow or native brown trout, is one that hasn't come all flaccid out of a tank. Or frozen out of a commercial deep-freeze. In restaurants – unless the restaurateur gets his trout straight from river or lake, and most can't – the only trout worth eating and paying for is a smoked one.

The best trout of all would be one that had jumped straight from the stream or lake or reservoir into the pan, ready to be eaten within minutes of being caught. But trout caught today should still be delicious if eaten within 24 hours – for breakfast tomorrow or even for supper.

From many people's point of view this may seem so restrictive that there's no point in reading this bit of the book at all. But in fact more and more fresh trout are being caught by more and more people, not rich men with expensive fishing rights, but ordinary fishermen, particularly in the Midlands, who have access to the big reservoirs. Needing more water, we are likely to be cooking more trout, as a bonus. And not only more, but bigger ones as well.

Trout being such a delicately flavoured fish, it follows that accompaniments should be delicate too, and of the first quality. They should be subservient, or at the most complementary to the flavour of the fish. Avoid colourful little mounds of this and that, and serve the trout straight. As you will see from the recipes below for *truite á la meunière* and *truite au bleu*, butter is all that's required for really fresh fish. Almonds, or a few boiled new potatoes, belong to the longer caught fish that begins to need some help. Surplus trout can either be potted, or deep-frozen, and, eventually, baked. There is an excellent cream, butter and herb sauce suitable for trout on p. 213, but as a change try the less usual walnut sauce of Escoffier's given below.

Note: all the recipes following may be used for grayling, without adaptation.

Truite à la meunière

I had always pictured a young miller's wife cooking trout from her husband's mill pool in this way. But it seems that the real story was quite different. At Royat, near Clermont-Ferrand in the Auvergne, a town of many streams, there is an old inn called La Belle Meunière. Its speciality used to be – perhaps still is – fresh trout, floured and fried in butter. One day Napoleon stopped there. He ate his trout with enthusiasm, declaring that this way of cooking fish should be called *à la belle meunière* (the 'belle' has, most unfairly, been dropped with time).

It sounds to me like the apocryphal tale of Sir Loin, but perhaps it is true. I would like to think so. It's certainly true that Napoleon liked simple food of high quality. He would have enjoyed the crisp golden skin of the *trout à la meunière*, which sets off so well the light flavour of the flesh.

> 4 trout, about 8 oz. each
> 3 oz. butter

plus 4 tablespoons butter
milk
seasoned flour
lemon quarters

First clarify the 3 oz. butter by bringing it to the boil in a small pan. It will separate into white froth and clear yellow oil. Strain through a muslin-lined strainer, directly into the frying pan. The froth will be caught in the muslin, and there will be enough clarified butter for frying the fish. This process is most important and very simple. Trout or any other fish fried in unclarified butter stick to the pan, with the result that their skin (and sometimes their flesh) is broken and spoilt.

Rinse the trout quickly, wipe them dry and dip each one in milk. Turn them over firmly in the flour, while the frying pan is heating up. Shake off the surplus flour and slide them straightaway into the hot butter. Fry at a moderate heat for 5 minutes on each side, for ½ lb. fish. Larger fish will take longer, and the heat should be reduced after the first two minutes so that the fat does not blacken. The result should be golden brown fish.

Meanwhile, in a separate frying pan, bring the four tablespoons of butter to the boil. Cook until brown, a nice golden brown not a burnt semi-black. Put the trout on a hot serving dish, sprinkle with a seasoning of pepper, and pour over the foaming butter. Arrange the lemon quarters around the fish and rush to the table. Like a soufflé, *truite à la meunière* should not be kept waiting.

Trout with almonds

This is not entirely a dish to be despised, especially for trout eaten the day after they're caught. The flavour of almonds is welcome without being too obtrusive; their milky mealy texture going well with firm-fleshed but delicate fish like trout and sole.

Ingredients are the same as for *truite à la meunière*, plus 1 tablespoon of almonds for each fish, blanched and split.

A word about the almonds. It is not worth buying ready

blanched and split ones. Half their flavour seems to have disappeared with their skins. Buy ones with the skins still on, put them in a pan of water and bring to the boil. Drain and you'll find that the skins slip off easily. Use a sharp knife to split the almonds into halves.

Follow the method for *truite à la meunière*, but when the four tablespoons of butter are put into a separate frying pan, put in the almonds as well. By the time the butter is golden brown, the almonds will be slightly browned too.

Note: sole à la meunière and sole with almonds are cooked in exactly the same way, except that soles should first be skinned. The fishmonger will do this for you, but if he hasn't, ease off a corner of skin at the tail end and pull. Do the same thing with the other side.

Baked trout

This excellent method of baking trout (or other whole fish such as red mullet, bass, sea bream, etc.) allows none of the flavours to escape. For this reason it's the best way to cook trout from the deep-freeze.

Incidentally why do we import frozen trout from Japan? Could we not produce our own? There must be a fortune in it for some enterprising native of our islands.

> 4 trout, about 8 oz. each
> 4 oz. breadcrumbs
> 3 oz. mushrooms, roughly chopped
> 2 oz. onion, finely chopped
> 1 lemon
> heaped tablespoon chopped parsley
> salt, pepper, plenty of butter

Melt the onion gently in 2 oz. of butter over a low heat. In 10 minutes it will be golden butter coloured, not brown. Mix in a bowl with breadcrumbs, mushrooms, and parsley. Season well with salt, pepper and lemon juice, having first grated the lemon rind into the stuffing.

Cut pieces of foil about 12 inches square. In the centre of each spread a 5 inch line of butter – allow a generous tablespoon for each trout. Put the stuffing on top of the butter, dividing it between the four squares, and the trout on top of the stuffing. Twist the edge of the foil to form sealed, oblong, baggy packages. Place then on a baking sheet and put in an oven at Mark 3, 325°F, for about 30 minutes.

This method can be adapted for larger trout. A 2–4 lb. fish will take 1–1½ hours to cook.

Jellied trout

Bring to the boil in a covered pan, and simmer for 30 minutes the following ingredients:

> ¾ pint water
> ¼ pint dry white wine
> tablespoon wine vinegar
> 2 oz. sliced onion
> ½ bay leaf
> 2 sprigs each thyme and parsley
> scant ½ teaspoon salt
> 6 peppercorns

Leave to cool. Place up to 8 half-pound trout close together in a pan or oval casserole. Strain over them the water and wine mixture. Bring slowly to the boil, taking about 10 minutes, either on top of the stove or in the oven. When the liquid boils, remove the pan from the heat and leave in a cool place. The coddled trout will be firm but cooked, and of an excellent flavour. (The method can be used for large fish as they need more liquid to cover them, which takes longer to come to the boil and longer to cool – it even works for salmon.)

When the trout are cold, place them in an oval or oblong serving dish. Boil the cooking liquor down by half, cool again, and pour over the fish. It will set to a delicious jelly. Mayonnaise or horseradish-flavoured cream can be served with the trout, but this is not necessary. Chill the trout before serving.

Truite au bleu

If you can bring trout home alive, this is the best way of cooking them. Bring to the boil 2 pints of salted water, with 3 tablespoons of wine vinegar. Pick the trout from their bucket of water one by one, kill them humanely by banging their heads smartly on the table and clean them quickly. *Do not rinse them.* If you do, they will fail to turn the required bluish-grey. Slip them into the boiling water, and simmer for 10 minutes. Serve with melted butter.

If you wish to eat the trout cold simmer them for 3 or 4 minutes only and leave to cool in the cooking liquid. Serve with home-made mayonnaise, or whipped cream flavoured with lemon juice and chopped parsley.

Potted trout

Any cooked, left-over trout can be broken into pieces of about ¼ inch (remove all skin and bone first). Mix with an equal weight of cool melted butter, seasoned to taste with mace and nutmeg. Put into small pots. When firm, cover with a ¼ inch layer of clarified butter (see *truite à la meunière*). Cover with foil and store in the refrigerator.

Horseradish and walnut sauce

This unusually delicious sauce may be eaten with salmon as well as with trout. It comes from Escoffier's *Ma Cuisine*, and the only alteration I've made is to halve the quantities. There will still be plenty for six people.

> 2 oz. shelled walnuts
> 2 oz. grated horseradish

pinch salt
1 teaspoon caster sugar
1 tablespoon white breadcrumbs
¼ pint double cream
1 teaspoon wine vinegar or lemon juice

Pour boiling water over the walnuts and leave them for a moment or two. You will then be able to remove their fine skins, which can add a bitter taste to this sauce. Chop the nuts finely, then mix with the rest of the ingredients. Add the vinegar or lemon juice gradually – the whole teaspoon may not be to your taste, or you may like to add a little more.

Meat and Game

Meat Pies

1. Raised pies

Most of us have a weakness for meat pies. Or should I say for a
platonic ideal of meat pies? It's a weakness that has, surprisingly,
stood firm despite some of the works of the assembly line, with
their yellow-and-white cylinders of denatured egg piercing a mass
of ill-seasoned pork. In our optimism (or for convenience) we still
buy meat pies. And of course make them. One way and another,
we eat them by the million.

What is a meat pie? A hash of meat enclosed in pastry, is the
obvious answer. But really the matter's more complex. A pie, particularly a double-crust or raised pie, is an ingenious device
whereby bird or beast (or both) develops the finest flavour possible by being cooked in its own juices. (Lidded casseroles started
as a labour-saving substitute for pastry cases: many of them were,

and some even nowadays are, made to imitate a raised pie.)

Some experts may claim that the crust is unimportant once the pie is cooked, that it should be pushed to the side of the plate, but I can't agree. The right crust, succulent and crisp, is an important contribution to the success of any pie. Whether hot or cold, it sets off the meat perfectly.

The flexibility of the meat pie is another reason for its long popularity. The filling may be simply chopped pork with a seasoning of herbs and spices, and perhaps an embellishment of hard-boiled eggs, pieces of rabbit, a few mushrooms, whatever family and local circumstances may provide. On the other hand elaborate combinations of meat and game have delighted the rich for nearly two millennia. According to Apicius the Roman Emperor Verus, co-Emperor with Marcus Aurelius, himself concocted an 'amalgamation of sow's flank, pheasant, peacock, spiced ham, and wild boar's flesh ... within the thick casing of a laboriously worked crust.'

In the eighteenth century special poultry and game pies were sent to London from Yorkshire for Christmas feasting. Their pastry walls, made extra thick to withstand the jolting miles, contained a turkey stuffed with a goose, a chicken, a partridge and a pigeon, all boned and one inside the other, Russian doll fashion. The cavities round this innocent looking creature were filled with hare, woodcock, and wild fowl, plus 4 lb. of butter (a similar confection of many layers of game is made in Burgundy, most notably at the Côte d'or in Saulieu by Monsieur François Minot – because of its shape, it is called the *Oreiller de la belle Aurore*, Aurora's pillow).

We don't make such pies these days: they'd cost too much. They're not to modern taste. But when I think of their descendants, the wonderful game pies of Britain and France, I conclude that north of the Alps we've been able to bring such things to near perfection. Pies need plenty of fat in their filling: we've bred the pigs. Pies need a good crust: we've bred the pastry cooks. At this standard – let's forget the plastic and pork pies – we have achieved a certain grandeur, however elegiac and transitory that grandeur may be. 'Graceful monuments, delicious fortresses, seductive ramparts, which as soon as they are on all sides attacked,' wrote one great chef of the last century, 'totter, crumble, and no longer present anything but glorious and ephemeral ruins, like every work of man – all pass away whether they be temples, columns, pyramids or pies.'*

Pastry for hot-water crust or raised pies

---

       1 lb. plain flour
       7 oz. water
       6 oz. lard
       ¼ teaspoon salt
       scant tablespoon icing sugar (optional)
       beaten egg

Sift flour, salt and sugar if used (it gives a richness to the pastry), into a bowl. Make a well in the middle. Bring water and lard to the boil and pour into the well immediately, bringing in the flour with a wooden spoon until the dough forms a smooth ball. Cover and leave in a warm place for the pastry to cool a little. When it's malleable and still warm, remove about a quarter for the pie lid and put the rest into a greased hinged pie mould of 2 pint capacity (or a cake tin with a removable base). Shape the dough up the sides with light firm movements, taking care to leave no cracks through which the pie juices will be able to escape. If the pastry slides down the mould, it's still a little hot: leave it for a while, then start again.

Pack the filling gently into the corners and undulations of the pastry-lined mould, and mound it up nicely at the top to support the lid. Moisten the pastry rim with water or beaten egg, and lay on the reserved pastry which has been rolled out, as a lid. Trim and knock up the edges, make a hole in the centre and decorate with pastry leaves and roses, or whatever your fancy dictates. Cut a strip of stiff paper, or use a small piece of card (a 'Bristol' to the French), to roll up and push into the hole: this keeps it open during cooking. Brush lid and decorations with beaten egg.

A wooden pie mould, or a 2 lb. jam jar, may be used instead of a hinged pie tin or cake tin. In this case the pastry must be shaped or 'raised' on the outside. Flour the wooden mould very well before you start, or you won't be able to remove it from the pastry

*Alexis Soyer: *Pantropheon*, Simpkin, Marshal & Co., 1853.

Making raised pies with
wooden pie moulds

when it's cool. Tie a piece of thick paper (e.g. brown paper) round
the warm raised pastry to help keep the shape. When the pastry is
cold and set, remove the wooden mould but not the paper, which
should remain in place until the pie has been baked and has
cooled down. Now pack the filling in gently and cover with a
pastry lid. This is the way pies were and are still made in parts of
the Midlands and East Anglia, but it's undeniably trickier than
using a hinged pie mould, which can be bought from any good
kitchen suppliers.

Bake 30 minutes at Mark 6, 400°F, then 1½–2 hours at Mark 3,
325°F. Let the pie cool a little, then remove the mould, brush the
sides with beaten egg and return the pie to the oven for them to
brown (protect the lid with brown paper). Pour in the runny but
cool jellied stock (for recipe and quantity see recipe below)
through a funnel and the hole in the middle – first removing the
Bristol – and leave overnight before eating.

Raised pork pie

Unless you are lucky in knowing of a small family business which
makes good pork pies with a rich crust – not easy to find even in the

traditional Midland pie country – it's wise to make your own. Anybody who has ever watched the pastry being rolled, and rerolled, and rerolled, and rerolled (and picked up off the floor and rerolled) in a greying blanket all day in a pie factory will know what I mean.

In fact making a pork pie is not difficult. It takes time rather than any special skill. You need to remember three things: about a third of the meat must be fat to keep the filling and crust succulent; the filling must be well seasoned with herbs, spices and perhaps a dash of anchovy essence as in the Melton Mowbray area; the better the pork you use, the better the pie will be, and always include some bacon to improve the flavour and to give the filling an appetizing pink tinge from the saltpetre used in bacon curing.

hot-water crust as above

filling:

2 lb. boned shoulder or spareribs, with
    1 part fat to 2 parts lean
½ lb. very thinly cut green bacon rashers
teaspoon chopped sage
½ teaspoon each nutmeg, cinnamon,
    ground cloves, allspice
salt, freshly ground black pepper
1 teaspoon anchovy essence, or to taste

jelly:

bones from pork, plus veal knuckle or
    2 pig's trotters
large carrot, sliced
medium onion stuck with 2 cloves
bouquet garni
12 peppercorns

Make the jelly first. Put all ingredients into a large pan and fill with water to within an inch of the top. Simmer for 3–5 hours, adding no salt. Strain off the stock into a clean pan, and boil it down hard to about ¾ pint. Season with salt, and more pepper if necessary, and leave to cool. This jelly can be made a day in advance of the pie.

Next make the filling. Chop the pork, or mince it coarsely. Then mince half of it finely with 2 rashers of bacon. Mix all the pork well together; add the seasonings and anchovy essence. Fry a small piece of this mixture to test the flavour, remembering that dishes to be eaten cold always need a stronger seasoning than dishes to be eaten hot.

Make the hot-water crust, and line the mould as described above. Lay the remaining rashers of bacon over the bottom and lower sides to form an inner lining. Pack in the filling and finish in the usual way, see pp. 61–2. If the jelly has set firm, it should be melted to a state of cool runniness before being poured into a hot pie. Pour in a little of this jellied stock at a time, through the centre hole, using a kitchen funnel. Do this immediately the pie comes out of the oven finally, so that the stock sinks into the filling. Don't hurry this process, or you will flood the gap left by meat shrinkage. This will vary from one time to another, and it is impossible to predict accurately, but ¾ pint of jellied stock will be more than enough. Any left over can be used for soups, sauces, and for dishes such as *œufs en geleé*.

Game, chicken or rabbit pie

Follow the preceding recipe, but make the filling of:

> ¼ lb. hard back pork fat
> ¼ lb. lean pork
> ¼ lb. thin rashers
> 3 tablespoons brandy, or sherry, or
>   5 tablespoons dry white wine
> 1 lb. game, chicken or rabbit, cut from
>   the bone
> heaped tablespoon chopped parsley
> ¼ teaspoon each nutmeg, cinnamon, ground cloves
> salt, freshly ground black pepper
> ¼ teaspoon anchovy essence (for chicken and
>   rabbit only)

Mince fat and lean pork together finely with 2 rashers of bacon (use the rest for lining the pastry). Season with spices, salt and pepper. Cut the game, chicken or rabbit into nice pieces, not too large (mince the trimmings and mix into the pork mixture); leave for 2 hours in a dish with the brandy or wine, and some salt and pepper. When filling the pie, put some of the pork in first, then a layer of game pieces, then some more pork and some more game, finishing with a layer of pork. The wine should be included.

The bones from the game should be used when making the jelly. If venison is used, port may be substituted for the brandy – or one could use them both, about ¼ pint port and 1 tablespoon of brandy; the same applies to hare.

Cheshire pork and apple pie

This pork and apple pie is at least 200 years old (Hannah Glasse gives it in her *Art of Cookery*, first edition 1747), and probably very much older than that. When pigs were killed in the autumn on Cheshire farms – and on Leicestershire farms, too – the scraps left over from preparing hams, sausages, brawn, etc. were used in this kind of pie. It might be made of short or hot-water pastry. The apples were usually windfalls from the dessert pippin trees (if they were sour, the deficiency was made up with more sugar). In other words, the recipe was adjusted to circumstances.

> hot-water crust or short pastry, made with
> 1 lb. flour
>
> *filling:*
>
> 1 lb. lean and 1 lb. fat pork or
> 1¼ lb. lean and ¾lb. fat
> 1½ lb. Cox's orange pippins
> 8 oz. chopped onion
> brown sugar, salt, pepper, nutmeg
> 2 oz. butter
> 1 gill white wine, cider or light ale

Mince the pork coarsely (2 or 3 rashers of bacon can be included as well), and the onion finely. Mix them together and season well with salt, pepper and grated nutmeg. Peel, core and slice the apples; season them with sugar and nutmeg. Put a layer of pork into the pastry-lined mould, then apples, then pork, apples and pork. Dot with butter on top, pour on the wine, cider or ale. Finish in the usual way. Bake at Mark 4, 350°F for 1¼ hours. Eat hot or cold. Sage can be used instead of nutmeg.

---

2. Shortcrust Pies

Shortcrust meat pies may not have the castellated grandeur of the chef's raised pie — the curves, the flutings, the cornice, the roses, diamonds, circles and leaves — but they're the pies that people have loved. They belong to family life, to that stage of general civilized prosperity when home cooking becomes something more than handfuls of this and that, thrown into a pot over the fire. Their success depends on a certain skill, just enough to be both challenge and pleasure. Few moments in a cook's life can be more agreeable than cutting the first wedge from a beefsteak and kidney pie (particularly if it contains oysters) — the wonderful smell, the looks of anticipation around the table, the air of restlessness until the eating may begin, are the rewards of this skill.

Although these pies belong mainly to the eighteenth and nineteenth centuries, to the kitchens of farm and middle-class home, some of them are relics of a much older time. (And one, the Priddy Oggy, is a recent invention of style, in the pasty tradition.)

Ascribed now to different parts of the country, they were once eaten by everyone. Rabbit and oyster pies, for instance, are sometimes given to Shropshire, to Scotland, to the Kingdom of Fife, but when rabbits and oysters were abundant, the food of the poor, such pies were made everywhere. Sweet meat mixtures surviving the regional cookery of Pembrokeshire and North-West England, were once a nationwide solution to the problem of meat that was just beginning to go off. When lamb or beef in this condition was chopped small, and dowsed in sugar, alcohol, raisins, prunes and currants, it was absorbed into stronger flavours and need not be wasted (modern mincemeats, with beef suet, are their descendants).

Of all these shortcrust pies the masterpiece is, I think, the beefsteak, kidney and oyster pie (with Devonshire squab pie a close second). The recipe is based on one by Francatelli, Queen Victoria's French chef. He increased the flavour of our traditional recipe by browning the meat first in fat, and thickening the sauce with a roux (earlier cooks like Mrs Beeton and Eliza Acton just floured the meat before putting it into the pie dish and adding water).

Shortcrust pastry

> 1 lb. plain flour
> ¼ lb. each butter and lard
> 2 scant tablespoons icing sugar
>   (optional)
> ½ teaspoon salt
> cold water
> egg

Sift flour, sugar and salt into a bowl. Rub in the fat until the mixture is crumbly. Using as little water as possible, mix to a firm dough. Leave in a cool place for an hour at least. Roll out and line a greased loaf tin, or pie dish of about 2 pint capacity. Pack in the filling, mounding it up so that the lid will be nicely shaped, and moisten the rim of pastry. Lay on the pastry lid. Knock up the edges and make a central hole for the steam to escape (keep it open with a rolled card, or Bristol, see p. 61). Decorate with leaves and a rose (a roll of pastry rolled up, then pinched together at one side so that the other opens into a flower-shape). Brush with beaten egg and bake at Mark 2–3, 300–325°F, for ¾–2½ hours, according to the filling.

For single-crust pies, such as the steak and kidney and oyster pie that follows, use half the quantities given above.

Beefsteak, kidney and oyster pie (for 6)

An interesting thing about Roman cookery is the ubiquity in recipes, both sweet and savoury, of a substance known as *garum* or *liquamen*. It was the monosodium glutamate of ancient times, a taste-sharpener invented by the Greeks, but developed by the Romans to the point of being produced in factories, and sold in trademarked containers. The basis of this relish and its variants was the fermented liquor of salted-down fish entrails. Anchovies were used, so were mackerel and tunny, and even, in one luxurious recipe, the prized liver of red mullet.

Disgusting, you may say. But was it? I think that *liquamen* served the Romans better than monosodium glutamate serves us (it can cause headaches when overemployed in restaurants to conceal the lack of freshness and flavour in the food). Think of beefsteak, chicken or rabbit pie, all improved by oysters until the middle of the nineteenth century, when their rising price put them out of the seasoning category. Think of anchovy essence used in meat pâtés, and in pork pies around Melton Mowbray. These fishy additives lose identity in such dishes, giving up individual flavour to increase the general richness.

shortcrust pastry as above, half quantity

filling:
1½–2 lb. chuck steak
8 oz.–¾ lb. ox kidney
6 oz. chopped onion
1 oz. butter
heaped tablespoon flour
12–18 oysters
6 oz. mushrooms sliced
Harvey's, Worcester or soya sauce
salt, freshly ground black pepper
beef stock

First open the oysters, taking the precaution of wrapping your left hand in a tea towel. Put them with their liquor into a basin. Then cut the steak into cubes and the kidney into chunky slices, discarding all fat and skin. Season the meat with salt and pepper, and brown quickly in butter with the onion. Stir in the flour and cook for a moment or two until it has taken up the fat. Add the oysters and their liquor to the mushrooms, and enough stock until the consistency of the sauce is like thick cream (the mushrooms and meat will exude a certain amount of juice, bringing the sauce to a thinner consistency). Season with salt, pepper and a dash of Harvey's, Worcester or soya sauce. Transfer to a 2–2½ pint pie dish. Lay a strip of pastry round the rim, then moisten the pastry and lay on the lid. Finish in the usual way for shortcrust pies, baking for 2 hours at Mark 2–3, 300–325°F. Protect the crust with paper as it browns.

Alternatively the filling can be pre-cooked for an hour, in a covered casserole, and allowed to cool a little – or completely, overnight. Transfer to the pie dish, cover with pastry and bake for 30 minutes at Mark 5, 375–400°F. The first method is better from the point of view of flavour, I think, but the second may suit your convenience or your stove, better. It also gives you a more exact control over the cooking meat – beef can vary a great deal in toughness, so the time required in the oven can vary.

Rabbit and some fat bacon, cut in pieces, may be substituted for steak and kidney (this used to be done in Shropshire, and is still done in Scotland I believe). A longer cooking time will be required if the rabbit is mature; less time if it is very young and tender.

Easter Pie from Berry (for 6)

I remember once in Paris buying a wedge from a steaming wheel of pie, labelled *Gâteau Berrichonne*. It was obviously just sausage-meat in pastry, but it was cheap and we were hard up. Wandering into the Palais Royal near by to see where Colette had lived, we started chewing unenthusiastically. We took time to appreciate how delicious that pie was. Ever since I've had much respect for food from Berry, a province unharmed by too many visitors in spite of the reputation of Georges Sand, Alain Fournier and Bourges Cathedral – and of the flinty wines of Sancerre. The 'Easter' part of the title is not obligatory – just part of the Easter egg tradition.

> shortcrust pastry, made with 1 lb. flour
>
> *filling:*
>
> 1½ lb. pork from throat, about ⅔ lean
>   to ⅓ fat
> large clove garlic
> 2 rashers unsmoked bacon
> handful parsley

tablespoon chopped chives
teaspoon salt
plenty of black pepper
¼ teaspoon each nutmeg, cinnamon,
    ginger and cloves (or more,
    according to taste)

plus: 4 oz. chopped mushrooms
6 hardboiled eggs
beaten raw egg

Roll out the pasty into a rectangle a little longer than a baking sheet, but about the same width. Line a baking sheet with foil and grease it well. Cut the pastry to fit inside it, keeping the trimmings (to be used for the lid).

Now make the filling: mince pork and bacon coarsely, then mince half of it again finely. Season well with garlic, herbs and spices.

Lay half this sausagemeat on the pastry in a rectangle, leaving a clear 2–3 inch margin all the way round. Spread the mushrooms evenly over the meat. Cut the eggs in half and place the halves, cut-side down, on top of the mushrooms to make a double row of little white domes. Tuck the remaining sausagemeat in between the eggs and over the top, so that they are completely enclosed.

Nick triangles from the corners of the pastry margin to the filling, and moisten the cut edges so that you can bring them up together to make a box which encloses the sausagemeat, etc. Press them firmly. Roll out all the pastry trimmings and cut an oblong lid to cover the pastry. Moisten the edges of the lid and invert it over the pie. Press the lid edges together with the box edges, making scallops with your fingers. Cut some pastry leaves and arrange in two parallel rows the length of the lid, and make some decorative slashes in the middle to let the steam escape. Brush the whole thing over with beaten egg (or top of the milk), and bake for 1¼ hours at Mark 4, 350°F.

Eat cold or just warm, with a green salad.

Priddy Oggies (to make 8)

The other recipes in this chapter are old, genuine antiques mostly, from well before 1820 in origin at least, even if more recent adjustments have been made, to fit the recipe to modern life. Here's a modern upstart, a delicious pasty with no ancestors at all, invented by Mr Paul Leyton, for his restaurant at Priddy in Somerset, the Miner's Arms. He uses local Cheddar, local pork tenderloin, and his own smoked pork. The shape of it is based on the Cornish oggy or pasty, that convenient arrangement which enabled a miner – or a schoolboy – to take his lunch to work in his pocket. When through poverty resulting from the decay of the tin mines some or most of the original steak filling was replaced by potatoes, the Cornish pasty was often known as a tiddy oggy, tiddy being the local name for a potato. So by assonance and analogy, Mr Leyton found a name for his invention. (If you're feeling lazy, he will supply them in special containers for storage in the deepfreeze.)

cheese pastry:

½ lb. plain flour
1 oz. each butter and lard
1 small egg yolk
3½ oz. grated mature Cheddar
    (or ½ parmesan, ½ less mature Cheddar)
2½ tablespoons water
pinch salt

meat:

1 pork tenderloin (fillet), weighing about
    1¼ lb.
generous oz. very thinly sliced smoked
    pork, smoked bacon or Bayonne ham

stuffing:

3 oz. grated mature Cheddar (or
    ½ parmesan, ½ mild Cheddar)
sprig parsley, chopped
good pinch salt
8 drops tabasco (or Cayenne, or
    freshly ground black pepper)
large egg

Make the pastry first. Mix all the ingredients, *except the flour*, in a bowl. It helps to warm the butter and lard slightly. Cool the mixture in the refrigerator until firm. Sieve the flour, and rub the cooled mixture in roughly. Take about 3–4 oz. of this crumble pastry and roll it two or three times into a half-inch slab. Repeat, placing each slab upon the other: moisten the top of the pile before putting another slab of pastry on it. Press down firmly and cut down into several 3–4 oz. lumps. Repeat the rolling process twice more. Leave 30 minutes in a cold place. Cut into eight pieces. Squeeze each one into a sausage shape, and roll out to measure 4–6 inches. Leave to rest for an hour.

Trim tenderloin of fat and skin. Slice it lengthways into two halves and beat gently until they are $\frac{1}{4}$–$\frac{3}{8}$ inch thick. Cut the smoked pork, ham or bacon into 8 strips.

Make the cheese stuffing. Beat the egg, and put half of it aside. Mix in the cheese, parsley, salt and tabasco. Spread evenly over the two cut sides of the tenderloin. Roll each piece up, press down firmly, and leave in the icebox of a refrigerator to harden.

To assemble the oggies, cut each roll of tenderloin into 4 pieces. Wrap them round with a strip of smoked pork, ham or bacon. Lay each little parcel in the middle of a piece of pastry, which should be moistened round the edge with milk. Bring the pastry up and over the pork, pressing the two edges together in a scalloped crest, like a Cornish pasty. Press down to flatten the base, and trim where necessary. Brush over with the rest of the beaten egg and bake for 10 minutes at Mark 3–4, 325–350°F, until the pastry begins to brown. Finish in deep fat; or fry in lard, turning the oggies over until they are golden brown. Before cooking they can be stored in a refrigerator for 3 days, or in a deep-freeze for 3 months. In the latter case give them 15–20 minutes in the oven, before frying.

Sweet lamb pie, from North-West England

This recipe is based on one I heard during the war, when we were living at Casterton, in Westmorland. Our landlady was a farmer's daughter, and I remember her nostalgia when she described the pie she used to make, I think at Easter, before rationing, before the war. I remember, too, my childish, townbred disgust at the ingredients she listed – fat and lean mutton or lamb, sugar, currants . . . Similar recipes are found in Cumberland, and in Wales as well, where at Templeton Fair in November they şell Katt pies. These are small raised pies, filled with layers of minced Welsh mutton, brown sugar and currants – in equal quantities.

In fact such recipes belong to the days when everybody made sweet meat pies. In two fifteenth-century cookery books there is hardly a meat pie recipe that does not contain sugar, raisins and dates, not to mention prunes and ginger, all layered with veal or chicken or pork in 'coffins' of pastry. The predominantly sweet pies contain marrow and sometimes parsley. In some of these ancient recipes the sweetness was as mild as in the Devonshire squab pie on p. 75, or in the fidget pie which follows. In others – like this one – lamb or beef was so dominated by sweetness that it disappeared into a mixture we'd recognize as Christmas mincemeat:

shortcrust pastry, made with 1 lb. flour

filling:

1 lb. mutton or lamb, weighed without
    bones, half lean and half fat
¾–1 lb. apples
8 oz. each currants, raisins, sultanas
4 oz. candied peel
juice of 1 orange and 1 lemon
4 oz. blended almonds
¼ pint rum or brandy
½ teaspoon salt
freshly ground black pepper
teaspoon each mace, nutmeg,
    cinnamon (or more, to taste)

Mince lean and fat meat coarsely. Peel, core and grate the apples. Mix all the filling ingredients together, stirring well, and adding spices to taste. Use some of the mixture to make a double-crust pie (serve with single cream or a proper egg custard). Put the rest up in pots for Christmas, or the store cupboard.

Note: ½ lb. beef suet, and ½ lb. chuck or rump steak may be substituted for the lamb. Weigh without skin in the case of the suet, and without fat and skin in the case of the steak.

Fitchet, fidget or figet pie

Before the machine age, harvest brought to the farmer's wife her biggest problem of the year. She had to cope in hot, or at least warm, weather, with feeding her husband's army of reapers from the farm's resources five times a day. Cheese was the only 'convenience' food she could rely on with confidence (though cheese-making could go seriously wrong, too, before the chemistry of the business was properly understood). The autumn-cured bacon might have acquired 'a disagreeable rankness of Taste', it might have been spoilt by blowflies. Pork pickled in the late spring ran the risks of humidity and sudden changes of temperature. But with luck she was able to make a pie of this kind (a frugal version of the Cheshire pork and apple raised pie, p. 65) to be eaten hot at the harvest home.

> shortcrust pastry to cover
>
> *filling:*
> $\frac{3}{4}$ lb. green back rashers
> 1 lb. Cox's orange pippins, or cookers
> $\frac{1}{2}$ lb. onions, chopped
> 2 tablespoons stock or water
> salt, pepper and nutmeg
> sugar (see recipe)

Cut the bacon into $\frac{1}{4}$ inch dice, discarding the rind. Peel, core and slice the apples. Put bacon, apple and onion in layers into the pie dish, seasoning with salt, pepper and nutmeg (a little sugar should be sprinkled over the apples if they are very tart). Add the stock, and a lid of shortcrust pastry. Bake in the usual way for about 40 minutes; $\frac{1}{2}$ lb. very thinly sliced potatoes may be included, as in parts of Wales, but the flavour is better without them, I think.

Devonshire squab pie

The excellent flavour of this dish depends on using plenty of spices. Prunes are not always included, but I think they are important. How the pie got its name I don't know. I've tried, unsuccessfully, to find out: 'squab' meaning young pigeon, seems unsatisfactory, unless the pie was made with pigeons in the days of manorial dovecotes. But recipes for pigeon pies make no mention of apple and sugar. On the other hand, the recipe for pigeons and rice, on p. 116, does indicate a connection of a kind between the two – the pigeons are stewed in mutton broth. Perhaps there was felt to be a similarity between the two meats, so that the decidedly unmanorial cottager ennobled his mutton and apple pie with the name of 'squab'. Stories have been invented to explain the name, but they have no truth at all.

> shortcrust pastry to cover, made with
>   8 oz. flour (and ¼ lb. mutton fat, if
>   possible)
>
> *filling:*
>
> 1¼ lb. of lamb or mutton chops, or
>   2 lb. best end of neck
> 2 lb. Cox's orange pippins
> 2 medium onions, finely chopped
> 16 unsoaked prunes
> ¼ nutmeg, grated
> level teaspoon each mace, cinnamon
>   and salt
> freshly ground black pepper
> ¼ pint meat stock
> brown sugar

Cut meat off the bones, into slices. Trim away bits of skin or gristle, but not fat. Peel and core the apples, then slice them. Cut the prunes into pieces, discarding the stones.

Grease a pie dish. Arrange meat, apples and onion in layers, spicing each layer well and sprinkling a little brown sugar and prune pieces over apple layers (if you have to make use of

cookers, or windfalls, use more sugar). Add salt, pepper, stock and
a pastry lid. Bake at Mark 5, 375°F, for about an hour and a
quarter. Protect the crust with brown paper, if necessary. Eat this
pie with clotted cream, from Devonshire.

Salting Meat

England is covered with forgotten 'saltways' radiating from ancient salt pans on the coast or from the salt districts of Cheshire. Along them salt-merchants and trains of packhorses brought the salt that used to be needed in every household, to keep life going through the winter and spring. (The salt merchants, conveniently travelling on, became the heroes of Chaucerian episodes of love; poems recount how they outwitted watchful elderly husbands and satisfied young wives in all the bustle of a busy farm.) Cattle couldn't all be kept alive between autumn and summer, and had to be killed and salted. Mutton and fish were salted too, so was pork (think of the three little boys St Nicholas found in the wicked innkeeper's salt tub).

This was long-term salting. Short-term salting, in the 1970s, remains worthwhile for two reasons – it keeps meat on hand and ready to cook, and at no great cost or trouble it makes a difference to meat I find little short of miraculous. All cuts of pork, some of beef, and also such things as lamb and deep-frozen duckling are improved. And improvement is all the more necessary now that butchers are not hanging meat long enough to develop the flavour. Salting rescues the Sunday lunch.

If you use the brine recipe I give below, you won't find the meat salty so much as flavoured in a pleasant way. The texture will change slightly and for the better, and some of the grossness (especially of pork) will disappear. I would say that this pre-salting is the *sine qua non* for first-class pork cookery. Also for beef, pork or lamb you intend to eat cold.

Meat can also be cured by dry salting, but this needs more attention from the cook. It also takes longer to achieve a comparable result, brine penetrating the meat much more quickly than salt alone. The method was convenient when many hams were to be salted away – the Gauls used it for the famous hams they sent to Rome, and so did the Romans themselves.

Whichever method is used, all the home salter requires is a deep stoneware (not earthenware, which is too porous) vessel or plastic bucket, unrefined salt (preferably sea salt from health food stores), dark brown sugar, and saltpetre (from the chemist). Saltpetre is essential; it gives an appetizing rosy glow to meat, which the salting would otherwise make a dingy grey. The sugar counteracts the hardening effect of saltpetre.

In home conditions, in a cool larder, meat can be kept in brine for up to a fortnight or three weeks. Sometimes longer. The moment that islands of white mould begin to float on the surface, remove the meat and throw away the brine. The crock too will need washing with boiling soda water. The meat will be all right.

Brine

Bring to the boil:

> 7 pints water
> 1½ lb. sea or coarse salt
> 1 lb. dark brown sugar
> 2 oz. saltpetre
> 1 bay leaf

1 sprig thyme
10 crushed juniper berries
10 crushed peppercorns

Boil hard for 5 minutes. Leave to cool. Clean crock or bucket and lid with soda dissolved in boiling water, rinse well and leave to drain dry. Pour the cold brine in, through a muslin-lined strainer. Immerse the meat and keep it below the surface by laying a piece of boiled wood, or a scrupulously clean plate on top. Cover and keep in a dry place, at a temperature below 60°F. When removing pieces of meat from brine, always use clean metal tongs; this way the brine will stay good, and other pieces of meat can be put in to salt. Keep a separate pot for pork, beef and duck, etc.; they should never be salted together, or in brine which might contain the sediments of another meat. It is possible to strain off the brine, and reboil it adding a refresher of about half the above quantities. Naturally the crock or bucket will need a complete cleansing. This should be done before mould appears.

Salting time

Salting time depends on the thickness of the meat – pig's trotters are ready in 24 hours, a sizeable leg of pork can take about ten days. But don't worry. When salting is carried out to improve rather than to preserve meat, there is a certain amount of give and take over timing. Excess salt can always be corrected by soaking, or by changing the cooking water.

Note: joints required for roasting rather than boiling, will be improved by a 12-hour soak in brine, without tasting too salty.

> *Duck* (giblets removed): 36–48 hours
> *Pork* (leg, shoulder, loin): 3–10 days
> *Beef* (silverside, brisket): 7–10 days
> *Lamb, or, preferably, mutton*
>   (shoulder, leg, loin): 7–10 days

Salt duck

Remove from brine, rinse quickly under the cold tap and put into a deep pan. Cover the duck with half water, half dry cider, and add the giblets apart from the liver (which can be used up in a pâté). Put on the lid, or cover with foil, and cook 2 hours in a slow oven (Mark 3, 325°F) or until the bird is cooked.

If, as I do, you prefer cold duck, let it cool in the water-and-cider. Serve it with an orange and tomato salad, seasoned with sugar, salt and pepper, and dressed with wine vinegar and olive oil.

For hot duck, serve an onion sauce in the Welsh style:

> 1 lb. onions
> about 1 pint milk
> 1 oz. butter
> 1 oz. flour
> salt, pepper, nutmeg

Cook the sliced onions in enough milk to cover. When they are almost cooked, melt the butter in another pan, stir in the flour and cook for 2 minutes. Add ½ pint hot milk, stirring, until you have a smooth white sauce. Transfer to the onion pan. Simmer for 30 minutes, seasoning well with salt, pepper and nutmeg.

Picnic ham

Use a boned shoulder of ham, weighing up to 5 lb., and salted for 7–10 days. Remove from brine, rinse quickly, dry and weigh. Calculate cooking time at 30 minutes to the pound, plus 30 minutes. Tie the meat into a firm, sausage-like shape, using plenty of string.

Put the joint into a large pan with

> 2 onions, each stuck with 3 cloves
> 2 medium carrots, sliced

bouquet garni
8 crushed peppercorns
enough water to cover

Bring slowly to the boil. If the water tastes much too salty, drain it off and start again. Simmer on top of the stove or in the oven until the end of cooking time. Leave the meat until next day to cool in its liquid, putting a plate and a clean stone (or some tins) on top to press it lightly. Untie the joint, remove the skin and roll in hot toasted crumbs.

Glazed salt pork

Salt boned or unboned loin, shoulder or leg for 5–7 days. Follow cooking method for Picnic Ham above, but remove meat from pan 20 minutes before the end of cooking time. Remove the skin, which will peel off fairly easily, without removing the string.

Mix together:

1 tablespoon French mustard
1 tablespoon brown sugar
1 tablespoon double cream
1 teaspoon ground cloves, or cinnamon
2 oz. white breadcrumbs (optional)

Smear this paste over the salt pork fat; the joint should be placed in a roasting tin and put into a moderately hot oven to glaze for 20 minutes. Watch the heat – sugar catches quickly. Remove when it looks glazed and brown, to a warm serving dish.

Sauce can be made by stirring a ladleful of the simmering liquid into the juices left from glazing the meat. When this is bubbling nicely add some cream and/or Madeira or port to finish the sauce. Let it reduce a little, then correct the seasoning and strain into a hot sauceboat.

This is just one of many possible glazes. Others, using red-currant jelly or marmalade or apricot jam, etc., are easy to invent, but make sure there's a good balance of sharp – mustard, vinegar or lemon juice – to sweet.

Note: the liquid from boiling salt duck, pork and beef, makes excellent stock for soup.

Boiled beef and carrots

Boiled beef tastes much better and less dry if you lard it before cooking. This means drawing thin strips of bacon fat, or hard back fat, through the beef by means of a long open-ended larding needle. (As these needles only cost a few pence or so, it's worth buying one – steak, rabbit, hare, pheasant and pigeons and other lean meats are all improved by larding.)

A large joint of topside, silverside or brisket will benefit from 10 days salting in brine. Then cook it as for picnic ham above, putting 4 carrots into the pot instead of 2.

Serve hot with separately cooked glazed carrots, see p. 154, or red cabbage, or sauerkraut, and boiled potatoes.

To serve cold, cool the beef and press it like picnic ham; accompaniments are thinly sliced sweet-sour cucumber, sea salt and mustard, or horseradish sauce – mix 1 tablespoon grated horseradish into 3–4 oz. double cream, season with sugar, salt and lemon juice. A potato salad, dressed with an olive oil vinaigrette and plenty of parsley, chopped chives and shallot or mild onion, is also delicious with cold salt beef.

Salt beef sandwiches

Fourteen or fifteen years ago we often bought salt beef sandwiches at a Jewish restaurant at 114 Baker Street. They were the best sandwiches I've ever eaten. Thick slices of beef were cut off an immense steaming joint, slapped quickly between thick slices of rye bread, and handed out to us on the pavement.

Homemade beef sandwiches can never taste quite as good – to enjoy beef at its best, it must be cooked in huge joints – but it's worth following the restaurant's practice of making sandwiches

while the beef is still warm, and full of juice. If rye bread is unob-
tainable, the best substitute is a granary loaf. Unsalted butter and
horseradish or mustard can be spread on the slices of bread, but
all that's really required is hot beef and rye bread.

Salt mutton or lamb

Use a shoulder or leg; follow cooking instructions for picnic ham
above.

> *Serve hot* with caper sauce:
>
> 1 oz. butter
> 1 oz. flour
> ¾ pint hot milk
> 3 tablespoons double cream
> 1 tablespoon capers

Melt the butter, stir in the flour and cook for two or three
minutes. Add the hot milk gradually, until you have a smooth
béchamel sauce. Cook very gently for 30 minutes, stirring from
time to time, so that the sauce has a chance to develop a mellow
flavour. Stir in the cream, and at the very last moment the capers.
Correct the seasoning.

Serve cold (cool and press like picnic ham), sliced thin, with a
green salad and new potatoes.

Three recipes for dry salting:

The Hermit of Gower's salt duck

In 1867 Lady Llanover's *Good Cookery* appeared. More of a fic-
tionalized tract than a cookery book, it is interesting mainly for an
appendix of Welsh recipes. The mouthpiece for Lady Llanover's
ideas on diet (he could not be described as the hero) is an un-
lovable prig called the Hermit of Gower. He expounds his notions

– no butter for making the soup, no strong drink to keep harvesters going, etc. – to a Traveller from our corrupt world. Fortunately for the Traveller, the Hermit supports his opinions with some excellent dishes of which salt duck is, I think, the best:

> 1 duck
> ¼ lb. sea salt

Lay the duck in a dish in a cool place, and rub it over with the salt. Do this twice a day for three days, turning the duck over each time. Rinse the salt from the duck, put it into a deep pot, and add water almost to cover. Simmer for 2 hours in a moderate oven. Serve with onion sauce, see p. 80, or cold with a salad.

Welsh hams

In other words salted mutton hams. They were sold in London until nearly the end of the last century. Francatelli, in *The Cook's Guide* of 1880, gives a recipe for curing Welsh hams. Mutton hams were also made in Scotland to much the same recipe:

> 1 large leg of mutton cut into a ham shape
>
> For a 6 lb. joint:
>
> 4 oz. brown sugar
> 8 oz. sea or coarse salt
> ½ oz. saltpetre
> 1 oz. each black peppercorns and allspice
> ¼ oz. coriander seeds

Crush the spices, mix with salt, saltpetre and sugar. Rub the meat all over with this mixture and put into a deep covered dish. Leave in a cool place. Every day turn the ham and rub the mixture into it well. Leave for 12–14 days. With a larger joint the curing mixture must be increased proportionately, and it will take up to 14 days.

It can now be covered with cold water, brought to the boil and simmered gently for 2 hours. Cool under a weight (see picnic ham, p. 80).

In the old days, the uncooked joint would lie for 24 hours

under a weight. Then it would be smoked over oak sawdust for 15 days. 'In the Highlands,' says F. Marian McNeill in *The Scots Kitchen*, 'dried junipers are used in curing mutton-hams.'

Note: a leg of pork may be cured in the same way. But cook it in a covered pot with ¾ pint of water only. Turn the joint 4 times during cooking. 45–50 minutes per pound cooking time, Mark 1, 275°F.

Spiced salt beef

This used to be a great Christmas dish all over the British Isles, and recipes come from Scotland, Wales, Ireland and England. The curing mixture is almost exactly the same as for mutton hams above, but Elizabeth David adds juniper berries to the mixture itself, and has worked out an exact and successful method of cooking the joint:

> 5 or 6 lb. joint of silverside or round,
>   cut and tied for pickling
> 3 oz. brown sugar
> ¼ oz. saltpetre
> 4 oz. sea or kitchen salt
> 1 oz. black peppercorns
> ¼ oz. allspice berries
> 1 oz. juniper berries

First rub the beef all over with sugar. Leave it for 2 days in a deep pot. Crush the other pickling ingredients together, and rub the beef over every day for 9 days (11 in all). The salt and so on turns liquid, but continue to rub it into the meat just the same. Keep the dish covered. (A larger joint will need a proportionate increase in spices and in curing time – e.g. a 12 lb. joint will take 16 days in all.)

To cook the beef, rinse quickly to remove bits of spice. Put it into a close-fitting pot with about 8–10 oz. water. Cover the top of the meat with shredded suet to keep it moist during cooking time. Fix on the lid with two layers of greaseproof paper or foil, so that the juices cannot evaporate. Bake in a very low oven, Mark 1, 275° F, for 45–50 minutes per pound. Leave in the pot to cool undisturbed for 2 or 3 hours. Then remove it to a board (drain off all the fatty liquid first), cover it completely with greaseproof paper and put a 2–4 lb. weight on top. Leave for 24 hours. Serve with horseradish sauce, see p. 82, and a green salad, or diced avocado pears with a vinaigrette, and wholemeal bread and butter or jacket potatoes.

Quick spiced beef

Some butchers, and good grocers such as Sainsbury's, sell joints of beef which has been so lightly salted that it needs no soaking. It can be turned into the most delicious spiced beef with very little trouble. An ideal summer dish.

For a 2 lb. piece of salt beef, mix up the following ingredients:

> 2 heaped tablespoons brown sugar
> 1 rounded dessertspoon juniper berries, crushed
> 1 rounded dessertspoon peppercorns, crushed
> 1 heaped teaspoon allspice berries, crushed

Put half in the base of a deep dish. Place the beef on it and scatter the rest of the spice mixture thickly on top, rubbing and pressing it in. Cover the dish and leave for 3–7 days in the refrigerator. Scrape off the spices and sugar, and cook and press the beef as in the recipe above.

The spices can be varied to your own taste. Sometimes I use ground cumin and coriander seeds instead of allspice berries.

Snails

When we first went to stay in France, I was amazed to see the village come alive on wet summer and autumn evenings. As the rain grew steadier, the paths of the steep cliff – the houses are layered up and into this cliff – attracted more and more people, old men and children mostly. Wrapped to pear shapes in sacking and plastic, they peered into bushes and walls. In their hands, they carried sticks and those openwork globes of metal normally used for draining salad greens. The snail hunters were out.

Soon converted by the shared and savoury results, I never go out now without keeping my eyes firmly on the crevices of the lane. Returning at night to the garden, I see in the beam of the torch snail after snail moving majestically up the mint plants, or over the wet gravel. When in England, I hear the tap-tap-tap-tap on the paving stones outside the window, I try to startle the thrush into dropping its prey before the shell is broken.

The snail hunter's aim – and occasional prize – is the 'gros Bourgogne', *Helix pomatia*, the apple or vine snail, which can

measure 2 inches. This beautiful brown and white creature flourishes in local patches of chalk and limestone country in southern
England, and is known here as the Roman snail. In spite of its
name, *Helix pomatia* was not introduced by the Romans: it was
here to welcome Julius Caesar when he first set his standard on
the Pevensey coast. Its most famous habitat is Burgundy, where it
may be found in the vines, but more likely in *escargotières*, miniature snail farms which supply the Paris market. (The casual
hunter is not likely to be very successful, though things are not as
bad in Burgundy as in Neuchâtel in Switzerland where a licence
is now required; it's feared that snails may become extinct without these alarming precautions.) Burgundian cooks invented the
best way of dressing snails. They send them to table on specially
dimpled dishes of pottery, pyrex or metal, sizzling by the dozen in
garlic and parsley butter. A great treat.

Local savants, though, in our less opulent Touraine, claim that
the Bourgogne's close relative, *Helix aspersa*, the common garden
snail, or 'petit-gris' has a better flavour. They say, too, that it's
less inclined to toughness. I cannot judge between the two in this
respect, as I've never cooked or had the good fortune to find
Roman snails. And I can't often afford to eat them in restaurants,
either. But I do notice that recipe books give a three hour cooking
time for Roman snails, whereas the common garden snail takes
about 40 minutes only. So local opinion may be right, as size alone
would not account for the difference.

Helix aspersa is the snail you're most likely to find in your
garden in England. Its markings are dark grey and brown, less
glamorous than the Roman markings; the shell is about an inch
across. It seems to have a decided penchant for walls and hard
surfaces – in Bristol snails used to be sold as 'wall-fish' – and I
often find a dozen or 18 of them crawling about the porch and
doorstep at night.

The real devotee may profitably imitate the French *escargotière*, the snail enclosure, or snail bank if you like, into
which one deposits one's find, and from which one draws a festive
dozen or two or three for special occasions.

The most unusual *escargotière* I've ever seen was about 6
yards in from the mouth of a large cave used as a general store. It
consisted of a circle about 4 feet in diameter, of wood ash, with a
square concrete pillar sticking up in the middle like a lingam (to

give the snails exercise, the farmer explained). The wood ash kept them from wandering off, without the necessity of a closed-meshed wire roof. In the middle were plenty of cabbage leaves, and some thyme to improve their flavour. Naturally this is only suitable under cover, as rain would wash the wood ash away.

For temporary use a bucket does very well. Pierce it with small air holes, and weight the lid down – it's amazing how much lifting power a determined batch of snails can muster. Feed them with rosemary, thyme, lettuce. The idea is not only to make a collection, but also to give the snails ten days or a fortnight to get rid of any poisonous plants they may have eaten.

Or so it's said. One friend of ours – now seventy – maintains that this is nonsense, that he's eaten snails all his life without leaving them to fast. And without feeding them on flour or bran or cabbage leaves. He also pooh-poohs the idea that snails taken from hibernation are best. Too thin, he says, no good at all.

The French think we're odd about snails. 'To the Anglo-Saxon, the snail represents a curious French gastronomic habit,' says a recent article in a cookery periodical. But seeing that snails are on sale in tins, with accompanying bags of Roman shells, in quite unadventurous towns, places that no one could possibly regard as swinging or avant garde, I think the French are out of date. These tinned delicatessen snails may be the result of our modern travelling habits, but I suspect that the habit of eating snails, in some parts of Britain at least, has never quite died out, though it is much diminished in the last hundred years. Once glassblowers and glassmakers in Newcastle and Bristol used to consume them in quantity. They believed that the bubbly juice soothed their over-tired lungs. This was not superstition, but the survival of a medical opinion voiced as long ago as Pliny, and still maintained in the nineteenth century. Doctors had for centuries forced decoctions of snails (sometimes mixed with earthworms) on delicate children and chesty patients. As late as the 1880s Francatelli, the royal chef, gave a recipe for 'Mucilaginous Broth' in *The Cook's Guide*. It included chicken, crayfish and a pint of snails. 'This,' he said, 'is a powerful demulcent' – i.e. soother and loosener – 'and is much in use in France, in cases of phthisis, catarrh, bronchitis, etc.'

Less scrupulous dairymen of the time put these foaming gastropods to another use. They'd beat them up with milk and pass the thick result off as cream. Oh happy days, when business initiative and individual enterprise flourished, before food adulteration laws spoilt the fun.

Whether we eat snails in England now, or whether we don't, they've been part of Europe's diet since prehistoric times. They've been eaten because they were there, and free for the gathering, and not poisonous. For thousands of years the poor have been grateful for them, and the rich resourceful with them.

The habit has been dropped here very largely, I suspect, because we became more widely prosperous than the rest of Europe at an early stage. We've been able to buy easily prepared food for a long time; our low meat prices have appalled the rest of Europe for two centuries (pampered working classes of Britain). We've also suffered the defects of our eager adaptability in the almost complete loss of regional cooking. It's very noticeable in France, which is by no means a classless society or a particularly democratic one except in the narrowest sense of the word, that wealthy and poor in the same area eat the same food. All the grocers, for instance, are selling the same range of things whether they're supermarkets or family businesses. The wealthy eat more good things than the poor, and less bread, but their ideas of a good meal for a celebration are similar. Asparagus, ceps, morels and other mushrooms of the wood, oysters, squid, wine of quality and snails are consumed by everyone in our area. A contrast to England, where it seems that eating and drinking habits vary according to social class – we even give different names to our meals, or some of them, and eat them at different times. This the French would find even odder than our supposed antagonism towards snails.

Preparation

Having left your snails for a week, as a prudent measure, put them into a large bowl or bucket of water with a handful of coarse cooking salt. Leave them for half an hour, then put on rubber gloves and swirl the water and snails about until the juice of the snails begins noticeably to thicken the water. Throw the water away, and repeat four or five times, until the water is absolutely clear.

Meanwhile make a *court-bouillon*, of half water and half wine, about 1¾ pints of each (the very luxurious use champagne, but I think that supermarket wine is perfectly adequate, white or red), an onion, carrot, bouquet garni, peppercorns and other aromatics. Let it simmer for an hour, covered, then strain into a clean large pan. When cool, add the snails and bring slowly to the boil. Simmer for 3 hours (Roman snails) or for 40 minutes (garden snails).

Take them from the *bouillon*, and, using a needle stuck eye-end into a cork, remove each snail from its shell, discarding the hard round 'door' and the little black bit at the opposite end.

Now they are ready for various treatments.

Matelote of snails (1 dozen snails per person)

Use red wine for the *bouillon*. When the snails are cooked, remove them and reduce the *bouillon* by hard boiling until you have 1½ pints. Fork together a good ounce of butter and an ounce of flour, and divide it in little bits. Add to the *bouillon* stirring all the time, until it thickens. Put in the snails – without their shells – to re-heat gently for 20 minutes. Serve with triangles of fried bread, and a good sprinkling of parsley.

Snail soup (9 snails per person)

Use white wine (or chicken stock plus 2 tbspns wine vinegar) for the *court-bouillon*. Remove the snails when cooked and reduce the liquid to about 2½ pints. Meanwhile melt 1 oz. of butter in a pan, stir in 1 oz. of flour, and add the reduced snail liquid slowly. Simmer uncovered for 15 minutes, add the snails and simmer for 5 minutes.

In a bowl, beat up 2 egg yolks and the juice of a lemon. Pour on a ladle of soup, beat well and return to the pan. Don't allow the soup to boil. Serve with a good sprinkling of parsley, and croûtons.

Escargots farcis à la bourguignonne

Allow 1 dozen snails per person. Prepare them in a *court-bouillon*, as above, using white wine, and adding 2 large cloves of garlic to the aromatics. Stuff with snail butter, as follows (for 6 dozen snails):

> 1 lb. butter unsalted
> 1 large bunch parsley, chopped
> 2 oz. finely chopped shallot, or
>   mild onion
> 5 large cloves garlic
> 5 teaspoons salt
> 1 teaspoon freshly ground black pepper

Soften the butter in a slightly warm basin, with a wooden spoon (or with an electric beater). Crush the garlic to a cream with the salt. Mix everything together well.

Put a little butter into each empty snail shell (it's sensible to wash them under the hot tap first), then the snail, and pack in some more butter until it's level with the rim of the shell.

Dispose the stuffed snails on specially dinted snail plates. Or else cut slices of bread, half an inch thick, horizontally across a large loaf: in each slice, cut out 12 holes with an apple corer. Put these slices on a buttered baking tray, and rest the snails in the holes. Apart from the extra trouble required, this is a better system than snail plates, because the butter bubbles over and is efficiently soaked up by the bread, which can afterwards be eaten.

Sprinkle the snails with fine breadcrumbs, and put into a moderately hot oven, Mark 5, 375°F, until they are well heated through, brown and bubbling.

If you are making use of tinned snails for this recipe, very little salt will be required for the butter as they are well salted already.

Although this is the classic butter for stuffed snails, variations of flavour are worth trying. In parts of France aniseed, fennel or thyme provides a dominant flavour. Lemon juice and spices such as nutmeg are also popular. In his *Edible Molluscs* M. S. Lovell describes a delicious preparation of stuffed snails: 'A fine stuffing is made with snails previously cooked, fillets of anchovies, nutmeg, spice, fine herbs and a liaison of yolk of eggs. The snail-shells are filled with this stuffing, then placed before the fire,' – nowadays in the oven – 'and served *very* hot.'*

If you are likely to eat stuffed snails regularly, it's worth investing in snail tongs and forks (as well as in snail plates). One can manage quite efficiently, though, with a pile of paper napkins, and a set of needles stuck into corks.

Escargots à la grand'mère

An unusual recipe from a French periodical. Very good.

> 4 dozen prepared snails
> 2 tablespoons olive oil
> 3 oz. lean bacon, diced
> 3 oz. cooked ham, diced
> 3–5 anchovy fillets, crushed
> 4 oz. shelled walnuts, finely chopped
> 2 large cloves garlic, crushed
> bunch of parsley, chopped
> 1 large teaspoon flour
> 1 heaped tablespoon fine breadcrumbs
> 1 oz. butter
> salt, black pepper

Brown lightly in the oil the bacon and ham. Add nuts, anchovies, garlic and parsley. Stir in the flour and cook for a moment or two. Add a bare half pint of water (if canned snails are used), or of snail *bouillon*. Season. Simmer for 10 minutes, until the sauce has thickened a little. Put in the snails and simmer for about half an hour. Correct the seasoning. Divide the mixture between individual bowls and keep warm. Brown the crumbs lightly in the butter, sprinkle on top of the bowls and serve hot and bubbling.

*M. S. Lovell: *Edible Molluscs of Great Britain and Ireland*, Reeve & Co., 1857.

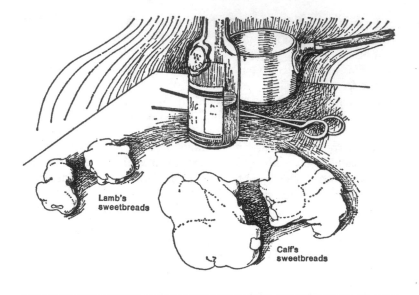

Lamb's
sweetbreads

Calf's
sweetbreads

Sweetbreads

I particularly like sweetbreads, either calf's or lamb's – it doesn't matter which. Although they may come deep-frozen from New Zealand at only 25p or 30p a lb, and although they are served as greyish-white lumps in a floury sauce by hospital cooks, I persist in regarding them as a luxury. They're delicate food, to be treated with ceremony, to be given to friends at dinner, to the family at some small domestic feast.

To start with, the name is charming: sweet describes their flavour well, and the round heart sweetbread of the calf looks like a nice round bun. Did some poetical butcher think of the name in the sixteenth century, when it was first recorded? It's unusually gracious for such a realistic trade (think of mudgeon, crow, tripe, shin, hock or ham – the only one that comes anywhere near sweetbread in feeling is tenderloin). In fact sweetbreads are the thymus gland of the animal, and the pancreas (the one that cooks prefer, for its convenient shape). They are known respectively as the throat and heart sweetbreads. One could not, I think, make a distinction in flavour between the two, or between lamb's and calf's sweetbreads.

Sweetbreads have often kept illustrious company (there is, after all, only one set to each carcase). They have made their appearance at most great European banquets of recent centuries. Along with cocks' combs, truffles, and other expensive bits and pieces, they've been threaded on ornamental skewers, or arranged in little piles around some grand centrepiece.

Who ate this delicious garniture? I feel sure it wasn't always the guests. One of the greatest of all cooks, Carême, castigated those mean rich men who want to make a show – without spending too much money. Their chefs were compelled to present the identical centrepieces at dinner after dinner, and their footmen had to make sure that visitors were served from the less important dishes on the table. Economy on the grand scale. For the first few days I expect the kitchen boys picked at the alternating piles of sweetbreads and truffles, white beside black, then rearranged them to deceive the master's eye with a dab of jelly or coating sauce.

Cooks in less princely circumstances often put sweetbreads into poultry stuffing. They would pattern a forcemeat (like the one in the sweetbread pie described later) with diced sweetbread, tongue and ham, and pistachio nuts, to make a good effect when the galantine was sliced. Families in comfortable middle-class homes probably had the best of the sweetbreads, as we do now. They ate them as a course on their own, set off to advantage by a well-made sauce or a single vegetable: sweetbreads with young peas, sweetbreads creamed and scalloped, sweetbreads with a mushroom and cream sauce, or an oyster and cream sauce, sweetbreads wrapped in fat bacon and cooked on a spit in front of a lively kitchen fire.

One thing: if you are using an old recipe, or a modern French or Italian one, you'll find that sweetbreads, after their initial preparation, are sometimes baked or braised in the oven for about 30 minutes. This is because the large calf's sweetbreads are intended. Lamb's sweetbreads (for many of us the only ones available) are tiny by comparison and they need no more than the brief cooking I've indicated in the recipes. The same applies to calf's sweetbreads, if they're sliced up.

Another problem. Some recipes specify 'a pair' of sweetbreads, i.e. the throat and heart sweetbread. This is muddling. A pair can vary so in weight from two to the pound in England, to one pair – or less – in France. I recently bought a pair weighing 1 lb. 6 oz. in the small butcher's shop in our Touraine village. These are things to be borne in mind. I've stuck to measurements of weight, and allowed 4–6 oz. per person to the recipe.

Preparation

Whatever size, weight or type of sweetbreads you are dealing with, the initial stages are always the same. It sounds laborious, but it isn't really. The various stages needn't be timed exactly – fit them in with your other activities. Never be tempted to skimp the preparation, whatever any recipe book may indicate. If you do, you'll end up with a rubbery, inedible mass.

Soak the sweetbreads in a bowl of cold water with a handful of salt for at least one hour, preferably three, or even longer if they are frozen solid. This removes traces of blood, and any bits and pieces that shouldn't be there. Drain them, rinse them and put into a saucepan. Now, cover with water, or chicken, veal or vegetable stock and a dessertspoonful of wine vinegar or lemon juice. (Even if the dish does not require a sauce, it's worth using stock rather than water if you can: it acquires gelatine from the sweetbreads and will make beautiful soup or sauce for another meal.)

Bring to the boil slowly and simmer until the sweetbreads become firm and white, losing their raw pinkish look – 2 minutes for lamb's sweetbreads, up to 10 minutes for calf's. Don't overcook them. Strain off the liquid, run the sweetbreads under the cold tap and remove hard bits, tubes etc., as soon as they're cool enough to handle. Be careful not to take off too much of the transparent elastic skin that holds the sweetbreads together.

Put them between two boards, or plates, with a light weight on top. Leave for 1–2 hours in a cool place, or overnight in the refrigerator.

Sweetbreads in the English style (for 4)

Carême, who cooked for Talleyrand, Napoleon, the Rothschilds, and the Tsar of Russia, spent some time with the Prince Regent. He was amazed at the sumptuous china and furnishings of the royal household at Brighton and London; he got on well with the appreciative Prince; but in the end he returned to France, driven away from England by fogs, loneliness and the lack of conversation. However he'd come to admire quite a lot of food in our country, including the beef, a number of puddings, and seakale. In his great books on cookery, English recipes were included (and so were some of the lavish dishes he himself invented for the Prince Regent). Here's a simplified version of sweetbreads à l'anglaise, from his *Art of French Cookery in the 19th Century.*

> 1 lb. prepared sweetbreads
> 8 oz. very thinly cut smoked bacon
> 3 oz. breadcrumbs
> 2 oz. butter
> bread sauce

Cut the sweetbreads into thickish slices, suitable for threading on skewers. Remove rind from bacon, and stretch the rashers. Put them into pieces and wrap round the slices of sweetbread. Divide between four skewers.

Prepare the bread sauce in the usual way, and leave it simmering over a pan of hot water, while you grill the sweetbread and bacon skewers, under a medium heat. About 10–15 minutes. Meanwhile brown the crumbs in the butter. When the skewers are cooked, roll them firmly in the breadcrumbs and arrange on a serving dish, with the remaining crumbs scattered over them. Serve immediately, with the bread sauce separately in a sauce boat. This is most delicious.

Sweetbreads in the Italian style (for 4)

The Italians have a good way of cooking delicate pieces of lean meat such as turkey or chicken breasts, or poultry livers, or sweetbreads. The system is to brown them lightly in butter, then to stew them for a little with marsala until they are glazed and succulent. The result is delectable, sharply stimulating to the appetite, but not in the least heavy.

> 1 lb. prepared sweetbreads
> 4 thin slices lean smoked bacon, or, more correctly,
>   Italian *prosciutto*
> 6 fresh sage leaves (1 teaspoon dried sage)
> 3 oz. butter
> scant ¼ pint marsala (or madeira, port,
>   brown sherry)
> 4 large croûtons of bread, fried in butter

Divide the sweetbreads into nuggets. Cut the bacon into matchstick strips, discarding the rind. Snip the sage into tiny pieces with scissors. Fry the sweetbreads in butter quickly until they begin to brown (be careful not to burn the butter) with the sage. Add the bacon and cook for another 2 or 3 minutes. Pour in some of the marsala, and, as it boils down, add some more, and so on until it's used up. This takes about 10 minutes, and the heat should be turned up to evaporate the wine. Turn the sweetbreads over and over all the time, to acquire a brown, syrupy glaze. Serve them on the croûtons of bread, with the small amount of sauce left in the pan poured over them.

Sweetbreads à la Castillane (for 6)

The French way of cooking sweetbreads produces a richer result, with more sauce. The usual accompaniment is mushrooms, but in this recipe (which I've adapted from one given to me in Tours) the sweetbreads sit on a purée of apple and banana. Out of the ordinary and very good.

1½–2 lb. prepared sweetbreads
4 small, very ripe bananas
4 medium eating apples
4 oz. butter
4 oz. double cream
liqueur glass cognac
lemon juice, salt, pepper, sugar

Slice the sweetbreads into pieces about ½ inch thick. Cut up the apples and stew them in 2 oz of butter in a covered pan; sieve them and throw away remains of peel and core. Mash the bananas thoroughly and mix them with the apple purée. Sweeten if necessary, and add a little lemon juice – very good apples and scented bananas will need hardly any additions. Keep the purée warm. Brown the sweetbreads in the rest of the butter; pour in about ¼ to ½ a pint of their cooking liquor little by little, so that it reduces to a rich glaze on the sweetbreads (see preceding recipe). Arrange the sweetbreads on the fruit purée, swill the pan juices round with the cognac and scrape all the nice brown bits into the sauce as it bubbles. Stir in the cream and cook gently for a few moments. Season this smooth rich mixture with salt, pepper and lemon juice to taste, pour over the sweetbreads and serve immediately. Boiled rice is a good accompaniment.

Sweetbread pie or pâté (for 6 to 8)

On a recent trip into Burgundy, we visited the town of Avallon, not far from Vézelay. After looking at the carved portal of the church, we wandered down the small main street in search of picnic food. As we waited to be served in the *charcuterie*, we gazed at the wonderful display, at the puff pastry pies slashed and shaped like an Elizabethan hat, at the hunks of farm-made butter, at the many sausages and hams – and then, with astonishment, at the pâtés. The cheapest was 22 francs the kilo, and the most expensive – a sweetbread pâté – bore a ticket marked 44 francs (in English terms £1 for 8oz.). How, I wondered, could the burghers of this small town of about 7,000 inhabitants, pay such prices? Even if some of them do happen to be prosperous biscuit manufacturers? The pâté didn't look at all as if it was made once a year, and dusted off daily, for show only. I still haven't worked out the answer, and we bought brawn. But I've a new respect for this recipe:

Shortcrust pastry:

12 oz. flour
6 oz. butter and lard mixed
rounded tablespoon icing sugar
water to bind

filling:

1 lb. prepared sweetbreads
¾ lb. lean pork, or veal and pork mixed
½ lb. hard back pork fat
2 rashers green back bacon
2 large eggs
heaped tablespoon flour
4 oz. mushrooms, roughly chopped
2 tablespoons onion, finely chopped
1 clove garlic, crushed
4 oz. cream, double or single
3 oz. butter
salt, pepper, thyme

Make the pastry in the usual way. Separate the sweetbreads into neat, even-sized pieces. Make a forcemeat by mincing the pork and bacon, first coarsely, then finely. Add beaten eggs, flour and cream. Cook mushrooms, onion and garlic in the butter slowly for 15 minutes. Mix into meat and season well.

Line a 2 pint capacity loaf tin with the pastry, keeping aside enough for the lid. Lay in about a third of the forcemeat; arrange half the sweetbreads on top in two parallel rows. Use another third of the forcemeat to tuck round and over the sweetbreads. Arrange the rest of the sweetbreads on top in the same way, and cover them with the last of the forcemeat. Mound it up nicely above the height of the loaf tin, to support the pastry lid. Moisten the pastry rim, lay on the lid and finish in the usual way, brushing finally with an egg-yolk and water glaze, or with the top of the milk. Decorate with leaves, and roses, etc. Bake for an hour and a half in a moderately hot oven (protect the lid with greaseproof paper, when it gets brown). Eat warm.

If you decide to make a pâté, rather than a pie, omit the pastry. Cover with a double layer of silver foil, removing it for the last 20 minutes of cooking time to brown the top. Cool under a light weight overnight.

Bouchées à la reine (for 6)

If you have to stretch a few sweetbreads (or use some left over from another meal), make these *bouchées à la reine*, which have no hint of frugality about them. Cold chicken is the meat often used, but I've noticed that sweetbreads are usually included. Sometimes they're the only meat used. These *bouchées*, these queenly mouthfuls, were named for Marie Leszczinska, gourmet daughter of Stanislaus Leszczinsky, King of Poland, and wife of Louis XV of France.

Should you feel disinclined to make puff pastry, bake shortcrust tartlets instead, or one large pastry case. Alternatively 2-inch thick slices of bread can be deep-fried (cut the crusts off, and hollow out the middle part to contain the sweetbreads first). The filling can be put into scallop shells or small pots, covered with buttered crumbs and set in a hot oven, or under the grill, until browned and bubbling. None of these will be *bouchées à la reine*, but they'll be appetizing all the same.

> 12 baked vol-au-vent cases, or 1 large puff
>   pastry case baked blind
> 10 oz. diced, prepared sweetbreads, or mixed
>   sweetbreads and chicken
> 1 oz. butter
> heaped tablespoon flour
> ½ pint sweetbread cooking liquor, hot
> ¼ pint hot milk
> ¼ pint double cream
> 6 oz. mushrooms, sliced thinly
> salt, pepper, lemon juice

Melt butter, stir in flour and cook for 2 minutes. Gradually incorporate sweetbread liquor and milk. Simmer this sauce until it's reduced to a thick consistency. Add the mushrooms, and cook for another 10 minutes, then add the cream. Simmer again until the sauce is thick without being gluey. Season well with salt, pepper and lemon juice. Reheat the sweetbreads, or sweetbreads and chicken, in the sauce carefully so that they don't disintegrate. Be sure to bring it to the boil, then simmer for 5 minutes.

Meanwhile put the vol-au-vent cases into the oven to heat up. Arrange them on a serving dish and pour in the filling. Replace the lids and serve immediately.

Sweetbreads with oysters (for 4)

This American recipe is in the old European tradition of oysters with meat, from the days when oysters were a poor man's food and able to be used as a seasoning.

> 1 lb. prepared sweetbreads
> 2 tablespoons flour
> ½ teaspoon paprika
> 1 oz. butter
> ¼ pint double cream
> 2–3 dozen oysters with their liquor
> salt and mace to taste
> 3 tablespoons dry sherry

Divide the sweetbreads into small pieces. Roll them in the flour and paprika mixed together, then fry them in the butter until they're a nice golden brown. Pour in the cream and make a sauce by stirring it well into the pan juices. Add the oysters and their liquor; when the edges begin to curl up the dish is ready. Season with salt, mace and sherry to taste.

Serve with triangles of bread fried in butter.

Rabbit and Hare

Rabbit, or at any rate wild rabbit, needn't be so much undervalued as a poor relation of the hare. Rabbit was introduced late in the twelfth century from Norman France as rather a lordly meat, raised not in hutches in the modern European back-yard style, but in long artificial mounded burrows or conygers, which, like the dovecot, formed part of the perquisite of the lord of the manor. The rabbits flourished and escaped to provide, in due time, and up to myxomatosis 18 years ago, some of the only meat regularly eaten by the poor.

The hare has always been game, not an adjunct of feudal economy, and highly regarded as a richly flavoured food. That's really the difference – the hare rich and gamey in flavour, the rabbit (good wild rabbit) fresh and succulent. The hare makes one think of port, burgundy, redcurrant jelly, spices and cream; the rabbit needs onions, mustard, white wine, dry cider and thyme.

Every year wild rabbits increase, though there is little hope that they will ever again be sold at low pre-myxomatosis prices. But they are still cheap. And so is hare, which can provide two or three dishes for a family of four. Ask the poulterer to hang hare for at least three days (longer hanging time depends on taste and humidity, ten days being in our climate the maximum), and to save its blood, to which a few drops of vinegar should be added to prevent it coagulating. The poulterer will also skin and joint both animals, and split the head.

A number of recipes can be used interchangeably for both creatures. For instance rabbit can be jugged or turned into a civet. Hare is delicious cooked in the sweet-sour style (recipes below). A point to notice is that extra fat often needs to be added when cooking hare and rabbit, as they both have dry-textured meat. Cubes of fat bacon are often used, slices of pork belly, hard back fat tied round the joints jacket-fashion, or introduced into the meat as strips, with a larding needle.

Rabbit with mustard

This is one of the best meat dishes I know for piquant contrast of flavours. For four people, you need the saddle cut in two, and the hindquarters. The forequarters and head can be used for soup, or a pâté. You will also need:

> 1½ lb. pork belly
> 3 medium carrots, chopped
> ½–¾ lb. chopped onions
> 1 tablespoon thyme, or wild thyme
> 1 bay leaf
> 1 tablespoon chopped parsley
> 1 large clove garlic, crushed
> ¼ pint dry white wine (or chicken stock
>   plus dessertspoon wine vinegar)
> 2 liqueur glasses brandy
> 1 egg yolk
> 1 tablespoon Dijon mustard
> 3 tablespoons double cream
> Extra parsley to garnish, salt, black pepper

Skin, bone and slice pork. Mix carrot, onion, garlic and herbs. Lay half the pork in a casserole, then half the vegetable mixture. Season well. Add the rabbit, then the rest of the vegetables, then the rest of the pork. Season. Lay the pork skin on top. Pour over wine and brandy, cover tightly and cook in a slow oven, Mark 2, 300°F, for 2½–3 hours, until the rabbit is tender. Arrange meat and vegetables, well drained, on a serving dish, and keep them warm. Skim fat off the cooking juices. Beat yolk and cream together, add the skimmed juices and cook gently. Stir this sauce well, but don't let it boil. When it's thick, add the mustard. Pour over the rabbit, etc., sprinkle with parsley, and serve with some plainly boiled potatoes.

Young rabbit with chives

Although this French recipe is intended for domestic rabbit, it can be used most successfully with young wild rabbit. But be sure it's young. Older rabbits need the slow stewing of the recipe above.

> 1 rabbit, jointed, or 3 lb. rabbit joints
> seasoned flour
> 2 oz. butter
> ¼ pint chicken or veal stock
> liqueur glass Calvados or brandy
> 6 oz. cream
> thick bunch chives
> 16 small onions
> salt, black pepper, Cayenne pepper

Cut the hind legs of the rabbit into two joints. Turn all the rabbit pieces in seasoned flour, and fry to golden brown in butter. Use a large heavy frying pan, cast-iron is best. Warm the Calvados or brandy, set light to it and pour over the rabbit, turning the pieces about in the flames. Add the onions, giving them a few moments to colour slightly in the pan juices. Stir in the stock, cover the pan (silver foil will do, if it has no lid) and simmer for 40 minutes or until the rabbit is cooked. Remove meat and onions to a warm serving dish. Reduce the liquid in the pan by boiling it down, then stir in the cream. After a few moments' bubbling, the sauce will have thickened nicely. Add salt and pepper if required; then a pinch of Cayenne pepper and the chives snipped into tiny pieces. Pour the boiling sauce over the rabbit and onions and serve.

Note: chicken can be substituted for rabbit, and tarragon for the chives. Add a teaspoon of tarragon to the pan with the stock.

Rabbit with mushrooms

Wild rabbit and wild mushrooms – ceps, horns of plenty or field mushrooms – make a fine combination in this Breton dish. It's worth making the effort to find out where fungi grow in your area, as they are often allowed to rot by the thousand in English woods. All those wonderful flavours entirely wasted (see p. 198).

> 1–2 lb. mushrooms (or 1 lb. cultivated mushrooms)
> 1 rabbit, jointed
> seasoned flour
> 3 oz. butter
> ½ lb. streaky bacon, cubed
> ½ lb. chopped onions
> large glass dry white wine, or cider
> bouquet garni
> 1 large clove garlic, crushed
> beef stock
> extra parsley to garnish
> triangles of toast or fried bread

To prepare mushrooms: cut off the earthy parts, then rinse them quickly under the cold tap. With ceps, remove the spongy under-layer of tubes from the cap, unless they are very young, and cut out the wormy bits. Slice all mushrooms except horns of plenty. If you wish to use dried ceps, follow the soaking instructions on the packet – i.e. about 20 minutes in plenty of hot water.

Brown bacon, rabbit rolled in seasoned flour, and onions in the butter. Transfer to casserole with mushrooms, bouquet garni, wine and garlic. Pour ½ pint stock into the frying pan, bring to the boil, scraping in all the little brown bits. Pour over rabbit. Add more stock to cover, if necessary. Simmer gently, Mark 2, 300°F, until cooked. Strain off liquid, and reduce by boiling until the taste is well concentrated. Pour over rabbit and mushrooms, sprinkle with chopped parsley and serve with toast or fried bread.

Rabbit rillettes

This light-textured form of potted meat will keep for months in a cool place. Serve it as an hors d'œuvre, accompanied by good bread and sea salt, or as a teatime snack for children. The true basis of *rillettes* is pork, but rabbit, goose, pigeon, duck or turkey are often added for variety.

> 2 lb. rabbit joints
> 1½ lb. pork belly
> ¾ lb. hard back fat
> nutmeg, cinnamon, black pepper, salt
> good sprig thyme
> lard

Cut pork and pork fat into 1½-inch cubes. Put into a heavy-bottomed pan with the rabbit and thyme, and a ladle of water. Cook, covered, over a low heat or in a low oven, Mark 1, 290°F, for four hours, or until the meat falls off the bones. Pour contents of the pan into a large strainer set over a bowl. Remove bones, pork skin and thyme stalks. Crush the meat with a pestle, then tear it into shreds with a couple of forks. This demands a little patience. One shortcut is to drop the meat on the whirling blades of a liquidizer, but it must not be pulverised to sludge. (Whatever you do, *don't mince it*.) The final result should be unctuous and thready. Season the meat generously with spices, add some of the strained fat and juices, but be discreet or the *rillettes* will congeal too solidly as they cool. Re heat to boiling point, add salt to taste, and pack into sterilized bottling jars or stoneware *rillettes* mugs (from Elizabeth David Ltd, 46 Bourne Street, S.W.1, and branches of Habitat). Cool. Cover with ½ inch melted lard, then with jam pot covers or cooking film. Keep in a refrigerator if possible.

Hannah Glasse's rabbit casserole with orange

A good recipe to try when Seville oranges come into the shops
after Christmas. The bitter-sweet flavour goes well with wild
rabbit:

> 1 rabbit, jointed
> seasoned flour
> 3 oz. butter or lard
> ¼ pint dry white wine
> beef stock
> pepper, salt
> bouquet garni
> 1 oz. butter
> 1 tablespoon flour
> juice of 1 Seville orange
> 2 Seville oranges

If the rabbit is on the mature side, it's prudent to lard it (see Hare
with cream in the German style, p. 110). Turn the joints in
seasoned flour and brown lightly in the butter or lard. Put into a
casserole (Hannah Glasse advises an 'earthenware Pipkin'), and
add the wine and enough stock just to cover the meat. Season
with pepper and salt. Put in the bouquet garni. Cover and simmer
until the rabbit is cooked. Meanwhile mash the flour into the
butter, and divide it into a number of small knobs. Strain off the
sauce into a small pan, reduce it by boiling to a good flavour, then
keep it under boiling point and whisk in the knobs of flour and
butter. This makes the sauce thick and slightly shiny. Cook for
about five minutes, flavouring the sauce to taste with orange
juice.

Cut the two oranges into thin slices, and notch the peel all
round, cutting out tiny triangles which should be carefully kept.
Put the rabbit pieces on a warm serving dish, pour over the sauce
and scatter the little bits of peel on top. The slices of orange
should go round the edge of the dish.

Sweet-sour rabbit (or hare) Italian style, with chocolate

It may need an act of faith to include the chocolate, but please don't leave it out. And make sure it's the bitter kind. Pine kernels can be bought at delicatessen or health food shops.

> 1 rabbit, jointed (or 1 young hare)
> seasoned flour
>
> *marinade:*
>
> ¾ pint red wine
> 2 heaped tablespoons each onion and carrot
> 1 tablespoon each parsley and thyme
> 1 bay leaf
> 3 cloves
> plenty of black pepper
> half teaspoon salt
>
> *sauce:*
>
> 2 oz. lard
> 2 oz. fat bacon, diced
> 3 oz. chopped onion
> beef stock
> heaped tablespoon sugar
> 3 oz. wine vinegar
> 2 oz. sultanas
> 2 oz. pine kernels
> 2 oz. candied peel, cut in strips
> 1 oz. grated bitter chocolate
> salt, pepper, lemon juice

Soak the rabbit or hare in the marinade ingredients for at least 4 hours. Drain and dry the meat, roll in seasoned flour and brown in the lard, together with bacon and onion. Put into a casserole. Strain the marinade liquid over the rabbit and add enough beef stock to cover it. Season well and simmer for 1½ hours, or until the meat is cooked. Melt sugar in a thick saucepan until it turns pale brown, add vinegar, stirring vigorously – the mixture will become a brown syrup. Pour into the casserole, and add the sultanas, pine kernels, candied peel and half the chocolate. Simmer 5 minutes. Correct the seasoning with salt, pepper, lemon juice and remaining chocolate to taste. No accompanying vegetables are needed.

Hare with cream in the German style

Only the saddle is needed for this recipe; the rest can be used up in a civet (see p. 112). Be careful to remove the pearly skin. The saddle should be larded to keep it moist during the cooking. This is not at all difficult to do – buy a fat end of bacon, or a piece of hard back pork fat, and chill it well. Cut into strips about 2 inches long and ¼-inch wide. Thread the first strip into the open end of a larding needle, and take a stitch into the meat, parallel to the backbone, as if you were sewing. The ends of fat will protrude. With a little practice, one can do this quite elegantly so that the slices of meat are neatly patterned with the bits of fat. This excellent and decorative way of making dry meats such as pigeon, fillet steak, venison and hare more succulent certainly justifies the 15p spent on a larding needle.

> saddle of hare, larded
> ½ pint double cream
> ¼ pint sour cream
> 2 oz. chopped mild onion
> 2 oz. chopped carrot
> 2 teaspoons wine vinegar
> redcurrant jelly
> 1–2 glasses red wine or port

Choose an ovenproof cooking pot that just accommodates the hare. First put in the vegetables, then lay the saddle on top. Pour over cream and vinegar, which should ideally come well up the saddle of hare. Roast in a moderate oven, Mark 4, 350°F, for about ¾ hour or until the hare is cooked. Baste frequently with the juice. Remove hare to serving dish and keep warm. Strain cooking liquid into a heavy pan. Boil gently, adding jelly and wine to taste. This dish is often served with chestnut pureé, but I prefer whole boiled chestnuts mixed with Brussels sprouts.

Jugged hare (or rabbit) with forcemeat balls

We've been eating stewed hare for hundreds of years, but we've only been calling it 'jugged' hare (which sounds so traditional) for a couple of centuries. 'Jugged' means, precisely, cooked in a jug. You could use one of the brown stoneware 4 pint milk jugs, sold by Elizabeth David and other good cookery equipment shops, but an ordinary casserole does perfectly well.

> 1 hare, jointed
> seasoned flour
> hare's blood, brain, liver (optional)
> ½ lb. streaky bacon, cubed
> ½ lb. chopped, or pickling onions
> 3 oz. lard
> ½ tablespoon thyme
> 1 heaped tablespoon chopped parsley
> bay leaf
> beef stock
> glass of port
> redcurrant jelly

Brown hare, which should first be rolled in seasoned flour, bacon and onion in lard. Pour off surplus fat, add herbs, cover with stock and bring to boil. Transfer to a jug, cover with foil, and stand in a large saucepan of hot water. Put into a slow oven, Mark 2, 300°F, until the meat parts easily from the bone. Mash brain and liver, pour on some of the hot liquid and cook in a little pan for five minutes, stirring. Add blood, off the heat, and stir the whole thing into the jug of hare. Keep it just under boiling point for five minutes. Stir in port and redcurrant jelly to taste. Serve with forcemeat balls:

> 4 oz. fresh white breadcrumbs
> 2 oz. chopped suet or melted butter
> about ½ tablespoon thyme
> about 1 tablespoon parsley
> grated rind half a lemon
> 1 beaten egg

Mix together, form into balls and fry in lard until golden brown.

Civet of hare, or rabbit

Civet is really just another word for stew, a French word which has been naturalized in England since the middle ages. It's said to derive from *cive*, chive, indicating that essential flavouring of most stews – onion. More recently, a civet has been used to describe a stew thickened with the blood of the animal being cooked.

> hare, or rabbit, jointed
> blood, brains and liver
> ¾ pint dry white wine
> nutmeg, cinnamon, black pepper
> seasoned flour
> 3 oz. lard
> ½ lb. bacon cubed
> liqueur glass brandy
> ½ lb. chopped onion
> beef stock
> 1 tablespoon thyme
> 20 small whole mushrooms (½ lb.)
> 20 pickling onions
> 2 oz. butter
> 1 tablespoon sugar
> 3 tablespoons cream
> about 1 tablespoon redcurrant jelly
> parsley to garnish
> pieces of fried bread

Marinade the hare for 48 hours in wine, well seasoned with spices. Drain and dry it well, roll in seasoned flour and brown, with bacon and chopped onion in the lard. Heat the brandy, set it alight and pour into the frying pan – turn the pieces of hare over in the flames. Transfer to a casserole, pour in the marinade with enough beef stock just to cover the meat. Wedge the lid firmly on to the pot with kitchen foil. Simmer, either on top of the stove or in the oven, for an hour, then add mushrooms. In another pan brown the pickling onions in butter, add the sugar and shake the onions about until they are caramelized. Add them to the pot and complete the cooking; the onions will need at least 20 minutes, but can have longer. Mash brains and liver, mix blood with cream;

incorporate them with the stew following the Jugged Hare recipe above. Season with redcurrant jelly, black pepper and more salt if necessary. Served with fried bread and a garnish of chopped parsley.

Pigeon

One of the pleasures of autumn is the arrival of woodpigeons at the poulterer's. They taste delicious – and even better when the winter is over, if the spring is mild enough to allow them to grow fat on young corn. Also they can cost as little as 10p apiece, if you are prepared to pluck and dress them yourself. This is not so trying as it sounds. But remember to dampen the feathers before you start, to stop them flying all over the kitchen. As an extra precaution, it's wise to pluck them inside a paper sack, with a bowl of water alongside to rinse your cluttered hands in from time to time.

The woodpigeon's gamey flavour makes it suitable, along with wild rabbits, and with hares and the more expensive game, for cold game pâtés and pies. Patience is needed, rather than any special skill; and nerve enough to suppress a feeling that only Fortnum's or the kitchens of Castle Howard can cope with such lordly specialities.

Lark was another fat, gamey-flavoured, autumnally eaten bird, but to enjoy lark in pâtés – since Shelley and ornithology – you have to go to Chartres, Orléans or Pithiviers, on the edge of the Beauce, the great farm plain of northern France.

Incidentally, from March to September, domestic pigeons can be bought from Harrod's poultry counter, or from John Baily & Son, 116 Mount Street, London W.1. These birds are American squabs, bred in Kent. They're similar to the pigeons which cooed in the dovecots of medieval lords of the manor, or modern French *pigeonneaux*, or for that matter, to the pigeons which were given nesting boxes by early Mesopotamian farmers 6,000 years ago. They are bland and tender, take less time to cook than wild pigeon, and can be roasted without larding – but they are not cheap. (It follows that if you adapt American or French pigeon recipes to woodpigeons, you must increase cooking time.) I believe that there is only one breeder of these squabs in Britain, which seems a pity. Like venison, these delicious birds could add a welcome variety to our meat dishes, if they were produced in greater quantity for the home market.

As a feudal perk of the big houses, dovecot pigeons were a source of meat in the days when cattle could not be fed through the winter. Turnip culture and winter beef in the eighteenth century saved the cattle and introduced winter steaks and sirloin. And it had long been thought intolerable that privileged pigeons should fatten on other people's fields and gardens. So exit the squab.

Woodpigeon's are just as much of a nuisance, an enormously successful species. All the same it isn't impossible that woodpigeons as well will disappear from the kitchen. Farmers say it won't be economical to shoot them much longer, with the present high price of cartridges. So make the most of these fat birds while they are still on the poulterer's slab.

Pigeon with grapes

This dish comes from the Bas-Vendômois, where pigeons in autumn are fat with maize, and grapes ripen on house walls and south-facing hills.

4 pigeons
3 oz. chopped mild onion
3 oz. butter
1½–2 lb. white or black grapes
3 tablespoons *marc* or brandy

Soften onion for 10 minutes in half the butter. Put into the casserole (which should be just large enough to hold the pigeons) with a layer of grapes. Brown the pigeons in the rest of the butter; warm the *marc*, set it alight and pour over the pigeons, turning them about in the flames. Tuck them breast down into the casserole, filling the gaps with grapes. Keep a few back for garnishing. Season lightly and cover. Cook in a hot oven (Mark 7 or 8, 425–450°F) for 10 or 15 minutes, then lower the heat to Mark 3, 325°F, or even less, to keep the pigeons at a gentle simmer. Cook for 1–2½ hours according to the age of the pigeons; remove them as their flesh begins to part from the breastbone.

Sieve the sauce into a clean pan. Boil down to about ¾ pint. Adust seasoning and skim off the fat. Carve pigeons (keep carcases for soup, see p. 126), arrange with the reserved grapes on a bed of boiled rice, and pour some of the sauce over them. Serve the rest of the sauce in a separate jug.

To boil pigeon with rice (for 4)

A dish from Shakespeare's day, from a cookery book of 1609. Unusual and good.

mutton stock:

meaty mutton or lamb bones
2 pints water
bouquet garni
medium carrot, sliced
medium onion, sliced

pigeons:

4 pigeons
4 bunches of thyme, parsley, marjoram
1 oz. butter and 1 tablespoon oil

rice:

1¼ oz. rice
1 pint single cream (or cream and milk)
about ¼ teaspoon mace
sugar
1 lemon, large and juicy

Simmer the stock ingredients for 3–4 hours (this can be done in advance). Strain and reduce to 1¼ pints. Season with salt and black pepper.

Put the rice, single cream, thinly pared lemon peel and mace into a casserole. Cook in the oven, Mark ¼–1, 250–275°F. Stir in the crust occasionally, and should it become too dry, add some creamy milk. Leave for 2–3 hours – the slower a rice pudding is cooked, the better it tastes.

Insert the bunches of sweet herbs into the pigeons' cavities. Then brown them all over in the butter and oil. Next tuck them closely together in a casserole, breast down, and pour on the boiling stock which should barely cover them. Simmer until cooked either on top of the stove, or in the oven with the rice – in the latter case, it's important that the casserole should be at the boil when you put it in.

When the flesh begins to show signs of parting from the breastbone, separate completely, so that each pigeon is divided into two large pieces. Lay them on a serving dish and keep warm.

Reduce the stock until it has a good strong flavour. It can be thickened a little if you like, but I think that a strongly flavoured thin gravy is preferable as the rice provides the desirable thickness.

Season the rice pudding with sugar, and more mace to taste. Smother the pigeons with it, and squeeze a lemon over the rice.

No green vegetables should be served with this dish. They could come beforehand, or afterwards, as an entirely separate course.

Pigeon with cabbage (for 4)

Cabbage-growing is a British national sport as well as an industry. Yet we cook it appallingly. (How often do you meet anyone who really likes cabbage?) We ignore its wonderful quality of absorbing meat flavours while retaining an agreeable crispness and bite, as in this recipe.

> 4 pigeons
> 1 tablespoon butter
> ½ lb. fat bacon diced
> 20 small onions (about ¾ lb.)
> ¼ pint each dry white wine and beef stock
> Savoy cabbage

Fry bacon gently in butter until its fat flows. Add pigeons and onions, and brown them. Transfer to casserole, pigeons breast down. Pour off remaining fat. Bring wine and stock to the boil in the frying pan, scraping in all the brown bits, then pour over the pigeons. (Woodpigeons should be almost covered, so you may need to add more hot stock.) Put on the lid. Simmer gently. Meanwhile plunge the cabbage into a pan of boiling salted water for 10 minutes. Drain and open out into a nest-shape. Half an hour before the pigeons are likely to be cooked, remove them from the casserole, place them breast down in the cabbage, and return the whole thing to the casserole. When cooked, arrange pigeons, cabbage, onions and bacon on a serving dish. Skim fat off the sauce and reduce to a concentrated flavour. Pour over the pigeons, etc., and serve.

Note: some recipes put the blanched cabbage into the casserole with the pigeons immediately after the browning stage. But the above method leaves the cabbage crisper. It also has the advantage, particularly with woodpigeons, that most of the cooking can be done in advance without spoiling the fresh flavour added by more lightly cooked cabbage.

Pigeon pie (for 4)

Woodpigeons can quite well be used for this very English pie, which was originally intended for dovecot pigeons.

> shortcrust or puff pastry

filling:

4 pigeons
2 oz. butter
beef stock
6 oz. piece rump steak
4 hard-boiled egg yolks
1 tablespoon finely chopped mild onions
¼ lb. sliced mushrooms
parsley, salt, pepper

Brown pigeons in butter, and then, if they are woodpigeons, simmer them for 1¼ hours, covered in beef stock. Halve the pigeons along breastbone. Lay steak on the bottom of a buttered pie dish, season and lay pigeon halves on top. Season again and fill the gaps with hard-boiled egg yolk, crumbled. Add onion, mushrooms, plenty of parsley and stock to cover the meat. Put a band of pastry round the rim of the dish, moisten it, then cover with a lid of pastry. Knock up the edges, decorate and brush with beaten egg. Put into a good hot oven to start with (puff pastry, Mark 7, 425°F; shortcrust, Mark 6, 400°F) for 20 minutes, then reduce the heat to Mark 4, 350°F. Protect the pastry when it begins to look nicely browned with thick paper, or several layers of grease-proof paper. Total cooking time for the pie 1½ hours.

Spanish pigeons with chocolate sauce (for 4)

Chocolate makes an excellent seasoning for game sauces. Italian dishes of hare with chocolate and pine nut sauce are famous; here's a Spanish recipe of a similar but lighter kind. Don't be nervous of the chocolate if you've not come across this kind of recipe before: so little is used that it is unidentifiable, yet the difference it makes in richness of flavour is surprising. Another important point of the dish is the glazed onions. Their moist sweetness goes well with dark close pigeon meat. In Spain plump squabs would be used, so I've had to adapt the recipe to our tougher wild birds.

4 pigeons, larded
1 large onion, sliced

5 tablespoons olive oil
¼ pint dry white wine
about 1 pint chicken stock, lightly seasoned
12–16 pickling (small white) onions
2 teaspoons sugar
7 tablespoons butter
1¼ tablespoons flour
1½–2 teaspoons grated Bournville chocolate
1 lemon, cut down into wedges

Brown the pigeons and sliced onion in the oil. Fit them into a casserole, the pigeons breast down. Pour in the white wine, then enough chicken stock to cover the birds. Bring to the boil and simmer for 1½–2 hours until the pigeons are cooked.

One hour before the pigeons are cooked, prepare the small onions: prepare enough to make a single layer in a large heavy saucepan. Cover with water. Add the sugar and 4 tablespoons of the butter. Boil hard so that the liquid evaporates to a golden brown glaze. Keep a careful eye on the onions towards the end of the cooking, as they must not burn. Shake the pan gently so that they are coated in the caramel.

When the birds are almost done, i.e. when the legs move loosely and the meat begins to part from the breastbone, remove 2 cups of stock from the casserole. Reduce it by boiling to just over a cup (this concentrates the flavour, which is why you must start with lightly seasoned chicken stock). Skim off fat and foam as it rises. Mash the remaining butter with the flour (*beurre manié*), and add it in small knobs to the reduced stock, which should now be kept at simmering point. When the sauce has thickened, correct the seasoning and stir in the chocolate gradually to taste.

Arrange the cooked pigeons on a warm serving dish, with the glazed onions round them. Pour a little of the sauce over the birds, and put the rest into a sauceboat. Arrange the lemon wedges among the onions.

Pigeons au soleil (for 4)

'Pigeons in the sun' were very popular in England and France in the eighteenth century. The recipe occurs in most of the cookery books of the time. And I'm not surprised. It's worth taking trouble to lard the pigeons – particularly when, as in this recipe, they are being served without a sauce. Fried parsley is not much used these days, but its agreeable sandiness goes well with the pigeons in their sunburnt coating of crisp batter.

batter:

2 oz. plain flour
pinch salt
1 tablespoon olive oil
about ¼ pint lukewarm water or beer
1 large egg white

4 pigeons
½ lb. piece of fat bacon, chilled
1 large onion, sliced
1 large carrot, sliced
bouquet garni
1-1½ pints chicken or veal stock
salt, black pepper
oil or lard for frying
2 bunches parsley
garnish with 1 lemon, cut into wedges

First of all make the batter, so that it has time to stand. Mix flour and salt with the oil and water or beer, beating the ingredients well together. Cover and leave in the kitchen, not in the refrigerator or other cold place. The egg white is not added until the batter is required.

Cut the chilled bacon into 2-inch strips, and lard the pigeons (see p. 110).

Put a thin layer of oil or melted lard into a heavy frying pan, and brown the birds and the vegetables in it. Transfer them to a casserole (pigeons breast down). Add the bouquet garni and enough stock to cover the birds. Season well, as this stock will not be reduced to make a sauce. Simmer for 1½–2 hours, until the birds are cooked. Remove the large breast fillets – carcases and remaining meat on the legs, etc., can be used with the cooking stock to make pigeon soup for another meal.

Whisk the egg white until stiff, fold into the batter. Coat the pigeon fillets (it doesn't make any difference if they're still warm) and fry in olive oil or lard, which should be about ¼ inch deep in the frying pan. When they're golden brown on both sides, and crisp, put them on to a warm serving dish. Fry the parsley until dark green, drain and arrange round the pigeons with the lemon quarters. Serve immediately.

Note: 8 oz. white wine may be added to the cooking liquor (reduce the amount of stock). Wine always has a good effect on meat which is likely to be dry or tough, and the flavour of your pigeon soup will be improved. In this case use water for the batter, not beer.

Pigeon with olives (for 4)

We could, I think, make more use than we do of olives in cookery. They're in every grocer's shop and delicatessen – black olives, green olives and stuffed olives, large olives, small olives, olives in bottles and olives in barrels – yet how rarely they appear once the aperitifs are finished. This is a pity. In stuffings and sauces, they add a light sharpness to meat, their firm flesh gives bite and richness.

The kind of olives chosen for a dish will depend on personal taste (and, in some places, on what happens to be available). I've a preference for small black shiny olives, though my eye is often seduced by the green ones stuffed with red pimento. Many varieties are grown in Mediterranean countries, but the main division is a matter of ripeness – green olives are picked when fully grown but unripe, black olives have been left on the tree to darken in the sun. This obviously makes for difference in texture as well as in flavour. Very occasionally one may buy olives which taste unpleasantly of brine: the remedy is to pour boiling water over them, and to leave them for 5 minutes before draining.

> 4 pigeons larded
> 1 large carrot, sliced
> 1 large onion sliced
> 4 oz. butter
> 8 oz. white wine
> bouquet garni
> chicken or veal stock, lightly seasoned

heaped tablespoon flour
4 oz. olives

serve with: boiled rice or egg noodles

Brown pigeons and vegetables in 2 oz. of butter. Transfer to a
casserole. Add wine, bouquet garni and enough stock to cover the
birds. Simmer for 1½–2 hours, until they are cooked.

About half an hour before the end of cooking time, remove 1
pint of liquid from the casserole. Reduce it by hard boiling to just
over ½ pint – let flavour be your guide, remembering that the
olives will add sharpness to the final result. In a small, heavy
saucepan, melt the remaining butter, stir in the flour and cook for
two or three minutes. Add the reduced stock bit by bit until you
have a sauce the consistency of heavy cream. When the pigeons
are cooked, add the olives to the simmering sauce and correct the
seasoning (give the olives a chance to heat through before you do
this). Pour a little of the sauce over the birds, and serve the rest in
a sauceboat.

Choose boiled rice or egg noodles to go with this dish, rather
than potatoes.

Matelote of pigeon (for 4)

The red wine dishes of France, or to be precise of Burgundy, have
the most comforting effect in winter – eggs *en meurette*, matelote
of fish, beef *à la bourguignonne*. Pigeons cooked in the same way
are delicious. Apart from the wine, the little pieces of fat pork, the
button mushrooms, and tiny glazed onions make this stew into a
special dish for Sunday lunch, or dinner on a cold night.

4 pigeons, preferably larded
¾ lb. belly of pork
1 large carrot, chopped small
1 large onion, chopped small
2 oz. butter
2 cloves garlic, crushed
1 heaped tablespoon flour
½ pint red wine

chicken or veal stock
salt, black pepper
nutmeg, ginger, ground cloves
¼ lb. button mushrooms
16–24 pickling (small white) onions
2–3 lumps of sugar
dash of wine vinegar
2 tablespoons chopped parsley

serve with: either 12 triangles of bread, fried
in butter, or boiled potatoes

Remove skin and any bones from the belly of pork, then cut into small strips, about 1½ inches long and ¼ inch wide and thick. Brown pigeons, pork, carrot and onion in the butter with the garlic: do this at a moderate heat, so as not to burn the butter. Put into a casserole (pigeons breast down). Stir the flour into the remaining fat. Cook for 2 or 3 minutes, then add the red wine and about 1 cup of stock. Pour into the casserole, adding more stock if necessary to cover the pigeons. Season with salt and pepper. Add a grating of nutmeg, and a good pinch of ginger and powdered cloves. Simmer for 1½ hours.

Now put the mushrooms into the pot, pushing them down below the simmering liquid. The onions can be added at the same time – or else they can be cooked and glazed separately (see Spanish pigeons with chocolate sauce, p. 119), which gives more flavour to the dish as well as improving its final appearance.

After a further ½ hour pigeons and mushrooms, etc., should all be cooked. Strain off the sauce into a clean pan, skim and reduce it by boiling if necessary. Use the sugar, wine vinegar and additional spices, if necessary, to improve the flavour.

Arrange the pigeons and vegetables in a large round serving dish. Pour the sauce over, sprinkle with parsley and put triangles of fried bread or boiled potatoes in a ring round the edge of the dish.

Note: this delicious way of cooking pigeons may be further improved by flaming the birds with a glass of brandy, after they've been browned and before they're put into the casserole.

Pigeon or game pâté

6–8 oz. boned pigeon, rabbit, hare or venison
liver of pigeon, rabbit or hare
3 oz. hard back pork fat
8 oz. belly pork
2 oz. veal or rump steak
2 rashers back bacon
1 egg
parsley and thyme
½ inch slice of bread, crumbled
3 oz. chopped onion and 1 large clove
   garlic crushed
2 oz. butter
1 liqueur glass cognac, or ½ gill sherry or port

Dice hard fat, liver and half the game. Finely mince the rest of the game, plus the pork belly, bacon and veal or steak (more game may be used; it depends how strong a flavour you like). Add breadcrumbs, herbs. Simmer onion and garlic in the butter without browning them, until soft and golden. Add to the pâté mixture with the beaten egg and brandy or wine. Season well with salt and pepper. Mix everything thoroughly with your hands. If you aren't sure about the seasoning, fry a little knob of the mixture and taste it.

Pack into a 1¼ pint terrine, or 2 small ones – which is more practical, as one may be stored in the freezing compartment of a refrigerator for later use. Cover with a double layer of foil, stand in a pan of hot water and bake for 1–1½ hours (time depends on the *depth* of the pâté, rather than its extent) at Mark 3, 325°F) remove the foil about 10 minutes before the end of cooking time for the pâté to brown. It is done when it swims in fat, clear of the terrine, or when a steel knitting needle is pushed in and comes out clean. Leave to cool under a light weight, until next day at least. It takes 2 days for the full flavour to develop.

Game pie

The pâté mixture above can be turned into a delicious game pie, if it's baked in shortcrust or hot-water crust pastry. Allow some extra pieces of game, nicely cut into strips, to be layered in with it.

For recipes, see pp. 61–5.

Pigeon or game soup (for 4)

This excellent but simple soup is a good way of using up small amounts of game and the carcases.

> legs and carcases of 4 or more pigeons
> *or*
> head and forequarters of rabbit or hare
> *or*
> mixture of game
> *plus*
> about 2 pints beef stock
> medium carrot, sliced
> medium onion, sliced
> bouquet garni
> port
> lemon juice, salt, pepper
> forcemeat balls (p. 111), or small
>   croûtons fried bread

Simmer game, carrot, onion, herbs and stock until meat begins to fall off the bones. Pour through a sieve into a clean pan, remove the herbs and bones and vegetables from the debris; liquidize the rest with some of the strained soup. Season with port wine, lemon juice, pepper and salt. The lemon juice is particularly important, if you have no port. Redcurrant jelly may also be used as a seasoning.

Serve with tiny forcemeat balls, or with croûtons.

Note: for a clear soup, add ½ lb. shin of beef and 1 pig's trotter to the game, and omit the liquidizing process. Strain through a muslin-lined sieve, and skim well.

Venison steak en croûte

Venison

In the past noble lords and rich men – when they could get a licence from the Crown – built themselves a living larder in the shape of a deer park with high fences and walls. They went out and formally hunted the deer inside, and then, to mix metaphors, pigged on the venison. Now some of them are glad to sell their venison to the people, you and me, who used to poach it – if we could. Most of the venison comes from fallow deer, the kind that drop their horns in April and May in the park at Richmond – these are the traditional inhabitants of deer parks. At Richmond, too, one may see red deer, which also provide venison, though more particularly in Scotland than in England.

French chefs have often complained that they could get nothing but venison from roe deer. The flesh, said Escoffier, was 'very often mediocre in quality' and he thought that the fallow deer from an English park 'has no equal as far as delicacy and tenderness are concerned'. They devised very good recipes all the same.

When you eat venison, reflect that it was an integral part of living it up in the Middle Ages. The menu survives of a feast given in 1443, at the installation of John Stafford, Archbishop of Canterbury. The game – strange list – included pheasant, swan, heron, crane, curlew, partridge, plover, rails and quails, and no less than three different dishes of venison.

They knew, the cooks of those days, that venison is a rich and gamey meat which needs tempering a little. They served it with saffron-flavoured frumenty (p. 138), the wet ancestor of the packeted breakfast cereal, and with an early version of poivrade sauce (p. 135). Sometimes it was enclosed in pastry. Venison cooking by the Victorian age had multiplied accompaniments of fruit and berries – pears, apples, oranges, cherries, juniper berries, even bananas. In this country port wine was as essential as redcurrant jelly, the two being combined in Francatelli's deliciously simple sauce for venison (p. 135), and in the better known Cumberland sauce for cold venison (p. 137).

Venison is easy to cook. No problem there. The trouble may be to buy it. Some branches of Macfisheries will take an order for venison, so will butchers specializing in game. Bejam will supply venison for people with deep-freezers, when it is available, and so will some other companies supplying frozen meat. It is always worth inquiring.

Only persist. The venison is there on the hoof. The sad thing is that threequarters of it goes abroad (like our best scallops, pigs, horsemeat and lobsters), mainly to Germany. It seems, though, that our producers are beginning to meet tough competition from Russia and New Zealand, and may have to consider new markets. They might, who knows, consider us, their fellow countrymen. With intelligent and patient publicity – think of the avocado pear and chicory campaigns – venison could soon become part of our normal choice of meat. It's not, after all, an exotic, but part of our traditional food and folklore.

Venison soup (for 6)

A good nineteenth-century soup, using the cheapest parts of venison, and the bones. It's a recipe that can be easily adapted to other game, hare, pigeon, etc.

> 1 lb. stewing venison, plus bones
> 1 thin slice gammon
> 1 stalk celery, cut into 3 pieces
> 1 medium onion, quartered
> 4 oz. piece carrot
> bouquet garni
> scant teaspoon mace
> 3 pints water
> 1 tablespoon each butter and flour
> 1 gill port
> redcurrant jelly (optional)
> salt, black pepper

Put everything, except butter, flour, port and jelly, into a large pan. Simmer for about 2 hours until the venison is cooked (the time depends on the age of the venison). Skim and strain the soup. Pick a few nice pieces of meat out of the sieve and keep them warm; put the rest of the meat, without skin, bones, etc., back into the soup and liquidize or push through the *mouli-légumes*. Bring back to the boil, turn the heat down a little and add the butter and flour, which should be mashed together, in little knobs. Keep stirring as you do this, and the soup will thicken smoothly after about 4 or 5 minutes: it should not boil hard, but simmer. Add the port wine and the pieces of venison. Correct the seasoning with salt and pepper, adding a little redcurrant jelly if you like. As with all venison dishes, this soup should be served very hot, with very hot soup plates.

Venison cutlets in the Ardennes style (for 4)

If you've never cooked venison before, try this recipe from Elizabeth David's *French Provincial Cooking*. For one thing, it's an introduction to the fine combination of venison and juniper berries; for another, the method of baking the cutlets or chops gives one plenty of chance to make sure that all is well. The worst of trying some new things, a soufflé for example or a steak and kidney pudding, is that there's no way of knowing whether you've succeeded or flopped, until everyone starts eating. So build up confidence with this exceptionally delicious recipe, before committing yourself to the grander enterprise of a joint of roast venison:

> 8 cutlets or 4 thick loin chops
> 12 crushed juniper berries
> dried marjoram or thyme
> salt, freshly ground black pepper
> lemon juice
> 2 oz. butter
> 1 small onion, chopped
> 2 carrots, diced
> small glass white wine or vermouth
> small glass water
> about 4 dessertspoons chopped cooked ham
> 3 oz. breadcrumbs
> half a bunch of parsley, chopped
> extra butter
> dessertspoon redcurrant jelly
> juice of half a bitter orange

Mix juniper berries with some dried marjoram or thyme, salt and pepper. Pour lemon juice over the meat and rub with the juniper mixture. It's a good idea to do this an hour or two before you start the cooking. Melt 2 oz. butter in a shallow pan, add onion and carrot. When they are golden brown, put in the meat and brown it on both sides too. Pour in wine or vermouth, and boil steadily to reduce it a little. Add the water. Put some chopped ham on top of each cutlet or chop (transfer them, if more convenient, to a shallow ovenproof serving dish), then some breadcrumbs mixed with the chopped parsley. Dab a little butter on top of the breadcrumbs. Bake in a low oven, Mark 2, 300°F, uncovered. The time required will depend on the condition of the venison, varying from 1 to 2 hours. After about ¾ of an hour, pierce one of the chops gently with a larding needle or skewer to see if it's nearly ready.

When the meat is tender, pour off the juices into a wide pan (keeping the meat warm in the oven, at a reduced temperature) and boil them down until the flavour is well concentrated. Stir in the redcurrant jelly and bitter orange juice (one could use a little dark marmalade when Seville oranges are not in season). Pour over the cutlets. Serve very hot, with a few boiled potatoes.

Venison in the Villeneuve style (for 4)

We do not seem to have much of a habit in this country of wrapping chopped meat and seasonings into small delicious bundles, enclosed – and perpetually basted as they cook – by the web of fat known as the caul. Faggots, those good but hefty West country specialities, are the only example I can think of. They are really a rough pâté, eaten hot, and made most usefully from the liver and lights of freshly killed pigs. This recipe is a much finer affair from Escoffier, who was born at Villeneuve-Loubet, near Nice. He served these venison packages with Chasseur sauce and a purée of celery. You could try them without a sauce, accompanied by bananas split and fried in butter. Or with a potato and celeriac purée.

The finest meat from loin or haunch may be used; or the less noble parts, as long as they are well trimmed of fat, skin and gristly bits.

> ¾ lb. lean trimmed venison
> ¼ lb. melted but cool butter
> ¼ lb. white breadcrumbs
> milk
> 3 good tablespoons double cream
> salt, pepper
> piece of caul fat

Chop or mince the meat. Add a very little milk to the breadcrumbs and squeeze them out, so that the bread forms a thick paste. Mix meat, bread, cream and butter. Season well. Divide the mixture into 8 or 12 knobs. Soften and stretch the caul fat in warm water. Cut it into 8 or 12 squares and wrap up the venison knobs neatly, flattening them into ovals about ½-inch thick. Fry in butter on both sides until golden brown, about 15 minutes in all.

Civet of venison (for 8)

A dish for a banquet, or at least for a meal of celebration.

3 lb. stewing venison, diced and trimmed.

marinade:

½ bottle red wine
1 medium onion, sliced
3 tablespoons brandy
3 tablespoons olive oil
salt, black pepper

sauce:

½ lb. streaky bacon in a piece
2 oz. butter
2 large onions, chopped
1 large carrot, diced
2 tablespoons flour
beef or venison stock
bouquet garni
large clove garlic, crushed
¼ lb. mushrooms, sliced

garnish:

24 small mushrooms
24 small onions (pickling size)
1 dessertspoon sugar
beef or venison stock
8 slices bread
4 oz. butter
chopped parsley

Mix the marinade ingredients together, seasoning them well, and soak the venison in it overnight. Next day, melt the butter (sauce ingredients) in a heavy pan, and brown the bacon in it, which you have first cut into strips about 1 inch long and ¼ inch wide and thick. When the fat runs from the bacon, put onions and carrot and garlic into the pan to be browned lightly, then the well-drained venison. Stir the flour into the pan to take up the fat, and make a sauce by adding the strained marinade, plus enough stock to cover the ingredients (everything can be transferred to a deep casserole if this is more convenient). Add the mushrooms and simmer until the venison is cooked – about 1½ to 2 hours. Skim off any surplus fat. (The cooking up to this point may be done the day before the venison is to be eaten.)

Half an hour before the meal, prepare the garnish and reheat the civet if necessary. Melt 1 oz. of butter with the sugar in a heavy pan. Turn the small onions in this until they are well coated. Add just enough stock to cover them, and cook at a galloping boil. This will reduce the liquid to a spoonful or two of caramel. Be careful it doesn't burn, and keep shaking the onions about in it so that they are nicely glazed. Cook the mushrooms whole in 1 oz. of butter, with salt and pepper. Cut the bread into triangles, and fry in the last 2 oz. of butter.

Arrange the civet on a large hot serving dish, put the mushrooms and onions on top pushing them down a little so that they look naturally part of the dish (but not too far so that they disappear). The croûtons go round the edge. Sprinkle with parsley and serve very hot.

Venison chops grilled (for 4)

A simple recipe which shows off very well the flavour of venison.

> 4 loin chops, thick ones
> piece of caul fat
> ¾ lb. mushrooms, or 20 juniper berries
> 3 oz. butter
> salt, black pepper

Season the chops with salt and plenty of freshly ground black pepper. Soften the caul fat in tepid water, cut it into four pieces and wrap up the chops (trim off the surplus – the meat should not be swaddled). Grill for 20 minutes, turning once, keeping the heat high for 5 minutes then turning it down to medium. Stew the mushrooms or crushed juniper berries in the butter. Season and pour over the chops just before serving them.

Venison en croûte (for 4)

Venison steaks may be encased in puff or short pastry, in the same way as fillet of beef.

> ¾ lb. short or puff pastry
> 4 loin or rump steaks of venison
> (without bones)
> 4 oz. chopped mushrooms
> 1 large clove garlic, crushed
> 3 oz. butter
> about 2 oz. breadcrumbs
> egg yolk
> salt, black pepper

Roll out the pastry and cut into four oblong pieces large enough to enclose the steaks. Cook mushrooms and garlic in butter, then add enough breadcrumbs to make a moist stuffing. Sear the steaks quickly on both sides in a heavy pan which has been rubbed over with lard. Put some stuffing into the centre of each piece of pastry, lay the steaks on top, then the rest of the stuffing. Brush the pastry edges with egg yolk and bring them together to form turnovers. Brush the tops with egg yolk, and bake for 20 minutes at Mark 6, 400°F.

Roast venison

It's not necessary to marinade roasting joints of venison (should you wish to do so, use the marinade given with the civet recipe, p. 132), but they should be larded. Which is a reasonable precaution to take with any piece of very lean meat — hare, beef steaks, pigeons, etc., as well as venison. Buy a piece of fat end of bacon. Chill it firm, and cut it into strips 2 ins. long, and just over ⅛ in. wide and thick. Push a piece into the open end of a larding needle (10p or 15p from good kitchen suppliers) and take a stitch in the joint as if you were sewing, leaving the fat bacon behind. Repeat until the whole joint is nicely studded with fat.

To roast the venison, tie a jacket of thinly cut pork back fat round it (or a fatty piece of pork or bacon skin) and cook at Mark 4, 350°F. Venison should be slightly rare: the time required for a small joint is about 20 minutes per lb., plus 20 minutes. As the joints get larger, above 4 lbs., reduce the time per pound to 15 minutes. Should you ever have the good fortune to be presented with a haunch of venison, i.e. a leg plus half the saddle in one magnificent piece, it will require 3 to 4 hours cooking.

Serve roast venison with one of the following sauces:

Francatelli's venison sauce

Of all the sauces for venison, I think that this one, invented by Queen Victoria's chef, Francatelli, is the best. It happens to be easy to make as well.

> 2 tablespoons port wine
> ½ lb. redcurrant jelly
> small stick cinnamon, bruised
> thinly pared rind of a lemon

Simmer together for 5 minutes, stirring. Strain into a hot sauceboat.

Poivrade sauce (pepper sauce)

Poivrade sauce started out in the Middle Ages as a kind of bread sauce, with stock and wine or vinegar replacing the milk. The seasoning was of course pepper. It was still popular with people of old-fashioned tastes in 1846. But by that time this much more complex sauce had been developed by the great chefs. The quantities sound enormous, but as it forms the basis of several sauces to go not only with venison, but also with lamb and hare, it's worth making the full amount and storing the surplus in the freezing compartment of a refrigerator.

> 1 carrot and 1 onion diced
> 3 tablespoons corn oil
> 2 oz. flour
> 1½ pints beef stock
> 1 tablespoon tomato concentrate
> bouquet garni
> venison bones if possible
> ¼ pint each vinegar and marinade (see
>   civet recipe)
> 8 crushed peppercorns
> ¼ pint red wine

Brown carrot and onion in the oil. Add flour, and when it's browned, stir in stock and tomato concentrate. Put the herbs and bones, if used, into the pan, and simmer for 2 hours, covered. Skim off the fat. Meanwhile reduce vinegar and marinade in a small pan with the peppercorns. When it measures 6 oz., put into a larger pan and add the strained brown sauce. Simmer for a further half hour and then add the red wine.

Cherry sauce

Heat ¼ pint each poivrade sauce and redcurrant jelly together. Stir in 4 oz. drained black cherries (Swiss tinned ones are very good). An excellent sauce, too, for duck.

Cream sauce

Pour fat from the roasting pan, leaving the juices behind. Warm a liqueur glass of brandy or gin or other spirits, set it alight and pour into the pan, scraping in all the delicious brown bits. (If you've used gin, add 2 or 3 crushed juniper berries as well.) Pour in ¼ pint double cream and a generous tablespoon of poivrade sauce. Correct the seasoning.

If you've no alcohol, season the sauce with lemon juice and a little sugar at the end.

Venison sauce

¾ pint poivrade sauce and 1 teaspoon sugar boiled down to just over ½ a pint. Remove from the heat, and stir in 2 oz. butter in small pieces. Added at the last moment like this, without being too much heated or cooked, the butter gives a wonderful flavour and sheen to the sauce.

Cumberland sauce for cold venison

Melt half a pound of redcurrant jelly with the juice of two oranges and 1 lemon, a teaspoonful of mustard and a dash of Cayenne pepper and of ginger. Meanwhile cut finely into shreds the peel of 1 orange and 1 lemon (no pith) and simmer them in boiling water for 5 minutes. Drain and add to the jelly, with 2 or 3 tablespoons of port. Sometimes some glacé cherries are added, but they should be well washed first under the hot tap to remove the sticky syrup which coats them.

Accompaniments to venison

French beans, dressed with plenty of butter. Traditional British accompaniment.
Chestnuts or lentils, cooked whole, or served as a purée.
Celery or celeriac. The latter usually made into a purée with potatoes, see p. 167.
The edible fungi, from ceps and girolles through to cultivated mushrooms – and truffles.
Pears – the Baden Baden style of presenting venison, includes pears, cored and quartered, stewed with lemon rind and cinnamon in water, *without sugar* (though a little redcurrant jelly added towards the end of cooking time is an advantage).

Apples, sliced and fried in butter, or stewed with cloves.

Bitter oranges sliced, and *sauce bigarade*. Melt 1 oz. butter and stir into it 1 oz. flour. Cook until pale brownish colour. Stir in half a pint of hot venison or beef stock. Peel 2 Seville oranges thinly, cut into strips, and simmer in water for five minutes. Drain and add to the sauce with seasoning. Cook slowly for 5 minutes. Put in the juice of the two oranges and 5 or 6 teaspoons of sugar and the meat juices from the roasted venison.

Frumenty, flavoured and coloured with saffron, was a favourite accompaniment to venison in the Middle Ages, especially to salted venison. This recipe comes from a fifteenth-century manuscript in the British Museum:

'Take wheat and pick it clean. Put it into a mortar with a little water and pound it with a pestle to loosen the husks. Then fan away the husks and put it in a pot and let it simmer until it bursts. Drain it well, add some sweet milk, and simmer it again, stirring. When it's cooked colour it with saffron, and season it with salt.'

Other recipes enrich the frumenty with beaten egg yolks.

Vegetables

Asparagus

How would you describe the best asparagus? Thick, certainly. Fresh certainly, as, whatever kind is grown, its flavour will deteriorate with delay. No argument here.

But after that, would you prefer it to be blanched white? Or white with a yellowish head? Or green and white streaked with pinkish purple? Or as green as possible?

The answer will tell me more about you, than about absolute standards of asparagus perfection. Germans and Italians like white asparagus with a yellowish head (the most delicious asparagus I've ever eaten was in a restaurant at Bassano del Grappa – a rich little town, with a famous bridge, famous painters, famous brandy and famous asparagus). The French like their spears violet and green and white. And the English and Americans like unblanched, tender greenness. In our favour, I will modestly add that European chefs working in England have said, do still say, that our fresh asparagus beats all for flavour.

That's the theory anyway. In practice, your answer would more likely have been curt, rather than considered: 'The best asparagus is the asparagus I can afford – when I can find it.'

There is an aura of aristocracy, a mystique of asparagus which seems to stop gardeners growing it. And housewives buying it. Asparagus is not for us. Its past is long, cherished and peppered with great names. Pliny described asparagus spears weighing 4 oz. (Super Extra Selected Roman style). Louis XIV ate asparagus in January – did it, I wonder, have any flavour at all? – forced in his gardens at Versailles. Pepys bought 'sparrow-grass' (it's still called 'grass' in the trade) in 1667 in Fenchurch Street, a hundred spears for 1s. 6d. Proust's eye was caught by the rainbow asparagus lying on his aunt's kitchen table at Illiers.

I remember as a child being told by an elderly gardener in Gloucester that the huge bed we were contemplating had taken seven – or was it ten? – years to establish. I forget his exact figure, but recall that it exceeded the number of years it had taken to establish me in the same world. He was choosing the finest asparagus for a luncheon party during the Three Choirs Festival. Severn salmon and strawberries were to complete the meal. It all sounded very grand.

In fact the old man was quite wrong with his figures. With modern methods, planting one year old crowns, you can pick a little asparagus the first season, more the second, and as much as you like the third. This is because nowadays asparagus growing is better understood, thanks to Mr Kidner of Suffolk. He discovered that to be sure of asparagus producing a high proportion of fine fat heads (as opposed to the thin 'sprue'), he had to select it and breed it like cattle. He was one of a family of stockbreeders, and had first applied their methods to asparagus in 1908 in his own kitchen garden. It was not until 1931 that he turned wholly to asparagus farming. Much work is still being done to produce more and more reliable asparagus: growers like Mr Paske of Regal Lodge, Kentford, Suffolk, import Dutch and French strains to improve their own stock. (He will supply both crowns and bunches of asparagus by post.)

Given all this hard work and intelligence, it seems ridiculous that in our country of cheap food, we can't buy good cheap asparagus. It makes me angry that we haven't encouraged growers to grow more. We have 1000 acres of asparagus in England, com-

mercial acres, and little or none in Scotland, Ireland and Wales.
Holland has twenty times as much. I wonder why this is? Are we
of all the people in Europe so cowed by past grandeur that we
cling to cabbages and to giant, stringy scarlet runners and olym-
pian marrows? What a waste of ground.

I have this image of early summer, May and June. We walk
home slowly up the village street, which runs across the cliff at a
kindly slope. The midday angelus rings from the church tower
above us. Children stream out of school, and flow politely past our
slower feet into open cottage doors. The air pulses with the warm
smell of lilac, but as we pass each door, the lilac dominance is
subdued by heady wafts of asparagus cooking.

This is not Utopia. It's a poorish village, less than 300 miles
south of London. The inhabitants have the sense to grow asparagus, that's all. If they haven't a garden patch across the river,
they can buy it at 35p the lb. bunch in the village shop. No aristo-
cratic aura. Not even a whiff of bourgeois privilege, just a universal smell of asparagus.

Yet in spite of this abundance, in spite of this daily luxury, it's
from village neighbours that I've learned.

How to make the most of asparagus (for 4–6)

---

        2 lb. bunch of asparagus
        1½ lb. new potatoes
        4–6 hard-boiled or mollet eggs

Scrape the new potatoes and leave them in water until required.
Peel the hard part from the asparagus stems, then trim 2–3 inches
from the bottom – this is the part usually left on the side of the
plate. Tie the asparagus into bunches.

Take a large saucepan. Put 2 inches of water into it with a
teaspoon of salt, and bring to the boil. Stand the bunches of asparagus upright in the pan, put the stem trimmings round them,
and the new potatoes on top. Put the lid on the pan, or arrange a
domed cover of silver foil on it if the asparagus heads come above
the rim. They will cook in the steam and be tender by the time the
lower part of the stalks is done. Allow at least 20 minutes.

Special pans with an internal strainer can be bought, in France, for cooking asparagus. One or two shops in London may be able to supply them, but usually one has to improvise with pan and foil. Unless you grow asparagus, the cost of a special pan is hardly justified.

Remove the asparagus, when cooked, to a colander to drain, or arrange it on an old-fashioned meat dish with a removable strainer. Put the potatoes, which will be delicately flavoured with asparagus, round the edge of the dish, together with the eggs cut in half. Serve hot, warm or cold, with one of the sauces given on pp. 145–7.

This dish makes an excellent main course for a summer lunch, but if you want to make it a little more substantial, wrap thin slices of Bayonne, Westphalian or Parma ham round bundles of asparagus. In Switzerland, air-dried beef from the Grisons is eaten with asparagus in this way.

You are left with the asparagus water and stalk trimmings, enough to transform the evening's soup into something unusually good:

8 oz. peeled and cubed potato
4 oz. chopped onion
1–2 cloves garlic, chopped
2 oz. butter
1 dessertspoon flour (see recipe)
asparagus water and trimmings
milk or chicken stock
cream to finish, or butter
chopped parsley and chervil, or a
    head or two of asparagus saved from lunch

Stew potato, onion and garlic gently in the butter, without browning them. If you intend to put the soup through a sieve or *mouli-légumes*, stir in the flour: if you're going to liquidize it, the flour is unnecessary. Pour in the asparagus water and simmer until the potatoes are just cooked. Add the asparagus trimmings, and when they are heated through sieve or liquidize the soup.

Return it to a clean pan, and bring it to the right consistency by stock. Reheat to just below boiling point, and finish the soup with a spoonful of cream per person, or a knob of butter. Sprinkle with the chopped herbs, or with the asparagus cut into pieces the size of peas.

Hot sauces for asparagus

Flemish sauce: serve each person with a hard-boiled or mollet egg (exactly 6 minutes in boiling water for a large one, leaving the yolk slightly liquid), and have a sauceboat of melted butter on the table (allow 1 oz. per person). The eggs should be crushed with a fork, seasoned, and then moistened with melted butter. The asparagus is dipped into this mixture before being eaten in the usual way.

A French version of this method serves each person with a boiled egg and a little pot of melted butter. First dip the asparagus into the butter, then into the runny egg yolk, as if it were a child's bread 'soldier'.

Maltese sauce: if Flemish sauce is the simplest, Maltese sauce is the best to serve with asparagus. It is really a variation of Hollandaise sauce:

>   3 tablespoons white wine vinegar
>   2 tablespoons water
>   10 white peppercorns
>   3 large egg yolks
>   6 oz. unsalted butter, cut into 12 pieces
>   juice and grated rind of an orange,
>   preferably a blood orange
>   salt and lemon juice to taste

Boil vinegar, water and peppercorns in a small pan until they're reduced to 1 tablespoon of liquid. Strain it into a large pudding basin, or the top of a double boiler, and leave to cool. Beat in the egg yolks with a wooden spoon, then set the basin over a pan of simmering water on a low heat. Add the butter knob by knob, stirring all the time. Remember that you are really making hot mayonnaise, so don't add more butter until the previous piece is absorbed. If the sauce curdles, the remedy is the same as for mayonnaise: put another yolk into a clean basin, and start again, adding the curdled mixture slowly. The sauce is finished and ready for its final seasoning when it coats the back of the spoon like a custard. Finish with the rind and juice of the orange, some salt and a little lemon juice if extra sharpness is needed.

The consistency of the sauce may be varied by using less butter, say 4 oz. to 3 yolks: Escoffier used 8 oz. of butter to 2 yolks.

This sauce is not difficult: it needs concentration, and calm patience. See that the water keeps at a bare simmer, if it begins to boil hard the eggs are likely to scramble. I recommend the following timetable: (1) peel the asparagus, (2) make the sauce and stand it at the side of the stove, over hot but not simmering water, while you (3) cook the asparagus. The sauce will come to no harm, so long as you give it an occasional stir and make sure it doesn't get too hot.

Sauce Hollandaise: the above recipe without the orange juice and rind. A basic sauce, for salmon, and other poached fish, eggs and vegetables to be served as a course on their own – true French beans, broccoli of all kinds, globe artichokes, sea kale, and of course asparagus.

Sauce Mousseline: beat 3½–4 oz. double cream until thick, and fold it carefully into sauce Hollandaise just before serving. Correct the seasoning.

Cold sauces for asparagus

Vinaigrette aux fines herbes: 1 tablespoon lemon juice, or tarragon wine vinegar, beaten up with salt, pepper, a teaspoon of sugar, and 5–6 tablespoons of olive oil. Flavour with plenty of chopped parsley, tarragon, chervil, and chives or spring onion tops.

Mayonnaise Maltese style: 2 egg yolks, salt, pepper, well beaten together with 1 teaspoon lemon juice or wine vinegar. Drop by drop, beat in ¼ pint olive oil; then another ¼ pint in a steady stream. Season with more lemon juice or vinegar, and the grated rind and juice of a blood orange.

Tarragon cream (a delicious, quickly-made sauce from *Food for the Greedy*, Nancy Shaw, published in 1936 by Cobden-Sanderson): 'Season some thick cream with salt and pepper, and a dust of curry powder; and whip it until thick. Then flavour it by adding gradually a few drops of white tarragon vinegar and place it on ice for a short time before being served. To be sent up in a sauce boat for cold asparagus.' Don't overdo the chilling: in the thirties, domestic refrigerators were the new kitchen toy, food was chilled whenever possible – not always a good thing for delicate flavours.

Dijon sauce: crush the yolk of a hard-boiled egg with 3 *petits suisses* cheeses, to a smooth paste. Add 2 tablespoons Dijon mustard, then drop by drop 4 oz. oil. Flavour with lemon juice. This sauce, which I've taken from a French periodical, is good with hard-boiled eggs on their own, and with other cold vegetables such as artichokes. It should be the consistency of mayonnaise.

Chicken, rabbit or lamb in the Argenteuil style (for 6)

I like the proud habit of calling a dish after the place where a main ingredient flourishes. Eggs Florentine (spinach), Crécy soup (carrots), omelette Lyonnaise (onions), sauce Maltaise (blood oranges). We could by the same token call this dish chicken Evesham style; or Battersea style, in memory of those acres and acres of early asparagus beds that now lie under rows of grey houses, a power station and a fun fair. Argenteuil, though, must be allowed, because it's unmistakably a French recipe and a good one. It also seems suitable that Argenteuil, where Monet set up his easel beside the Seine, should produce asparagus. Potatoes, carrots, onions, have solid merits, I agree, one could not imagine life without them, but asparagus is a most impressionist vegetable. Proust saw a pile of them lying on the kitchen table, 'tinged with ultramarine and rosy pink which ran from their heads, finely stippled in mauve and azure, through a series of imperceptible changes to their white feet, still stained a little by the soil of their garden-bed'.*

*A la recherche du temps perdu.

2–3 lb. asparagus
1 large chicken, or rabbit, jointed, or
   2lb. boned shoulder of lamb cut in
   2-inch pieces
2 oz. butter
4 new season's onions, chopped
1 large tablespoon flour
¼ pint cream
lemon juice, salt, pepper to taste

Clean and cook the asparagus in the usual way, and put a quarter of it through a sieve, or liquidize, to make a purée. Meanwhile brown the meat and onions lightly in the butter. Stir in the flour, then about 1½ gills of the asparagus water. Simmer until the meat is cooked, stirring it about every so often. Be careful that the liquid does not evaporate too quickly: if you cannot turn the heat down very low, it's a good idea to cover the pan with a lid or piece of foil, so that the liquid is conserved. More asparagus water can be added, but watch the saltiness.

When the meat is just cooked, stir the cream into the sauce and keep it boiling for 3 or 4 minutes until it begins to thicken nicely. Then add the asparagus purée and bring it back to the boil. Correct the seasoning with salt and pepper, and sharpen with a little lemon juice. The sauce should be well amalgamated and thick, without being heavy. It will also be a most beautiful green colour. There should not be too much of it (the English tend to souse meat in thin liquids).

Arrange the cooked asparagus on a hot serving dish, either in bunches or as a circle round the edge. Pour the meat and sauce into the centre. Serve immediately.

Out of season, this dish may be made successfully with frozen asparagus. Three packets are the minimum requirement, 4 are better. In either case, allow half a pound of cooked asparagus for the purée.

Asparagus and egg tart

This and the following recipe provide good ways of stretching a small quantity of asparagus (they both lend themselves to tactful adjustment according to the resources of the larder as well). Don't use the finest quality, thick asparagus, but the thinner kind with spears about ¼ inch thick: out of season, frozen asparagus may be used.

> shortcrust pastry case, 9 inch diameter
> ½–1 lb. asparagus
> 2 oz. butter
> 1 small clove garlic, crushed
> 8 eggs
> 2 tablespoons cream (optional)
> salt, pepper

Bake the shortcrust pastry blind, in the usual way; clean and boil and drain the asparagus, having first trimmed it to 4-inch lengths (use trimmings and asparagus water for soup, see p. 144). Beat the eggs just enough to amalgamate yolks and whites; melt the butter slowly in a heavy pan with the garlic, and add the eggs. Stir them with a wooden spoon over a very low heat until they start to look scrambled, but are still rather liquid. Then remove the pan from the heat and add the cream if used (the eggs will continue to cook in their own heat). Season with salt and pepper.

While the eggs are cooking, reheat the pastry case in the oven, and the asparagus in a little cooking water. Turn the scrambled eggs into the pastry case, and arrange the asparagus on top. Serve immediately.

If you wish to serve the tart cold, put all the ingredients together just before serving so that the pastry has no chance of becoming soggy.

Asparagus au gratin (for 4–6)

Vegetables *au gratin* – leeks, purple sprouting broccoli, sea kale, potatoes and so on – make a good supper dish, or a delicious first course for a dinner party. Vegetables and sauce can both be cooked and put together several hours before the meal, then reheated just before the meal begins.

> 1–2 lb. asparagus
> 4–6 hard-boiled eggs

generous tablespoon butter
heaped tablespoon flour
8 oz. hot milk
8 oz. hot asparagus water
4 tablespoons cream
2 slices cooked ham (optional)
2 oz. grated cheese, preferably Gruyère
1 heaped tablespoon breadcrumbs
1 oz. melted butter
nutmeg, salt, pepper to taste

Cook and drain the asparagus in the usual way. Melt the tablespoon of butter in a heavy pan, stir in the flour and leave to
bubble for a moment or two. Add the milk and asparagus water
gradually to make a smooth sauce. Simmer for 15 minutes or
more, until the sauce is thick. Chop the ham, if it's to be used, and
add to the sauce with the cream. Season with salt, pepper and
nutmeg.

Arrange the asparagus in an oval gratin dish, with the sliced
hard-boiled eggs on top. Pour the sauce over them, leaving a clear
¼ inch at the top of the dish or the sauce will boil over and make a
mess. Mix cheese and breadcrumbs and scatter them on top of the
sauce. Dribble the melted butter evenly over them, and put into a
hot oven, Mark 7, 425°F, for about 20 minutes until the dish is
bubbling and brown (this can also be done under the grill).

Sweet Carrots

Carrots are sweet. And carrots are a beautiful colour. And they are cheap.

It's impossible to imagine cooking without them; they've become a basic pot-herb of European kitchens. English, Irish, Scottish, French, German and Italian soups and stews demand carrots. So do Italian tomato and beef sauces for pasta (carrots were first cultivated in the Mediterranean gardens of Greece and Rome).

We rely on these fashionably-coloured roots without a thought. Except perhaps for a moment's gratitude when children nibble them raw, rather than sweets, even if they don't make their hair curl. Or when they arrive at the greengrocer's in late spring, yellow-orange bunches with plumed green leaves – and a higher price than we've been paying for carrots all winter.

They're worth more attention. I'm not suggesting carrots at every meal, as in our house when I was preparing this chapter; and as in nineteenth-century Vichy, where smart doctors still seemed to agree with Galen, the great second century Graeco-Roman physician to Marcus Aurelius, that carrots help to break wind and scour the digestion. It's their gayer virtues that need exploiting. For instance, carrots make vivid apricot-coloured jam, and good puddings like the angels' hair charlotte on p. 158, or Hannah Glasse's carrot pudding on p. 159. It's said that we've given up making such things, though a faint hint of them did come back during the last war. In those days anything sweet was welcomed and exploited. There was a popular Christmas pudding recipe containing grated carrot. And I remember a high spot of school catering, a carrot flan, when the bright orange rings, boiled with some sugar first, were set in lemon jelly discreetly flavoured with ginger. The strange pudding looked beautiful. After a moment or two of schoolgirl priggery, hunger overcame dislike of the unknown, and we found the flan delicious. Now I try all the sweet carrot recipes I can find. It's the combination of flavour, colour and agreeable chewiness that makes the carrot so successful a pudding ingredient.

To start with, though, we put carrots into soups or salads, their freshness stimulates tired appetites at the start of an evening meal.

Carrot salad (for 4)

Of all carrot recipes, this shows off the fresh sweetness and brilliant colour of the carrot to best advantage. I'm always surprised that it's not served more often in homes and restaurants. Children love it. It costs very little. It's the easiest dish in the world to prepare, and, by changing the green herb, the flavour can be varied quite simply.

Use old carrots for the richest, sweetest flavour, new carrots for the lightest. The best version of this salad I've ever eaten was seasoned with chopped new fennel leaves, and served on a bright pink oval dish.

> 1 lb. carrots
> about 2 tablespoons chopped fennel,
>   or parsley, or chives, or chervil, or
>   tarragon

4 tablespoons oil
tablespoon lemon juice
salt and sugar

The carrots may be grated to extreme fineness, or to the thickness of matches. Mix in the other ingredients, adding sugar and salt to taste. Chill for at least an hour, and before serving, turn the mass of carrots over; drain it well, the salad should be moist, not swimming in liquid.

Crécy soup (for 4)

Two small towns dispute the title to carrot soups and purées in France – Crécy-en-Ponthieu, the site of the English victory in 1346, up near Abbeville, and Crécy-en-Brie, to the east of Paris, in the cheese and sugar-beet district of the Marne. Both areas grow good root crops. I'm sure battle associations are not intended: the French – or any other nation – would never commemorate their own defeat, a notable defeat, with such a lasting monument as this excellent soup.

½ lb. carrots, sliced
medium onion, chopped
1 oz. rice
1¼ pints veal or chicken stock
sprig thyme
5 oz. butter
3 ½-inch slices bread, cubed

Simmer carrots and onion in a covered pan, with 2 oz. of the butter for about 10 mins. Don't let them brown. Add rice, stock and thyme – which is most important to the flavour. Cook gently for 20–30 minutes. Remove thyme stalk, and sieve or liquidize the soup, adding more stock if necessary. Reheat. Stir in 1 oz. butter just before serving. Meanwhile fry the bread dice in the last 2 oz. butter. Serve with the soup.

Wonderful flavour apart, the muted orange of the carrots and the golden cubes of bread makes this soup a beautiful start to an evening meal, however grand. If you use a good home-made stock, rather than a stock cube, the flavour will repay the extra trouble.

Carrottes à la Vichy (for 4)

The chilling reason for the title of this delicious recipe is that, 'At Vichy' (according to a turn-of-the-century doctor), 'where derangements of the liver and of the biliary digestion are particularly treated, carrots in one or another form are served at every meal . . .' Yellow carrots for the yellow results of indigestion, according to earlier theories of medical treatment.

Some cookery books give the impression that it's the water from Vichy's illustrious springs that makes all the difference to this way of cooking carrots. In fact I've used Vichy water, the recommended substitute for which is tap water and bicarbonate of soda, and tap water on its own, and could taste no difference in the results. It's not water magic, but butter and sugar and concentration of flavour by reducing the cooking liquid, that make Vichy carrots so much better than plain boiled ones. They could almost be eaten at every meal.

> 1 lb. carrots, old or new
> ¾–1 pint water
> 1 oz. sugar
> 2 oz. butter
> ½ teaspoon salt
> chopped parsley and lemon juice
> to finish

Scrape the carrots and slice them diagonally. Put with the other ingredients into a pan (the water should barely cover the carrots). Boil hard, without a lid on the pan, until the water is reduced to a spoonful or two of syrup, and the carrots are cooked. Old carrots may need another 5 or 10 minutes over a low gas, with the lid on the pan to prevent total evaporation and burning. Finish with chopped parsley and lemon juice to taste.

Note: if a little sauce is required, don't use béchamel. Put 3 tablespoons of cream into the pan at the end of the cooking time, and simmer for a few moments before adding parsley and lemon juice.

Bœuf à la mode (for 8–12)

Marriages of beef and carrots are a commonplace of European cookery. Think of most tripe recipes, beef stews, beef stock, beef sauces and boiled beef, and of the finest partnership of them all, *bœuf à la mode*.

Flavour and texture apart, it's the ideal for a Sunday lunch party. Served cold, with no extra accompaniments, it feeds 12 economically and satisfyingly. Served hot, with bread or a few boiled potatoes, it is generous for 8, and much more panic-free to cook than a roast joint.

> 3–5 lb. topside beef
> 4 oz. fat bacon (optional)
> 6 oz. chopped onion
> a little oil
> 4 pig's trotters, or 1 calf's foot
> 3 lb. carrots, sliced
> 2 oz. brandy
> $\frac{1}{2}$–$\frac{3}{4}$ pint red wine
> beef stock
> 2 crushed cloves garlic
> 1–2 bay leaves, 2 large sprigs thyme,
>   2 large sprigs parsley, tied together
>   in a bunch
> chopped parsley to finish

Chill bacon until firm, cut it into strips and lard the beef. This is not strictly necessary, but will improve the beef, counteracting any tendency to dryness.

Brown the beef in a little oil, with the onion. Transfer to a deep casserole or saucepan. Warm the brandy, set it alight and pour flaming over the beef. Add the wine when the flames have died down, the trotters or calf's foot, garlic, herbs and $\frac{1}{2}$ lb. of the carrots. Cover with beef stock; bring to the boil, or rather to a desultory simmer, fix the lid on tightly and cook for 4 hours. This can be done in the oven, but it's easier to listen to the simmering and see that it doesn't develop into a rolling boil, if the pan stays on top of the stove (use an asbestos mat over gas). Test the beef with a larding needle – a 3 lb. piece should be done after 4 hours.

Skim off as much fat as possible, and replace the lid if more cooking time is needed, as it may be for a 4 or 5 lb. piece. Meanwhile cook the rest of the carrots separately in beef stock, with a dessertspoon of sugar.

To serve hot: put the beef on a warm serving dish, arranging the separately cooked carrots round it. Sprinkle with chopped parsley. Strain and skim some of the cooking liquid and serve in a sauceboat (the rest can be used for soups and sauces, and to make brawn with the chopped meat from the trotters).

To serve cold: let the beef cool in the cooking liquid for 4 hours. Remove to a deep, close-fitting dish. Cut away the string, fit the separately cooked carrots round the meat, sliding them down under it and up the sides of the dish. Pour in carefully some of the beef cooking liquid which should have been strained, skimmed and boiled down to a rich flavour. Leave to set in the refrigerator before turning out onto a serving dish.

Chicken fricassée in the Berry style

The Berry lying between Touraine and Burgundy, and partly enclosed by a great sweep of the Loire, is not so famous for food as its two illustrious neighbours. Which is unfair. The wide farmlands centred on Bourges produce fine unpretentious dishes like this one, or the pork and egg pasty on p. 69.

> 3–4 lb. chicken, jointed
>
> *stock:*
> chicken giblets
> 1 medium carrot

1 leek
1 medium onion
bouquet garni
1 pint water

sauce:
2 shallots, or 1 mild onion, chopped
2 lb. carrots, cut into 1½ inch strips
2 oz. butter
1 clove garlic, crushed
heaped tablespoon flour
¼ pint double cream
1 tablespoon wine vinegar
2 egg yolks

Make the stock by simmering the ingredients together for 1 hour. Then blanch the carrots in boiling salted water for 5 minutes, pour them into a sieve and rinse under the cold tap. Drain them well.

Melt the butter in a large heavy pan, cook the carrots in it until they're lightly browned. Remove them, and put in the chicken, shallots or onion and garlic. When they are golden brown, stir in the flour, and then the strained stock. Bring to the boil, then add the carrots. Leave the chicken to simmer, uncovered, for about ¾ of an hour, or until it's cooked, removing the breast joints, when they are done, to a warm dish. Mix cream, vinegar and yolks together. Put the cooked chicken and carrots on to the serving dish with the breast joints. Pour a little boiling liquid into the cream and egg mixture, return to the pan and cook without boiling until thick. Pour over chicken, etc., and serve very hot.

Mrs Beeton's carrot jam to imitate apricot preserve

To every lb. of carrot pulp allow:
> 1 lb. granulated sugar
> grated rind of 1 lemon
> strained juice of 2 lemons
> 6 chopped bitter almonds
> 2 tablespoons brandy

'Select young carrots; wash and scrape them clean, cut them into round pieces, put them into a saucepan with sufficient water to cover them, and let them simmer until perfectly soft; then beat them through a sieve (or *mouli-légumes*). Weigh the pulp, and to every lb. allow the above ingredients. Put the pulp into a preserving-pan with the sugar, and let this boil for 5 minutes, stirring and skimming all the time. When cold, add the lemon-rind and juice, almonds and brandy; mix these well with the jam; then put it into pots, which must be well covered and kept in a dry place. The brandy may be omitted, but the preserve will then not keep: with the brandy it will remain good for months.'

Note: if you cannot get bitter almonds, use the ordinary ones rather than none at all. Blanch and split them.

Angels' Hair Charlotte (for 8)

We are, as I've said, out of the habit of using carrots for sweet dishes. One has to search older cookery books for baked or steamed puddings, for rich carrot tarts, for sweet carrot pickles or carrot and orange marmalade – or for the best of them all, angels' hair charlotte. At first it was the name I liked, the gay image of copper-nobbed angels in a blue sky. Then the taste proved to be as delicious as the title.

The angels' hair can be made several days, even months, before the charlotte, as it's really a carrot preserve or jam and keeps well.

> *Angels' hair:*
>
> 1 lb. old carrots, weighed when cleaned
> 1 lb. sugar
> lemon
> ¼ pint water

Cut the peel thinly from the lemon, and slice into thin shreds. Cut the carrots into matchstick strips (a mandoline, or moulipulienne saves time). Put carrots, lemon peel, lemon juice, sugar and water into a heavy pan. Boil until setting point is reached (220°F, on a sugar thermometer). Pour into sterilized jars and seal.

Charlotte:

32 boudoir biscuits (2 packets)
juice 1 large orange
6–8 oz. angels' hair (half a pot)
2 oz. blanched, split and toasted almonds
¼ pint each double and single cream

Use a charlotte mould, a soufflé dish, or a straight-sided bowl of 2–3 pints capacity. Make a 2-foot strap, 1½ inches wide, of doubled silver foil; fit it down, across and up the inside of the mould, so that the two ends stick up. Line the mould completely with silver foil. (This is not as arduous as it sounds, and ensures a perfect turn-out for the charlotte.)

To make the charlotte filling, whip the two creams together until light and firm, and fold in the angels' hair and almonds.

To assemble the charlotte, dip the smooth side of the boudoir biscuits, one by one into the orange juice. Fit them immediately into the mould to make a lining, sugar side outwards. Do the sides first, then cut biscuits to fit the bottom. Make sure they don't become too soggy. Pile in the filling. Biscuits, and bits of biscuit left over, can be used for a top layer, if there's enough room.

Cover and chill for at least 4 hours. Just before the meal, remove the cover, and ease the charlotte gently by moving the ends of the foil strap. Now place the serving dish, upside down, on top of the mould, and turn the whole thing the right way up. Finally, lift up the mould carefully, and peel off the foil strap and lining.

Hannah Glasse's carrot pudding (for 4)

I've often wondered why the English seem to have excelled in puddings and cakes, why earlier cookery books only come alive at the sweet sections (French bourgeois cookeries sparkle from soup through to vegetables, flagging slightly at dessert). A grandmotherly reminiscence gave me a possible explanation. She described the kitchen of a pre-war English middle-class household as forbidden territory, a silent battleground. Most cooks did not care at all to work under the eye of the mistress. A tactful house-wife, who wished to keep her cook, restrained her efforts to the 'frills' of the meal, to an occasional pudding or cake. One imagines two centuries of frustrated feminine creativity bursting out into the wonderful puddings which followed oven-roasted beef and aqueous cabbage.

> 4 oz. sweet shortcrust pastry (4 oz. flour,
>   1 tablespoon icing sugar, 2 oz. butter,
>   small egg)
>
> *filling:*
>
> 2 oz. finely grated carrot
> 2 oz. breadcrumbs
> 2 egg yolks
> 1 egg white
> ¼ pint cream
> 2 oz. melted but cool butter
> 1 liqueur glass brandy
> 1 tablespoon orange flower water
> 3–4 tablespoons sugar
> about ¼ of a nutmeg grated

Line an 8½ or 9½ inch tart tin, with a removable base, with the pastry (Hannah Glasse used puff pastry, but nowadays I think we prefer the crispness of sweet shortcrust for open tarts). Beat the filling ingredients together, adding sugar and nutmeg to taste. If you cannot find orange flower water at local chemists' or grocers' shops, add a little extra cream and more nutmeg. Bake in a mod-erate oven, Mark 3–4, 325–350°F, until the filling has risen a little and acquired a golden crust. Eat warm or cold. The filling is de-licious, with the texture though not the flavour of grated coco-nut.

Celery

The fine pleasure of buying celery in earthy heads, after the first improving frosts of winter, is gradually being eroded by the wash of enterprise and aviation. Almost the year round, cleaned and slightly flabby greenish celery, sometimes from America, is on sale at inviting prices. It's the wise cook who averts her eyes from this profuse and plastic display, and waits until November. Then crispness and flavour are at their peak, and celery can provide a perfect antidote to the heavy diet of dark months. Everyone feels better for something light, something simple. In any case one of the greatest luxuries you can have in Britain today is simple food of the best quality (how often do people in towns eat good boiled eggs?).

In the 12 days of Christmas particularly, it's worth exploiting celery, which is then in prime condition. 'This herb Celery is for its high and grateful taste ever placed in the middle of the grand sallet at our great men's tables, and our proctors' feasts, as the grace of the whole board.' That was John Evelyn writing in 1699, when the habit (introduced from Italy) of eating blanched celery as a salad had been common for 20 or 30 years. But the recipes I've chosen for celery – and for celeriac – are not for salad only. It's the most versatile of winter vegetables. Against other Christmas expenditure, celery at 9p or 12p a head is negligible, which makes experiment possible without anxiety. And it's quick to prepare, with little waste.

Celeriac is a turnip-rooted variety of the same species, much used in Germany and France. Commonly on sale in Britain, it is interchangeable in some of the recipes that follow – though it has a salad or two of its own. Its turnip root makes it keep much longer than sticks of celery. This is an advantage, but for me its rather solid texture puts it second to celery. However, a purée of celeriac goes well with strong-flavoured game – venison, pheasant, hare and so on – where you need something bland but more interestingly flavoured than potato. Like chestnut purée, which is often served with game as well, celeriac purée needs to be well flavoured, to be firm without being stodgy, creamy without being sloppy.

Celery and sea salt

This is the best way of eating first-class celery, but care must be taken with butter and salt. Marks and Spencer now stock the best, unsalted butter from Normandy (at half the price one pays in France). Unadulterated sea salt is harder to come by, but worth the trouble – and expense. Once you've tasted it, you won't want to return to the free-running varieties. Maldon or Tidman's sea salt can be bought at health food shops and good groceries.

Put on the table two or three heads of celery, outside stalks removed (use these for soup, or in stews), and the inner stalks separated, washed and chilled. Have a dish of unsalted butter at spreading temperature, and some sea salt (a salt mill isn't necessary). Each person puts butter fairly thickly into the channel of his celery sticks, then sprinkles a thin line of sea salt along it. Simple and delicious. Avoid embellishments. A good way to start a meal.

Céléri-rémoulade (for 4)

An excellent hors d'œuvre, which should be assembled not too long before the meal. Making the mayonnaise a day or two ahead, and storing it in the refrigerator, reduces the final work:

mayonnaise:

2 egg yolks
1 good teaspoon Dijon mustard
⅓ pint olive oil, or corn oil
wine vinegar, salt, pepper

plus:

1 celeriac
4 tablespoons vinegar or lemon juice
chopped parsley

For the mayonnaise, warm a sturdy bowl or mortar under the hot tap and dry it. Put in the yolks and mustard and beat well with a wooden spoon. As the yolks begin to thicken, begin pouring in the oil *drop by drop* until you've used up about half. The oil should be at warm room temperature. Advance cautiously to a steady trickle of oil until it's used up, and the mayonnaise is thick and firm. Flavour with vinegar, salt and pepper.

Trim, quarter and peel the celeriac. Grate rapidly, in matchstick shreds, into a bowl of water acidulated with tablespoons of vinegar. (A mandoline cutter, which can be set flat over the top of the bowl, copes well with this.) Bring 1½ pints water to the boil with 2 tablespoons of vinegar, add the drained celeriac and bring rapidly to the boil. Drain the celeriac again, dry well in a clean cloth and mix with the mayonnaise. Sprinkle with chopped parsley; serve well chilled. The vinegar (or lemon juice) in the water stops the celeriac turning grey – which is harmless, but unsightly.

Celery soup (for 4)

This simple soup tastes exceptionally good when flavoured with dill weed (available in the McCormick spice and herb range). Or with chopped fennel leaves.

>8 oz. chopped celery, outside stalks, or
>   celeriac
>4 oz. each chopped onion and diced potato
>3 oz. butter
>2 pints turkey or chicken stock, or 1½
>   pints plus ½ pint milk
>about 1 teaspoon dill weed
>2 tablespoons cream

Stew celery, onion and potato gently in the butter in a covered pan for 10 minutes. Don't let the vegetables brown. Add stock and ½ teaspoon of dill weed. Simmer for 20 minutes if you have a liquidizer, 40 minutes if you use a *mouli-légumes*. Liquidize or mouli the soup. Pour through a sieve into a clean pan (to remove the last few threads of celery), adding the milk if used. Bring slowly to just under the boil, seasoning with salt, pepper and more dill weed if required. Put the cream into the soup dish, and pour the soup in on top. Swirl round with the ladle before serving, to mix in the cream.

There will be enough soup for six, if the rest of the meal is fairly copious.

Two celery stuffings

(1) *with lemon and parsley*

This light and fresh-flavoured stuffing complements the flavour of turkey better than heavier mixtures of chestnuts and sausage-meat. It also goes well with chicken, and with large fish which are to be baked in the oven. Quantities given here are enough for a 10–12 lb. turkey:

8 oz. chopped onion
8 oz. chopped celery
4 oz. butter
12 oz. fresh white breadcrumbs
rind and juice 1 large lemon
4 tablespoons chopped parsley
2 small eggs
salt and pepper

Melt onion and celery in the butter over a low heat, covered, for about 20 minutes. The vegetables should not brown. Remove pan from the heat, and mix with the rest of the ingredients in a large bowl, seasoning to taste.

Never stuff poultry, or anything else, too tightly; the bread-crumbs need room to swell in the cooking.

(2) *with ham*

A variation on the stuffing above, with stronger flavours pre-dominating.

12 oz. fresh white breadcrumbs
milk
4 oz. butter
8 oz. chopped onion
4 large cloves garlic, crushed
6 tablespoons chopped celery
4 tablespoons chopped parsley
6 oz. lean cooked ham, or lean smoked
    bacon uncooked
dessertspoon thyme
rind and juice of 1 large lemon
2 medium eggs
salt, black pepper

Moisten the crumbs slightly with a little milk: they should be damp without surplus liquid. Melt butter and cook onion, garlic and celery in it for about 20 minutes. Don't let them brown. Meanwhile chop or mince the ham finely (or the bacon). Mix all the ingredients together with salt and pepper to taste.

Boiled turkey and celery sauce

A favourite dish of the Victorians. Quite rightly, too. Stuff the bird with the celery and lemon stuffing above, and sew up the openings firmly. You will need a ham kettle to cook the bird in, though a preserving pan could be used with a lid of silver foil if your turkey is a sizeable creature.

stock:
4 medium carrots, sliced
1 turnip, sliced
stick celery, sliced
3 onions, each stuck with 3 cloves
10 black peppercorns
heaped tablespoon salt
2 bay leaves
4 sprigs thyme
nice bundle of parsley stalks

sauce:
head of celery
3 oz. butter
béchamel sauce (2 oz. each butter and
    flour, ¾ pint hot milk)
¼ pint double cream

Put the stuffed turkey, breast down, in the pan. Add the stock ingredients, and enough cold water barely to cover the bird. Bring to the boil and simmer for 2 hours, or until the turkey is done (the legs will pull easily away from the body, and the flesh will start to break from the bones). Keep the stock for soup.

Meanwhile wash, trim and string the celery. Cut into strips, and blanch in boiling salted water for 20 minutes. Drain and simmer in butter, covered, for 15 minutes. Add the béchamel sauce, and cook slowly for another 10 minutes. Liquidize or put through a *mouli-légumes*. Sieve, stir in the cream and reheat. Adjust the seasoning.

Purée of celeriac

This purée goes well with game as I've mentioned, or with turkey or chicken. It's a recipe that can be adjusted to taste, but the result should never be watery.

> large celeriac
> ⅓ its weight in potatoes
> 4–6 oz. butter
> parsley, chervil, salt, pepper

Quarter, peel and cut the celeriac into 1-inch cubes. Cook in boiling salted water for 10 minutes. Drain well, then stew in 3 oz. butter (cover the pan) for 20 minutes, or until celeriac is cooked. Put through a sieve or *mouli-légumes* – don't liquidize the celeriac or it will be too soft and smooth.

Meanwhile scrub, boil and peel the potatoes. Sieve in the same way and add to the celeriac. Add chopped herbs, salt, pepper and more butter to taste. Reheat and serve.

Note: If you have some thick béchamel or cream sauce, this may be substituted for the potatoes.

Peking celery

Celery as a hot vegetable is often a watery disaster, as anyone who eats in railway dining cars will know. The French way of avoiding this is to blanch the celery, cut in strips, in boiling water for 20 minutes, then to drain it well and stew slowly in butter until cooked but biteable. Lemon juice and chopped parsley are stirred in with the final seasoning of salt and pepper. The same method can be applied to celeriac (see recipe above).

But here is another method, more economical and quite as good. The celery retains its crispness, acquires an extra piquant flavour, and can be eaten hot, warm or cold. The recipe was given me by a Chinese friend, who serves it with poultry; it shows a method which can be adapted to many other vegetables such as Florentine fennel, or chicory, or Savoy cabbage.

> head of celery
> corn or groundnut oil
> soya sauce
> freshly ground black pepper

Trim the celery (keep the leaves for soup), and separate, wash and string the sticks. Cut them into ¼-inch strips on the bias, i.e. at an angle of 45° when the stick is laid pointing towards you. Cover the bottom of a large heavy frying pan with a thin film of oil. When it begins to smoke, throw in the celery pieces and sizzle, stirring for 4 minutes. Add a good dash of soya sauce, and plenty of black pepper. Stir the celery about (ideally with chopsticks) until the sauce is absorbed. This takes about eight minutes. If you wish to serve the celery cold, keep it in a cool place but not the refrigerator.

Mixed celery salads

---

(1) *Celery and beetroot.* A good layer of sliced, boiled or baked beetroot, with a roughly equal quantity of sliced celery laid on top. Good with turkey, or chicken.
Dressing: 1 tablespoon wine vinegar, 4 tablespoons olive oil, salt, black pepper, i.e. vinaigrette.

(2) *Salad cauchoise,* i.e. from the Pays de Caux, the chalk country in northern Normandy, behind Rouen.
   1 washed, sliced head of celery, mixed with ¾ lb. potatoes, scrubbed, boiled and peeled, then sliced.
Dressing: 3 oz. double cream lightly whipped, and seasoned with salt, pepper, wine vinegar and lemon juice.
Garnish: 1 truffle, chopped, and 1 good slice of lean, raw smoked ham, chopped. Tinned truffles and raw ham can be bought from delicatessen shops.

(3) *Celery and turkey.* Equal quantities of diced, cold turkey (or

chicken), diced crisp unpeeled eating apples (Reinettes or Cox's), sliced celery, plus 3 oz. Gruyère cheese to each 8 oz. poultry.
Dressing: vinaigrette or mayonnaise (see above).

(4) *Celeriac and apple.* Another Normandy salad. Prepare celeriac. as for *céleri-rémoulade.* Weigh the blanched shreds, and add half the weight in strips of unpeeled Reinette apples (or Cox's).
Dressing: vinaigrette.

(5) *Waldorf.* This famous combination of diced, unpeeled eating apples and sliced celery, dressed with mayonnaise, was invented by the *maître d'hôtel* of the Waldorf-Astoria in New York. Walnuts were a later addition. Use equal quantities of celery and apple. Be sure to choose crisp eaters; the woolly kind are disastrous in this kind of dish. Serve chilled.

(6) *Celery and walnut.* 1 head of celery, trimmed, washed and sliced. Half its weight in shelled walnuts.
Dressing: 3 good tablespoons mayonnaise mixed with 3 good tablespoons of double cream.
Garnish: a ring of watercress, picked into sprigs. Serve chilled.

(7) *Cromwell salad.* ¾ lb. prepared celery, mixed with ½ lb. shelled walnuts. Put into a lettuce-lined bowl.
Dressing: ¼ pint mayonnaise mixed with 3 oz. well-mashed Roquefort cheese, and 3 tablespoons oil, 1 tablespoon wine vinegar, and up to 1 tablespoon Worcester sauce, depending on taste.
   Why Cromwell? In this salad the only ingredients he would have been familiar with are the walnuts, oil and vinegar. Perhaps there is a reference to his victory at Worcester, on 3 September 1651 in the last ingredient.

(8) *Celery and Florentine fennel.* 1 head of celery, prepared and sliced, mixed with 1 large head of fennel, sliced.
Dressing: vinaigrette (see salad 1).
Garnish: 2–3 oz. Gruyère cheese, in small dice.
Serve chilled.

(9) *Stuffed celery salad*. Make a thick pommade of ¾ lb. Roquefort, Stilton or cream cheese, with ¼ lb. unsalted butter (or 2 oz. unsalted and 2 tablespoons cream). Season with salt, pepper, and, in the case of cream cheese, with chives and parsley. Smooth this paste into the channels of celery sticks. Cut slantwise into short lengths, and put into a bowl without dressing.

Chicory

Some years ago now we were visiting the painted caves of France, and came at last to La Mouthe with its image of a thatched shelter, an inverted V, painted and scraped on to the rock face. After the grandeur of Lascaux, and the squeeze-belly narrows of Font-de-Gaume, La Mouthe was domestic, tamed, providing useful storage space for a busy farm (which also had an identical shelter to the one drawn in the cave, a design with 20,000 years success). A heavy wooden door barred the entrance. Inside were piles of potatoes, and further in a long hummock of reddish earth. It glimmered in the thin light with many pale points. 'Chicory,' said the farmer's wife, and raised her carbide lamp as she disappeared into the gallery opening off the cave.

It's strange to think that this chicory, the chicory we buy at the greengrocer's (and the chicory sometimes added to coffee) is the same as the slender plant of European fields and gardens. The flat blue rosettes with their square-ended petals which cling tightly to the stem do not at all make one think of crisp winter salads.

Although the shoots of chicory had long been eaten as a salad, it wasn't until about 1845 that market gardeners near Brussels began to blanch the shoots in banks of earth, like celery. This reduced the bitterness of the leaves. Belgium is still the largest producer in Europe, growing 90,000 tons a year on the rich light acres of Brabant (half is for export, mainly to France).

An interesting thing is that the producers evolved a system which includes the advantages of La Mouthe or any other cave – steady temperature of about 60°F, insulation from frost, and absence of light. Seeds are sown in the ordinary way in the spring, and the roots are taken up and trimmed of their leaves in the autumn. They are then packed together on the ground in long rows. Specially prepared soil is mounded up over them. These oblong beds are warmed from below by hot water pipes or electrically heated metal lattices. The weather is kept out by corrugated iron sheets, bent over them like miniature hangers, and lagged with straw. Very quickly the shoots grow to an ideal 6 inches of compact white leaves, ready to be forked out. Women and old people – chicory growing is a family business – trim and pack the heads for market. The strong cardboard boxes, often lined with waxy royal-blue paper, are not a luxury touch but a necessity: the blanched chicory must be protected from too much light or it will turn green and bitter.

Basic preparation and cooking of chicory

Allow a minimum of two heads per person when cooking chicory (salads are a different matter – one each is enough). Store, wrapped up, in a cool place, best of all – seeing that the exclusion of light is important – is the crisper drawer of a refrigerator, where it will keep in good condition for ten days.

Prepare chicory immediately before cooking it. Never leave it to soak in a bowl of cold water; just remove the brownish edges of the leaves, and a thin slice from the cut end, and rinse as briefly as possible under a cold tap. Pat dry with a clean tea towel. Take out the tiny, bitter core with a sharp pointed knife.

To cook chicory, put it into a large saucepan in flat layers, with 2 teaspoons of sugar, the juice of a lemon and enough boiling water to cover. Simmer until the chicory's almost cooked, about 20–30 minutes, testing it with a larding needle or sharp knife. Pour away the liquor. Add a good lump of butter, or the juices from roasting meat, and finish the cooking at a more vigorous temperature. Turn the heads over occasionally in the syrupy moisture so that they acquire a slight glaze. Sprinkle with parsley and serve as a hot vegetable, with meat.

Like many other vegetables, chicory can provide a delicious course on its own, particularly when presented in more elaborate ways.

Chicory with cream sauce (for 6)

A good but simple recipe. Try it on its own, or with chicken, boiled ham or salt pork:

> 12 heads chicory, prepared
> 3 oz. butter
> 4 oz. double cream
> 1 teaspoon sugar
> juice of half a lemon
> 6 lemon slices or quarters
> salt, pepper, chopped parsley

Melt the butter in a large heavy frying pan, and add the sugar, and chicory which should lie in a single layer. Turn the chicory over so that it's coated with butter. Pour in the lemon juice and cover the pan with a lid or silver foil. Simmer for about 40 minutes, by which time the chicory should be cooked (small heads will take 20–30 minutes). Remove it to serving dish and keep warm. Bring the cream to the boil in a small pan, then tip it into the chicory pan juices. After a few moments hard boiling, the sauce should have reduced to a smooth thickness. Taste and correct the seasoning.

Pour over the chicory, sprinkle with parsley, garnish with lemon slices or quarters and serve immediately. Cream sauces should never be allowed to hang around and become tepid: make sure, too, that the plates are well heated.

Chicory au gratin (for 4)

The French are clever at using piquant stuffings in unusual ways. No doubt this is the result of antique thrift – like our country habit of serving suet pudding before the meat – but it often seems more like inspiration. Nicely seasoned with herbs, ham and spices, the breadcrumbs don't just puff out the dish, they embellish it:

> 8 heads chicory, prepared
> 2 medium onions
> 1 large clove garlic
> 2 slices gammon, or 4 smoked back
>   rashers
> 4 oz. breadcrumbs
> milk
> 6 sprigs parsley, chopped
> 4 oz. grated cheese, preferably Gruyère
> 3 oz. butter
> salt, pepper, nutmeg

Blanch the chicory in boiling, salted water for 8 minutes. Remove and drain in a colander. Put onion, garlic, and gammon or bacon through the mincer. Soak the breadcrumbs in a very little milk to moisten them; squeeze out any surplus moisture. Mix with the minced gammon, etc., the parsley and 3 oz. of the cheese. Season well with salt, pepper and nutmeg. Use 1 oz. of butter to grease an oval gratin dish, then put in half the stuffing. Lay the chicory on top, head to tail, close together, and cover with the rest of the stuffing. Melt the remaining butter and pour it evenly over the top layer of stuffing. Bake in a moderately hot oven, Mark 5, 375°F, for about half an hour. Sprinkle the last ounce of cheese on top, and return to the oven to brown (or place under the grill).

Note: at Saint-Malo, large heads of chicory are hollowed out, and filled with the stuffing, then wrapped in slices of local smoked ham. A glass of muscadet, plenty of butter and a good scatter of cheese, and the dish goes into the oven to bake at a low temperature.

Baked chicory (for 4)

This attractive, easily made dish is a good way of introducing chicory to people who've never eaten it before. Bring it bubbling and brown to the table, and provide good wholemeal bread for everyone to mop up the delicious sauce.

> 8 heads of chicory, prepared
> 8 long rashers of smoked back bacon
> 2–3 oz. grated cheese (Parmesan,
>   Gruyère or Cheddar)
> generous teaspoon French mustard, or
>   nutmeg
> 1 tablespoon butter
> 1 tablespoon flour
> generous half pint hot milk
> salt, pepper

Wrap the bacon round the heads of chicory, so that each one has a spiral jacket. Lay them in a lightly buttered baking dish; they should fit comfortably into it with a little room to spare. Make a sauce by melting the butter, stirring in the flour, and adding the milk, little by little, to avoid lumps. Add ⅔ of the cheese, salt and pepper to taste, and either the mustard or the nutmeg. Plenty of pepper is a good idea, but go carefully with the salt as the bacon will add extra seasoning as the dish cooks. Pour over the chicory. Put into a moderately hot oven, Mark 5, 375°F, for about 40 minutes or until the chicory is cooked. Sprinkle the top with the remaining cheese and brown under the grill.

Note: ham may be substituted for the bacon. In this case, blanch the chicory first for 10 minutes in boiling salted water. Drain, then wrap in the ham and continue with the recipe. Cooking time 15–20 minutes at Mark 7, 425°F.

Curried chicory (for 6)

---

12 heads prepared chicory
2 tablespoons olive oil
1 oz. butter
¾ lb. piece bacon
1 medium onion, chopped
3 cloves garlic, crushed
1 tablespoon flour
1 heaped teaspoon curry powder
1 liqueur glass Calvados or brandy
¼ pint red or white wine (or stock)
1 lb. tomatoes, skinned and quartered
salt, pepper, sugar

Blanch the chicory in boiling, salted water for 15 minutes, until it's nearly cooked. Leave to drain while the sauce is being made. Cut the bacon into strips about 1 inch long and ¼ inch wide and thick (remove rind). Melt oil and butter in a heavy pan, and brown the bacon, onion and garlic lightly. Stir in the flour and curry powder to take up the fat. Add Calvados or brandy, wine or stock, and tomatoes. Season with salt, freshly ground black pepper, and a little sugar to compensate for the likely lack of flavour in the tomatoes. Simmer for half an hour with the lid off the pan. Correct the seasoning, add the chicory to heat through and finish cooking, and serve, very hot, with boiled rice.

Chicory in the Polish style (for 4)

Most recipes for chicory as a hot vegetable, certainly most of the ones in this chapter, use ham and bacon, or a sauce, to contrast with its watery but definite flavour. Here's something quite different. For its blend of crispness and smoothness, for its beautiful appearance, this is my starred dish. A good main course for supper, or first course to a grander meal.

> 8 fine large heads chicory, prepared
> 5 oz. butter
> 2 teaspoons sugar
> juice of 1 lemon
> 4 hard-boiled eggs
> half bunch of parsley, chopped
> 2 oz. white breadcrumbs

Cook the chicory in boiling water with the sugar and 1 ounce of butter and the lemon juice. Meanwhile shell the eggs. Fork them into crumbs, then mix in the parsley and set aside. Fry the breadcrumbs to golden brown in 1½ oz. butter, and keep them warm. Drain the cooked chicory, pressing it a little to get rid of as much moisture as possible, and fry in 1 oz. of butter to brown it lightly. Arrange the heads on a large round serving dish, like the spokes of a wheel: leave a hole in the centre, and put in the egg and parsley. Scatter the browned crumbs over the whole thing. Melt the last of the butter and when it bubbles up, pour it over the chicory, crumbs, etc., and serve immediately.

Two chicory salads

Chicory makes a much better winter salad than floppy lettuce from a plastic bag. It's crisp and juicy, and can quite well be served on its own with just a French dressing, and plenty of freshly ground black pepper. Of all salad vegetables, it combines best with other ingredients. In this respect it even tops celery.

> 6 heads prepared chicory
> 3 oz. shelled walnuts
> 2 oz. raisins, soaked in hot water for
>   1 hour
> 4 oz. mild cheese, diced
> 2 large eating apples

French dressing, mayonnaise or cream
seasoned with French mustard and
lemon juice

Slice the chicory into ½-inch pieces, and push out the half rings of
leaves. Core and dice the apples, but don't peel them. Drain the
raisins. Mix everything together, chill and serve.

4 large heads prepared chicory
5 hard-boiled eggs
2 tablespoons melted butter
2 tablespoons double cream
1 tablespoon chopped parsley
salt, black pepper
12 black olives

Carefully separate and remove the leaves from the chicory heads,
stopping when you come to a core of about 2 inches. Shell and
mash the eggs with a fork, then mix them with cream, parsley and
melted butter. This mass should be lightly coherent, not smooth
or paste-like. Season it well. Fill the chicory leaves with the mixture, arranging them on a serving dish. Put a few slices of olive on
each one, and the tiny cones of chicory in the centre.

Note: 8 oz. cottage cheese may be substituted for the eggs.

Haricot Beans

Every civilization has its special beans. Europe's classical bean, back to the Greeks, was the broad bean. The bean of the Incas, and the Mexicans, was the kidney-bean, which Peruvian Indians were eating several thousand years ago.

When Europe obtained these new kidney-beans quite early in the sixteenth century, they were soon everybody's eating – especially dried, for winter food. It was the French, I think, and the Italians (so we say French bean, and used to say Roman bean) who devised most of the special bean dishes. Variously called haricot beans, butter beans, navy beans, Boston beans, the dried beans were haricots first of all because the French added them, with small turnips, to a haricot or ragoût of mutton.

Don't despise them. Beans may not be the pinnacle of Wine and Food Society living, but it is wonderful what can be made out of a packet of pallid, dull-looking butter beans (from a variety whose pods are yellow or butter coloured) or the smaller haricot beans.

It is wonderful how they combine without ceasing to be beans –
particularly with olive oil. There is a basic marriage for you – if
you like to mix history with your meals – of the two civilizations,
Andean and Mediterranean.

My starred dishes are the last two. One is really a version of an
ancient haricot; the other, from the Southern States, is an improvement of Boston baked beans, which in turn is another haricot with a New World seasoning of molasses.

You can keep haricot and butter beans indefinitely, like other
dried vegetables, but it's better not to. With time they become
drier, harder, increasingly tasteless. To enjoy them at their best,
see if you can find new season Soissons beans in the autumn
(called after the main town of a famous bean-growing district of
France); if you can visit Soho, this should not be too difficult. For
baked bean dishes, from cassoulet to the Southern baked beans on
p. 188, they are especially good. This is aiming at perfection,
though, because the quality of branded beans on every supermarket shelf can be relied upon.

I find haricot beans more useful than the larger butter beans,
whose coarse skins can be obtrusive. Whichever you are using,
disregard instructions to soak overnight. Unless they've been in
the store cupboard for months, this is far too long. Two, three
hours is often enough. Be guided by the fact that dried beans will
absorb enough water to double their weight, more or less. If you
are short of time, cover the beans with cold water in the proportion of 1 lb. beans to 3 pints of water, bring them to the boil,
then leave them to cool for 40 minutes; drain them well, before
continuing with the recipe.

An important point. When cooking beans, add salt at the end of
the cooking time, never at the beginning, or they will harden.

Bean soup (for 6)

The people of Tuscany are the great bean-eaters, the *mangia-
fagioli*, of Europe. They have so many bean dishes that I'm
surprised they've never invented any bean cakes, or buns, in the

Japanese style. But they have invented a special pot for cooking beans in, a *fagiolara*. Apart from being a beautiful object, the *fagiolara* is practical: it can be used over low, direct heat, or in the oven, and, on account of its chianti-flask shape, the top is easily sealed against loss of heat and flavour. In these pots beans simmer in water seasoned with olive oil, garlic, sage, tomato, and perhaps some pickled pork, to make Tuscan – not Boston – baked beans. But for a small party of tired urban stomachs this is the Tuscan recipe I would choose:

> ½ lb. dried haricot, or butter beans
> 2 pints water
> 5 or 6 tablespoons olive oil
> 2 large cloves garlic, chopped not crushed
> bunch parsley, chopped
> salt, black pepper

Soak, then simmer the beans in the water *without salt* until cooked. When they are soft, remove ¼ to ⅓ of the beans, and liquidize or mouli the rest. Season well, diluting the soup with more water if necessary. Reheat, with the whole beans. In a separate pan cook the garlic slowly in 2 tablespoons of the olive oil, until it turns golden. Add to the soup, with the parsley and the rest of the oil. Serve immediately.

Note: if you can't buy good olive oil, don't make do with corn oil, which is tasteless. Use butter instead. The result will be quite different, more like a French soup, but still very good.

Soissons soup

Soissons, a town about 65 miles north-east of Paris, is the centre of an important bean-growing district. So French bean soups have a tendency to be called after it, just as carrot soups are inevitably Crécy, and pea soups are likely to be St Germain.

> ½ lb. dried haricot beans
> 1 medium carrot

1 medium onion, stuck with 3 cloves
bouquet garni
salt, pepper
3–4 oz. cream
1 oz. butter
croûtons of bread fried in butter

Soak the beans. Put them into a large pan with the carrot, onion and herbs, and cover them with water. Simmer, without salting the beans, until they are cooked. Sieve or liquidize them (remove carrot, onion and herbs first) and return to the pan. Season and add more water if the soup is too thick for your liking. Reheat, adding the cream at the end. Pour into the soup tureen and stir in the butter. Serve with croûtons.

Cream of Haricot beans in the Berry style

½ lb. dried haricot beans, soaked
1 large onion
4 oz. potatoes, peeled
water
salt, pepper
3 oz. cream
1 oz. butter
parsley to garnish, and croûtons of bread

Cover beans, onion and potatoes with water. Simmer until cooked. Liquidize or sieve, then season and reheat. Finish as above.

Napoleon's bean salad

Napoleon, when he was on St Helena, used to eat this bean salad at lunchtime every other day. As with Tuscan bean soup, the important ingredient, after the beans, is olive oil.

½ lb. dried haricot beans
good handful of green herbs: chervil,
     tarragon, chives, parsley, etc.
5 tablespoons good olive oil
1 tablespoon tarragon vinegar
teaspoon French mustard (*moutarde
     de Maille*)
salt, freshly ground black pepper

Soak the beans, and simmer in water until they are soft but not disintegrating. Add salt when the beans are nearly ready. Drain and cool. Chop the herbs (cooks of Napoleon's time included the astringent salad burnet) into a salad bowl, and mix in the beans. Leave for an hour or two, for the beans to absorb the flavour of the herbs. Add the rest of the ingredients (which can be adjusted to taste) just before serving.

A tablespoon of chopped mild onion or shallot makes a good addition to the green herbs.

Note: liquidize half a tin of anchovy fillets, with olive oil and a little wine vinegar to make a different but deliciously piquant dressing for haricot beans.

Beans with cream and celery (for 4)

A delicious example of the elegance of French vegetable cookery. Here's something quite ordinary, not rare or luxurious, a subsistence food if you like, treated with love and intelligence. Serve these beans on their own, or as an accompaniment to chicken and turkey: the trick is to cook the celery at the very last moment. Beans and cream can be kept warm for a while, but not the celery.

½ lb. haricot or butter beans
2 oz. butter
nutmeg
3–4 oz. double cream
lemon juice

2 stalks celery
2 oz. extra butter
salt, black pepper

Soak the beans in the usual way. Drain them, and put into a pan with just enough water to cover them. Add 2 oz. butter, pepper and a good grating of nutmeg, but no salt. Simmer with the lid off the pan until the beans are nearly cooked. Put in ¼ teaspoon salt, and finish the cooking. The liquid should almost have disappeared. Stir in the cream, bring back to the boil and cook until the beans are bathed in a thick sauce (it's important not to overcook the beans in the first place). Correct the seasoning with a little lemon juice, salt and pepper.

String the celery well. Slice it across, at an angle, into thin strips. Just before serving the beans, fry the celery in the extra butter until it's lightly browned but still crisp. Keep stirring it about, and don't let the butter burn. Scatter on top of the beans as a garnish.

Chirashi-zushi with sweet beans (for 4–6)

The Japanese are famous for their bean cakes and buns, which are often sold in the most exquisite wrappings and boxes. They also cook beans in syrup and serve them with savoury rice dishes. Beans prepared this way are so good that I sometimes serve an anglicized version of *chirashi-zushi* as an hors d'œuvre, to give us an excuse for eating them. People who are fortunate enough to live near an oriental foodstore might like to substitute the Japanese ingredients (in brackets) for capers, etc.

Choose a plain beautiful serving dish for *chirashi-zushi*, and take extra time to arrange the items elegantly. There are six of them to prepare:

1.

4 oz. haricot or butter beans
3 oz. sugar
½ gill water
½ teaspoon soya sauce (preferably
    Japanese)

Soak and simmer the beans in the usual way, adding a little salt at the end. Drain well. Make syrup of the sugar and ½ gill of water by bringing to the boil, and stirring until the sugar has dissolved. Add the beans and keep them below boiling point for 10 minutes. Stir in the soya sauce and leave to cool.

2.

> 8 oz. rice
> 2 tablespoons wine vinegar
> teaspoon sugar
> soya sauce to taste (or 2–3 tablespoons
>   *dashi*)
> 2 oz. cooked carrots, chopped small
> 1–2 tablespoons capers (or 2 oz.
>   *chirasu-boshi*)

Boil the rice in the usual way. Rinse well under the hot tap, then mix in the other ingredients. More sugar or vinegar or soya sauce – or less – may be added to taste.

3.

> 4 oz. mushrooms (or 1½ oz. dried
>   Japanese mushrooms)
> tablespoon soya sauce (preferably
>   Japanese)
> tablespoon sugar

Slice the stems of the mushrooms, and cut them in strips (dried mushrooms must be soaked in tepid water for about 20 minutes, before slicing). Simmer until cooked in soya sauce and sugar. Cool. Mix in with the rice.

4.

> 4 oz. cooked green beans, preferably
>   *haricots verts*
> teaspoon each soya sauce and wine
>   vinegar (or 2 tablespoons *dashi*, ⅛
>   teaspoon salt)

Mix the ingredients together and leave to soak for an hour.

5.

> 4 oz. cooked, peeled shrimps
> 2 tablespoons wine vinegar
> 1½ tablespoons sugar

Mix together, leave for half an hour, then drain.

6.

    2 eggs
    pinch salt
    teaspoon sugar
    teaspoon soya sauce (or 2 teaspoons
        dashi)
    corn oil

Beat the eggs well, add sugar and soya sauce or *dashi*. Brush a
heavy frying pan with a thin coating of oil, place over a moderate
heat for a few moments, then pour in a thin layer of beaten egg. It
will cook quickly, and should not be moved about but left in an
even layer. Remove with a palette knife or fish slice. Repeat until
the egg is finished and you have 3 or 4 pancakes. Roll them up,
then slice them downwards into thin shreds: they will look like
tiny slices of jam roll.
Serve with warm *saké*. Bowls of clear Japanese soup (with bean
curd and mushrooms) can accompany the dish – the soup is easily
prepared from dehydrated packages sold in oriental food shops.

Leg of lamb in peasant style (for 8)

Beans of all kinds are a favourite accompaniment to lamb in
France. In early summer there will be a dish of the beautiful
stringless *haricots verts*. They will be followed by shelled green
flageolet beans, first fresh, then half-dried as summer passes. In
winter the lamb will be served on a bed of white haricot beans.
Sometimes they will be cooked together:

        3–4 lb. leg of lamb, boned
        2 cloves garlic
        1 lb. haricot beans, soaked
        onion, stuck with 3 cloves
        large carrot, sliced
        bouquet garni

2 oz. butter
8 oz. piece smoked streaky bacon
2 large onions, sliced
1 lb. potatoes, peeled and cubed
1½ pints light stock, preferably prepared
from lamb bones
salt, pepper

Cut the garlic into slivers, and insert them into the lamb (make little cuts with a sharp pointed knife first). Season well and tie firmly into a roll. Put beans, onion stuck with cloves, carrot and herbs into a saucepan; cover with water and simmer for an hour. Meanwhile brown the lamb in butter, in a large oval, enamelled iron pot. Cut the rind from the bacon, then cut it downwards into strips, about 1 inch long by ¼ inch wide and thick. Add bacon to the lamb when it's browned, and transfer the pot to a moderate oven to roast (calculate cooking time according to whether you like lamb well-done or slightly underdone). Half an hour before the lamb is cooked remove the pot from the oven. Put in the sliced onions first, slipping them underneath the meat, then the beans cooked and drained, the potatoes and the stock which should be at boiling point. Cover the pot and return to the oven for about half an hour, or until beans and potatoes are done. Serve in the cooking pot.

Note: in Brittany, salt marsh lamb is often served with haricot beans, but the two are cooked separately. No potatoes or bacon are included. I think the peasant style is more succulent, particularly for our often inferior lamb.

Beans village style (for 6)

This is the easiest recipe for beans I know. It's a good one, and cheap. All you need are two or three homely ingredients, an oven-proof pot (the Italian *fagiolara* does well, or a French storage jar, or stoneware jug), and a collection of open-air appetites.

Beans village style are the antique basis from which cooks

evolved cassoulet in the Languedoc and Boston baked beans in north America. Locally produced French additions were tomatoes, onions, garlic, sausage, preserved goose and occasionally a ragoût of mutton. American additions reflected their trade – molasses, soft brown sugar and rum from the West Indies. People in the circumstances of those days, a century or two or three ago, could not consult books of international cookery for inspiration: they consulted their store cupboards and kitchen gardens and cellars instead.

> 1 lb. haricot beans
> 6–8 oz. streaky bacon in a piece
> bay leaf, sprig thyme, sprig parsley
> salt, pepper

Soak the beans in the usual way. Tie the herbs together. Put all ingredients, except salt, into the cooking pot and add just enough cold water to cover. Add a lid of double foil, firmly secured to prevent steam escaping. Simmer in a slow oven, Mark 2, 300°F until the beans are cooked (1½–2 hours). Season with salt, at the end, as required.

Baked beans Southern style (for 6)

Nearer the home of the kidney-bean, cooks make use of other Southern ingredients – peppers, molasses and tomatoes. Being a hot substantial dish, these baked beans are best followed by fruit, say a chilled pear, or chilled melon.

Follow the ingredients and method for beans village style, but remove them from the oven when they are half-cooked. Take out the herbs, and mix in:

> 1 green pepper, deseeded and chopped
> large onion, chopped
> 2 large tomatoes, chopped
> molasses (black treacle), salt and pepper
>   to taste

Remove the bacon and slice it. Turn the beans, etc., into a large wide dish, put the slices of bacon on top and finish cooking in the oven without a lid. Beans and bacon will develop a rich brown glaze, almost a crust.

Meat stew with beans (for 6)

This recipe, I know, reads unpromisingly. The main ingredients sound like a school stew. But please try it — both flavour and texture are unexpectedly delicious. The interesting thing is the way the beans come almost to dominate the meat. They also thicken the sauce so that the dish coheres agreeably, without stodginess. Don't leave out the garlic and allspice.

> 6 oz. haricot or butter beans
> 1 lb. chuck steak or stewing lamb
> medium onion, chopped
> large clove garlic, chopped
> 2 oz. butter
> large tomato, skinned and chopped
> 2 tablespoons tomato concentrate
> allspice
> salt and pepper

Soak the beans for as short a time as possible. Simmer in unsalted water for 20 minutes and drain. Meanwhile cut the meat into cubes (when buying lamb, allow extra for the weight of the bones), including the fat. Fry onion and garlic in butter gently for about 15 minutes, turn up the heat and brown beef or lamb. Add tomato, tomato concentrate, beans and enough water to cover. When bubbling nicely season with plenty of ground allspice and black pepper. Transfer to a casserole and cook in the oven at Mark 3, 325°F, until meat and beans are cooked (cover the casserole). This takes about an hour. Fifteen minutes before the end of cooking time, season with salt and more pepper and allspice if necessary.

As with baked beans Southern style, it's prudent to follow this dish with fruit on its own.

Leeks

Leeks must be one of the oldest vegetables. They grew leeks (and
still do) in Egypt. Leeks spread north, green and fresh in beastly
winters. They fed the English, the Welsh, the Irish, the Danes.
Simple food. When an Irish hermit 900 years ago wrote a poem to
boast of how simple and good it was to be a hermit, he talked of
having 'fresh leeks, green purity' outside his hut in the woods.
When Englishmen 1400 years ago spoke of a vegetable patch, they
called it a *leactun*, leek-enclosure, as we might speak of a cabbage patch or potato patch or, in Scotland, a kail yard. They
scattered England with leek-patch names – Leckhampstead,
Latton, Leighton Buzzard. Up north, Loughrigg was a Norseman's
laukr or leek ridge. Lawkland his leek-land. Green as a leek was a
standard phrase in our Middle Ages – a green leek again in frozen
winter.

Why are leeks associated with Welshmen, St David and St
David's Day? Books give legends, but none of them sound reason-

able. I suspect it was only because a primitive dependence on leeks, so hardy and so easily grown, lasted in poor, wet Wales when it was on the way out in England. Anyhow, John Parkinson, our great gardener of the time of James I and Charles I, records that leeks had become a poor man's food in England, though leek pottage was still 'a great and general feeding in Wales with the vulgar gentlemen' (before a bunch of Welsh *cennin* hits me in the eye, mud, leaves and all, I hurry to say that 'vulgar gentlemen' means no more than the run of gentlemen).

I think leeks remained a poor man's food till recently – or just a taken-for-granted everyday veg., or an ingredient only. You won't find much about them, say, in Mrs Beeton or Eliza Acton (or even in such a regional recipe book as *Farmhouse Fare*). For every mention of leek there is a dozen of cabbage. But then social attitudes often make fools of us in matters of food – and I shall swear that some of the leek soups are not easily surpassed, the French *Bonne Femme*, the French-American *Vichyssoise*, the soup above soups, Scotland's Cockie Leekie. Talleyrand, who knew more about good food than most politicians – or most cooks – gave a high mark to Cockie Leekie, or Cock-a-Leekie.

To prepare leeks: cut off the roots, the coarse green leaves (can be used up in stock making) and the damaged outer layer. Run under the tap to remove the earth and grit.

They can then be sliced into a colander, and rinsed again.

Or, if they are to be cooked whole, they can be placed, root end up, in a bowl of water for half an hour. Any obstinate pockets of earth can be removed through tiny cuts in the stem.

Potage à la Bonne Femme and Crème Vichyssoise Glacée

These two soups are now linked with the name of Louis Diat, the French chef who over 50 years ago invented the most delicious chilled soup from a commonplace of French peasant cookery. 'Of the many specialities I created for the old Ritz-Carlton,' (he was writing of the hotel in New York) 'none has gained the wide and lasting acclaim of *crème vichyssoise glacée*, the chilled cream of leek and potato soup now served in restaurants everywhere. I suspect that some of the *fins bec* who order it would be much surprised to learn of its humble origins as my mother's simple leek and potato soup. Casting about one day for a new cold soup, I remembered how *maman* used to cool our breakfast soup, on a warm morning, by adding cold milk to it. A cup of cream, an extra straining, and a sprinkle of chives, *et voilà*, I had my new soup. I named my version of *maman*'s soup after Vichy, the famous spa located not twenty miles from our Bourbonnais home, as a tribute to the fine cooking of the region.'*

> 2 fat leeks
> 1 small onion, chopped
> 2 oz. butter
> 1 teaspoon salt
> 2 potatoes (about ½–¾ lb.)
> 1 pint water
> ½ pint milk
>
> *plus* for *Bonne Femme*,
> extra butter or cream, and croûtons
>
> for *Vichyssoise*,
> 8 oz. single cream
> 8 oz. double cream
> chopped chives

Use the white part of the leeks only – there should be between 8 and 12 oz. Chop and put with the onion and butter into a heavy pan. Cover, then stew very gently for about 5 minutes, but do not let the vegetables brown. Add water and cleaned, peeled and diced potatoes, and salt. Simmer until the potatoes are well cooked. Put through the *mouli-légumes* or liquidize.

To finish Bonne Femme soup: Add the milk, heated, and reheat the soup to just under the boil. Correct the seasoning. Stir in a little cream or a good knob of butter to finish, and serve with croûtons of bread fried in butter.

To finish Crème Vichyssoise: Add the milk heated, and the single

* Louis Diat: *Gourmet's Basic French Cook Book*, Hamish Hamilton, 1961.

cream, also heated. Bring the soup back to the boil, stirring to prevent it catching. Strain the soup again, or liquidize again. Stir in the double cream, correct the seasoning, and chill thoroughly. To serve, sprinkle each bowl of soup with finely chopped chives.

The amount of cream may be reduced, and replaced by milk. Alternatively water can be replaced by chicken stock, in double the quantity. The versions above are from Louis Diat himself.

Leeks à la grecque (for 4)

3 or 4 medium leeks
¼ pint olive oil
½ pint water
heaped tablespoon tomato concentrate
heaped teaspoon sugar
2 oz. rice
12 small black olives
chopped parsley
lemon juice and 3 or 4 slices of lemon

Prepare the leeks in the usual way, cutting them into 1½-inch slices. Bring to the boil in a heavy pan with the water, oil, tomato paste and sugar. Season with salt and pepper, then cook, covered, for 5 minutes. Add the rice. Boil, covered, for another 8 minutes – the liquid should be almost entirely absorbed by the rice. Turn off the heat, but leave the pan covered for another 10 or 15 minutes. The rice should be cooked but firm, in agreeable contrast to the moist leeks. Add lemon juice to taste. Serve chilled, with olives, parsley and lemon slices arranged on top.

Poor Man's Asparagus (for 4)

8 thin leeks
2 hard-boiled eggs
1 tablespoon chopped parsley

vinaigrette:

1 tablespoon lemon juice
4 tablespoons olive oil
salt, pepper, sugar to taste

Clean the leeks as above, leaving them whole. Cook in just enough salted water to cover, until tender but firm. About 8–10 minutes. Leave to drain and cool. Mix the vinaigrette ingredients, seasoning well.

Arrange leeks on a serving dish, pour over the vinaigrette and chill. Just before serving, mash the eggs to crumbs with a fork, and arrange with the parsley on top of the leeks.

Cornish Leek Pie

Very similar leek pies and flans have been made for a long time in northern central France, in Flanders, in Wales and in Cornwall. Basic ingredients are the same – leeks, cream, eggs and short pastry – but in Cornwall and Wales and in French Berry, bacon is added as well. This improves the flavour.

Pastry goes either below the filling, as in the *Leek Flammiche* (flan) that Francatelli, Queen Victoria's chef, shaped like a soft leather money-bag purse; or above it, as in this Cornish recipe:

10 oz. prepared leeks, sliced
2 oz. butter
½ pint Cornish double cream
1 egg and 1 egg yolk
4 oz. back bacon rashers
Short pastry made with 4 oz. flour

Cook leeks gently in the butter for 10 minutes, in a covered pan, without browning them. Remove from the heat. Add bacon cut into ¼-inch-wide strips, and turn into a pie dish or plate. A good size is 8–9 inches in diameter, and 1½ inches deep. Mix cream and eggs well together, season – allowing for the bacon's saltiness – and pour over the leek mixture. Cover with a pastry lid. Brush with beaten egg or cream and bake for 20–30 minutes in a moderate oven Mark 4, 350°F. Like all custard mixtures, this pie tastes best warm, rather than hot.

Note: for a Welsh leek pie, put a layer of pastry below as well as above the filling.

Welsh mutton broth
(Cawl Mamgu–Granny's broth)

This is a dish for those who live in good mutton areas – in Wales, obviously, but also in parts of Scotland and England, where lean, fine-flavoured lamb can be bought, even if true mutton can't.

'Cawl' is Welsh for soup. It comes from *caulis* or *colis*, Latin for a plant stem or stalk – usually of the hollow, cabbage type. (Cabbage names such as kale, cole, cauliflower, broccoli, and the Scottish kail, have the same origin.) Although the recipe for Welsh Mutton Cawl was first published in 1867 in Lady Llanover's *Good Cookery*, the dish has a long history like other peasant soups of Europe: French *potée* and *garbure*, for instance, or Scottish Cock-a-Leekie which follows.

> 2 lb. best end of neck
> salt and pepper
> 1 large carrot, sliced (6–8 oz.)
> 4 oz. swede or turnip, diced
> 2 lb. leeks
> 4 medium potatoes, scrubbed
> 2 oz. pearl barley
> 1 heaped tablespoon chopped parsley

Put the meat (don't cut it into chops, but have the joint chined) into a deep pot. Cover with water, add salt and pepper and bring to the boil. Skim off the greyish-brown foam. Put in the pearl barley, carrot, swede, potatoes and 1 large leek, whole, from the 2 lb. of leeks. Simmer for 1½–2 hours, until the meat is cooked. Meanwhile clean and slice the rest of the leeks, discarding the coarse green part. When the meat is done, divide it into chops; remove and peel the potatoes, then return them with the meat to the pot. Take out the large leek and discard. Put in the sliced leeks and parsley, cook for 5 minutes only – the leeks should still be crisp. Serve in soup plates, with a marigold flower or two on top if it's the season. Fingers of bread should also be provided.

Cock-a-Leekie (for 6–8)

For centuries, souplike stews kept most of Europe alive – just. Within present memory 'stew' has still meant a great deal of water, barely flavoured with vegetables, and a scrap of meat on Sunday. Potatoes, pearl barley or bread, sometimes oatmeal, were added to deceive the belly into temporary quiescence. No wonder that stews have a poor reputation with many people today.

This is a pity. When these old survival recipes are well made, with enough meat, they can be delicious. Welsh mutton cawl (above) is one example. Cock-a-Leekie from Scotland an even better one. No doubt it often provided a last home for the ageing rooster, but made with a younger bird of flavour, it has earned smart gourmet approval, outside its country of origin, for over a century and a half. (Anyone who's only tried Cock-a-Leekie from a can may find this difficult to believe.)

A capon produces the finest flavoured cock-a-leekie. Next, in order of merit, come a roasting bird, a really good boiling fowl (cooking time will need to be increased), a deep-frozen chicken, and lastly those egg-tired birds euphemistically known as 'steamers'.

> 1 lb. prunes
> 1 capon or chicken
> 2–3 lb. leeks
> Beef stock, or a 2 lb. piece shin of beef
>   and water

Soak the prunes overnight. Next day fit the bird, breast down, into a pot, with the piece of beef if used. Cover with water, or beef stock, and bring slowly to the boil. Skim off any brownish-grey scum. Meanwhile prepare and slice half the leeks; wash the rest, leaving them whole, and tie into a bundle – add these to the chicken pot after skimming. Simmer until the meat is almost cooked (if a very young bird has been used, it's best to cook the beef for 1½–2 hours first before adding the chicken. The point being to have them ready together). Correct the seasoning, and add the prunes, stoned. Simmer for 20 minutes. Add the sliced leeks, and simmer for 5–10 minutes. Remove and discard the bunch of leeks before serving.

By tradition cock-a-leekie is served in bowls – a slice or two of chicken and beef, a few prunes and some leek, plus the delicious broth, everything all together. However the broth is so excellent that it can make a first course on its own (with an extra flavouring of freshly ground black pepper), followed by chicken, prunes and leeks as the main course. The beef can be left to cool in the remaining broth and provide a meal next day. Talleyrand, the French foreign minister, considered that the prunes should be removed before serving. While from the gourmet point of view this may be a good idea (the prunes having given up their flavour to the broth), I think this is a shame, because the prunes look so beautiful against the green of the leeks and the pale chicken.

Some modern recipes omit the prunes altogether. Was this considered a refinement, I wonder? To do so is a pity because they add a wonderful richness. A description of a knight's table in country Scotland in 1598, by Fynes Moryson, mentions that while the servants and lower tables had broth with a little bit of stewed meat, the 'upper messe, insteede ... had a Pullet with some prunes in the broth'. He did not consider, as Talleyrand did, that this dish came within the 'Art of Cookery', any more than the oatcakes baked on the hearth, which everyone below the 'best sort of citizens' ate.

Pleurotis ostreatus
Russula virescens
Hydnum repandum
Craterellus cornucopioides
Boletus edulis (cep)
Cantharellus cibarius

Edible Woodland Mushrooms

Thousands and thousands of the best edible mushrooms go to waste in the woods – on this side of the Channel – every good mushroom season. Inherited fear perhaps, at any rate a fear of the unknown? Or just the result of inertia?

Whatever the reason, it's a pity. One of the best of Sunday afternoon pleasures is to search the woods of your neighbourhood for edible mushrooms, to bring them home, and over a cup of tea to sort out the different kinds carefully before enjoying a mushroom supper.

As to whereabouts, all woods are worth exploring, but the best are old forests. Mushrooms don't grow much in the centre of woods, as Varenka remarked to Levin's half-brother in *Anna Karenina*. He agreed that ceps preferred the outskirts – and decided to discuss mushrooms rather than propose. 'The stem of a boletus,' he remarked calmly as they walked through the trees, 'looks rather like the growth on a dark man's face who's not shaved for a couple of days.' Which is true, of some boleti at any rate.

If Varenka hadn't been so abashed at the lost moment, she might have added that mushrooms also grow on or near the rides through a forest. A certain amount of light slipping through the trees helps to create the right conditions. Should you find too many for present use, allowing for the fact that they shrink in the pan more than commercial mushrooms, you can dry the most perfect ones for winter soups and stews and omelettes. Slightly blemished ones must be used straight away.

In late summer and autumn far and away the two best woodland kinds are, to my taste, the two which are most famous in cooking: the girolle or chanterelle (*Cantharellus cibarius*), bright apricot yellow, which looks very clean and appetizing growing in colonies often out of green moss under tawny leaves, and the cep, *Boletus edulis* – edible boletus (though other kinds of boletus are nearly as good). Both are easily recognized (remember that boletus mushrooms don't have gills below the cap, but closely packed, spongy tubes). Both are common in leafy woods, especially beech woods.

I like to eat four other kinds of woodland mushrooms. First, the one the French call *pied de mouton* (*Hydnum repandum*), another clean and sweet-looking mushroom of leafy woods, easy to identify by its hanging spines, in place of gills or tubes (sometimes this is called the Rubber Brush mushroom, on account of the appearance of these spines). Then the Oyster Mushroom (*Pleurotus ostreatus*) which grows out of trees such as ash and beech in a cluster of soft shelves. Then two of that large, gay coloured, mostly white gilled family, which go under the name of Russula. These two, well worth a trial, are the Verdigris Russula (*Russula virescens*) with a blue-green cap (the French call it the *bise verte*, or the *palomet*) and the *Russula cyanoxantha*, with a cap of darkish green blue to violet. (There is a simple, sure and inexpensive chemical way of identifying *cyanoxantha*, described – see below – in the *Collins Guide to Mushrooms and Toadstools*.) These two Russulas are often abundant in beech woods; and when cooked you will find their flesh firm, more bity than the run of fungi, and tasting of new potatoes.

All the kinds I've mentioned are illustrated in colour in *Collins Guide to Mushrooms and Toadstools*. If the colours and the drawing aren't always exact, illustration and text together should be quite enough to clinch identities. The thing to remember is that there's no substitute for accurate knowledge. Any bits of country lore, any generalizations should be ignored: while there are very few fatal mushrooms, there are a number which taste bitter or can cause indigestion.

Incidentally if you go on holiday to France or Germany, look out for the excellent mushroom charts on sale in most places: they can be kept in the car as a preliminary aid to identification. (Papers in France in the autumn are continually exhorting people to take the mushrooms they've picked to the chemist for inspection before eating them: an English chemist would be startled indeed at such a request, you would have more chance of success at the local natural history museum.)

Preparation: remove the earthy base of the stem, and cut out any damaged parts of the cap. No need, with ceps, to remove the spongy, under-layer of tubes, so long as they're firm and fresh-looking.

Never soak any mushrooms in water – it spoils the flavour. Large ones can be wiped over with damp cloth: small – or messy – ones should be put into a colander and rinsed as briefly as possible under a cold tap.

Many recipes for woodland (and field) mushrooms start with a preliminary cooking, to draw the juice. A thin layer of corn oil is put into a frying pan, and the mushrooms are cooked over a medium to high heat for about 5 minutes. When they're swimming in liquid, they're transferred to a sieve to drain (use up the juice in sauces and soups). Then the cooking is completed in a clean pan with butter or *olive* oil.

This is a good method for girolles, which have plenty of moisture to lose (with, alas, a considerable diminution in size). With other mushrooms, particularly in a dryish season, it's usually enough to cook them quickly to evaporate the juice. The risk of this method is overcooking. Sometimes one has to switch rapidly to the first method, if the mushrooms produce more liquid than expected (this can depend on the weather, as well as on the type of mushroom). But with very little experience, one learns to judge the best method for any particular batch of mushrooms.

Girolles on buttered toast (for 4–6)

The most treasured finds are the egg-yolk coloured girolles or chanterelles. Their trumpet heads are easy to see against green moss, less easy when partly concealed by a scatter of autumn leaves. They're quickly identified by their gills, a miniature of fan-vaulting. For beauty, their only rival is the black flaring horn of plenty (*Craterellus cornucopioides*): for flavour, for their slightly earthy yet perfumed flavour, they have no rival.

> 2–3 lb. girolles
> 3 oz. butter
> 1 clove garlic, crushed
> salt, black pepper, chopped parsley
> buttered toast, or *biscottes*, or rusks

Prepare and drain the girolles as above. Melt the butter in a clean pan, add garlic and mushrooms and stew until cooked – about 5 minutes. They will be slightly chewy but not tough. Season with salt, plenty of freshly ground black pepper, and parsley.

Serve on generously buttered toast – better still on buttered *biscottes* or Dutch rusks, whose crispness and flavour set the girolles off perfectly.

This simple recipe can be used for all edible mushrooms, as well as for russulas, oyster mushrooms, *pieds de mouton* and ceps mentioned in this chapter. Rice may be substituted for buttered toast, or a puff pastry vol-au-vent case (warm it in the oven); or the mushrooms can be used to stuff an omelette.

Champignons à la persillade

An excellent recipe from the Dordogne. Serve it with boiled potatoes, finished in butter and chopped parsley.

> 2–3 lbs. mushrooms, preferably ceps
> 4 oz. lean smoked bacon

    1 large clove garlic, crushed
    1 large bunch parsley, chopped
    2–3 oz. breadcrumbs
    3 oz. butter
    salt, black pepper, wine vinegar

Prepare the mushrooms as above. Chop the bacon, and mix it with the breadcrumbs, garlic and parsley. Cook the mushrooms for 2 minutes in the butter, season with salt and freshly ground black pepper, and sprinkle on the breadcrumbs mixture. Cook uncovered for a further 15 minutes. Correct the seasoning, add a dash of wine vinegar to sharpen, and serve very hot.

Champignons à la crème

The classic recipe for mushrooms – any mushrooms – in cream. I think, though, that it's not the best way to cook ceps: their rich texture demands olive oil, garlic, parsley, not butter and cream. Cooked in this way, mushrooms can be eaten as a course on their own with triangles of bread fried in butter, or as the filling for pastry cases. As vegetable-cum-sauce, they make a good partner for veal, chicken, turkey and grilled meat.

    3 lb. mushrooms
    3 oz. butter
    5 oz. heavy cream
    salt, pepper
    chopped parsley
    chopped chervil or chives

Prepare mushrooms as above. Stew them in butter for 10–20 minutes uncovered, allowing them to produce a small amount of concentrated liquid. When they're cooked, stir the cream into the pan juices, and simmer for a couple of minutes to form a sauce. Season with salt, pepper and the herbs.

Mushroom stuffing from Berry

Although this stuffing is usually made with the fine fat stalks left over from grilling cep caps (recipe following), any other edible mushroom may be substituted. It's a good way of using up small quantities of girolles or *pieds de mouton* or oyster mushrooms, after a lean expedition.

> ½ lb. good sausagemeat
> 1 large onion, chopped
> 1 large clove garlic, crushed
> 2 oz. breadcrumbs
> 2 tablespoons milk
> ½ lb. cep stalks, chopped
> parsley, salt, pepper
> lard or olive oil or butter
> 1 egg

Melt onion and garlic over a low heat in 2–3 tablespoons of fat, which should be chosen to suit the meat being stuffed – for instance, butter or olive oil for chicken, olive oil for lamb, lard for pork, and so on. Moisten the breadcrumbs with the milk. Mix all ingredients together.

Use with poultry, boned joints of all kinds, and for beef olives. For Christmas turkey, double the quantities and use 4–6 oz. dried ceps (see pages 207–8), which have been soaked and drained.

The mixture can also be used to stuff large cep caps – bake at Mark 7, 425°F for 15–20 minutes, in a well-greased dish. Or to make *crépinettes*: divide into 2 oz. knobs, and wrap each one up in a 5–6 inch square of caul fat (soften it first in tepid water), then grill or fry, and serve with mashed potatoes.

Grilled ceps

Ceps are unlike any other woodland mushroom in their thick fleshiness, which does not collapse entirely in cooking. This means they can be grilled or baked, or turned into a cold hors d'œuvre.

For grilling, choose large, evenly sized ceps. Put the stalks aside for a stuffing (see above recipe), and remove the underlayer of tubes unless the ceps are in exceptionally good condition. Place the caps, peel side up, on the grill rack. Brush generously with olive oil, and grill at a medium temperature for about 10 minutes. Turn them over, put some more olive oil into the centre cavities, and grill at a higher temperature for about 5 minutes. Sprinkle with pepper, salt, and chopped parsley. Serve on toast or *biscottes*, with any juice from the pan, or as a vegetable with grilled meat.

Ceps as hors d'œuvre

1 lb. small, firm ceps
2 pints water
1 tablespoon vinegar, wine or malt
heaped teaspoon salt

marinade ingredients:

5 tablespoons olive oil
8 whole peppercorns
bouquet garni
thinly cut peel of a lemon

garnish:

3 large cloves garlic, chopped
2 tablespoons chopped parsley

After cleaning the ceps, cut the caps into quarters, and the stalks across into sizeable slices. Blanch in 2 pints of boiling water, seasoned with 1 tablespoon vinegar and a heaped teaspoon of salt, for 2 minutes. Drain the ceps well in a sieve. Put into a serving dish and keep warm. Simmer marinade ingredients in a small pan for 5 minutes, then strain it, boiling, over the mushrooms. Sprinkle with the finely chopped garlic and parsley. Cover and leave for at least 24 hours. Serve well chilled.

Fricassée of chicken with ceps (for 4–6)

Ceps are the ideal mushroom for cooking with meat. From Brittany down to Italy and across to Yugoslavia, one comes across recipes for chicken or lamb or beef stewed with ceps, and with ceps and tomatoes (1 lb. of each to 2–3 lb. of meat). The great advantage of ceps is that prolonged cooking doesn't make them tough, nor does it reduce them to nullity.

> 1 chicken, jointed and turned in
>   seasoned flour
> 1 lb. ceps, cleaned
> about ¼ pint chicken stock
> 2 large cloves garlic
> parsley, salt, pepper
> olive oil

Cover the base of a heavy frying pan with a thin layer of olive oil, and put it over the heat. When it begins to smoke, add the chicken joints and brown them to a nice gold colour. Add the cep caps, sliced or quartered, and cover the pan. Simmer for 20–30 minutes, until the chicken is cooked, adding stock from time to time if necessary, so that there is always about half an inch depth of liquid in the pan. Meanwhile chop the cep stalks and the garlic, mix them together with a spoonful or two of chopped parsley.

Transfer the chicken to a serving dish with the pieces of cep. Put the stalk and garlic mixture into the pan juices and boil hard for 5 minutes to reduce the sauce. Correct the seasoning and pour over the chicken. Serve with triangles of bread fried in olive oil, or with plainly boiled potatoes which have been sliced thickly and reheated in the sauce at the last minute: either of these garnishes should be added to the dish of chicken, and not served separately.

Trout with ceps (for 6)

Ceps go well with fish. Surprisingly well. And though the recipe
was invented for the fine fresh trout of Pyrenean streams, I can
recommend it for fillets of salt water fish such as cod, plaice, brill,
turbot, etc.

>6 trout
>seasoned flour
>4 oz. butter
>16 ceps (use stalks for stuffing,
>   p. 203)
>1 glove garlic, crushed
>1 tablespoon aniseed aperitif (e.g. Pastis
>   Ricard)
>3–4 tablespoons double cream

First clarify the butter by bringing it to the boil in a small pan, and
then pouring it gently into a bowl through a cloth-lined sieve. This
removes a white sediment, and prevents the butter burning when
you fry fish (or anything else).

Put just about half this clarified butter into the frying pan.
Turn the trout in seasoned flour while the butter heats up, and
then add them to the pan. Four minutes on each side should give
them a crisp brown coating. Transfer them to a serving dish, and
keep them warm.

Add the rest of the butter to the pan, and stew the sliced cep
caps with the garlic for about 5 minutes, until they're cooked,
keeping the heat fairly high. Arrange them round the trout, and
put the dish back in the oven to keep warm. Pour the aniseed
aperitif into the pan, and bring it to the boil, scraping in the
appetizing brown bits and the juices. Then stir in the cream and
boil for a couple of minutes until the sauce is thick and smooth.
Season, pour over the trout, and serve at once.

Potatoes with ceps

Only a few ceps? This is what you do. Prepare enough potatoes to fill a heavy frying pan. Cook them in 2 or 3 tablespoons of olive oil, with the sliced cep caps. Stir them about until they're lightly browned, cover and lower the heat. Chop the cep stalks with a clove of garlic and some parsley, add them to the pan with some salt and pepper, and leave to continue cooking. You'll find that the potatoes have absorbed flavour from the ceps in a most agreeable way.

This recipe can also be used with russulas, and with any other mushroom that doesn't toughen with prolonged cooking. Girolles are best cooked very quickly with a few peeled and sliced tomatoes, if you want to stretch them.

How to dry mushrooms

After a successful mushroom expedition, it's a good idea to set aside the best ones for drying. Then in January and February, soups, stews and omelettes can be flavoured with the unexpected delight of ceps or russulas. Even when dried, they have more to offer than fresh commercial mushrooms.

Speed of drying is the thing to aim for – although temperatures needn't be constant – so that the mushrooms don't have a chance to go mouldy. It follows that they should not be washed: just cut off the earthy parts of the stems. In less humid climates mushrooms will dry perfectly in an airy room or verandah, but in Great Britain it's prudent to make use of artificial warmth. Remember that the enemies are steam and smoke. Avoid these two, and you can use any of the following methods, or a mixture of them according to convenience:

(a) Thread the mushrooms on to string, with knots in between like well-spaced beads, and hang them over a radiator, or in a warm, dry kitchen.

(b) Spread them out on newspaper or butter muslin, on the rack of an oil-fired stove. You can do the same with a solid-fuel cooker, but the mushrooms have to be removed, or swathed in newspaper, every time you stoke or clean it. I've never dried mushrooms on a night storage heater, but I don't see why you shouldn't.

(c) dry them in the oven, on trays made with four flat bits of wood and a sheet of wire gauze. Line the trays with newspaper before putting the mushrooms on it. Keep the oven door ajar (for evaporating moisture to escape) and the temperature below 140°F, or they will cook rather than dry. The most economical way of doing this is to put the tray into the switched-off oven every day, after cooking lunch or the evening meal.

The mushrooms are ready for packing away when they're leathery and dry (and much reduced in size). Store them in paper bags in a dry place, or, if you're confident that all moisture has gone, in plastic bags. 2–3 oz. per bag is a sensible amount.

When the mushrooms are required, put them into a bowl of tepid water to soak. Allow an hour at least, although you may find that some mushrooms take far less time to plump up to a semblance of their original size. Drain and rinse them quickly, and use as if they were fresh.

Note: one can buy packages of dried mushrooms in delicatessen shops. They are reconstituted and used in the same way as home-dried mushrooms.

Parsley

Has parsley really crossed to Britain? Or stopped short at Boulogne? Of course we have used it for centuries in medicine and in cooking. The Greeks and Romans taught us that it was a great plant for bladders and kidneys and driving out wykked wyndys – a great body opener (Shakespeare was sure of a laugh when he wrote in *The Taming of the Shrew* of a wench getting married on the way to the garden for parsley to stuff a rabbit).

But for the Greeks, and the Romans, parsley was part of life. You were crowned with parsley if you won a race. It was a herb of life at funerals. (By country superstition, parsley is never transplanted or there will be a death in the family.) It was given – though not at 4p a bunch – as a strengthening feed to Homeric chariot horses. It reminded Pliny of holidays away from Rome – 'You see sprigs of parsley swimming on milk everywhere in the country.'*

Natural History.

And it reminds us – of what? Boiled cod, on Good Friday, the relationship of centuries and civilizations reduced to green flecks in a white sauce. Sometimes I eat the parsley from the cold buffet dish in restaurants. Waiters look surprised. It isn't there for eating. Butchers decorate windows with plastic parsley (try stuffing some of that in a rabbit).

Parsley can be grown anywhere – window box, backyard tub or kitchen garden border – provided the soil is rich and moist. Sow April and September for an almost year-round supply. French cooks care for its taste, not for its looks alone, or for its richness in iron or richness in vitamin C. They know that curly-leaved parsley is the kind for strong taste and smooth-leaved parsley the kind for delicate taste: that there is as much flavour in the stalks as the leaves. And they know that, in cooking, parsley is a flavouring ingredient as basic as wine or brandy or cream or butter.

All the recipes in this chapter, with one important, and one less important exception, are French. All require parsley by the handful.

Green salad

It's difficult to think of a simpler dish than this one, yet it's invariably badly made – at least in public eating places. The first important ingredient is the lettuce. It should be crisp (avoid winter lettuces, flopping heartlessly in polythene bags, and use chicory instead), a lettuce of substance, of character, such as Webb's Wonder or long-headed Cos. Wash, shake dry and pull apart.

For the dressing:

1 heaped teaspoon sugar
sea salt and black pepper to taste
1 large crushed clove garlic
1 tablespoon wine vinegar
Blend these together in the salad bowl.

Add to them:

4 tablespoons olive oil

1 heaped tablespoon chopped shallot
(or mild onion, or onion sprouts)

Just before the meal (no sooner), stir in 3 tablespoons of chopped parsley (a Parsmint herb mill is cheap, and quicker than knife and board). Lay the salad servers in the bowl across each other to form a base for the lettuce leaves, keeping them separate from the dressing.

After the meat course, serve the salad, turning it over carefully at table until the leaves are shiny and coated with dressing. Many French families like eating a bland cheese with their salad (Camembert is the obvious choice, but some of the soft Scottish cheeses now on sale do very well instead), finishing the meal with fruit, or, on Sundays, a delicious cake or pudding.

Fines herbes

Ideally a mixture of parsley, chives, tarragon, chervil and watercress, *fines herbes* is often reduced to parsley and chives. Or, at the family table, to a bowl piled high with chopped parsley to be sprinkled individually over cold dishes – chicken and mayonnaise, herrings and potato salad, tomatoes layered with slices of egg. Here is a basic mixture, which may be varied according to taste and supply, and used in the recipes which follow:

3–4 tablespoons chopped parsley
1 tablespoon chopped chives (spring
   onion stems, or onion sprouts, or
   Welsh onions)
1 tablespoon chopped tarragon
1 tablespoon chopped watercress
1 large clove crushed garlic (optional)
grated rind of half a large lemon
   (optional)

Beurre aux fines herbes

Fork the mixture given above into about 6 oz. unsalted butter, until it's well distributed. Flavour with lemon juice to taste, form into a long roll and keep wrapped up in the refrigerator. Cut slices off as required, to serve with steak or lamb chops, or grilled fish. Toss summer vegetables in it – new potatoes, carrots, real French beans, young broad beans, spinach, asparagus. Or use it in sandwiches instead of plain butter.

Cream cheese aux fines herbes et l'ail

We're familiar now with those delicious cream cheeses from France which are blended with herbs and garlic. It's easy to make them at home, as many Frenchwomen do – and rather cheaper. Mix together:

> 8 oz. soft cream or milk cheese (cottage, Philadelphia, Gervais)
> 1–3 tablespoons double cream
> salt and pepper
> about half the *fines herbes* quantities above

If cottage cheese is used, it must be sieved, or liquidized with cream, to get rid of the granular texture. With other soft cheeses, mash them with a fork and add the cream gradually. Non-fat cheeses will require 3 tablespoons – or more if you can manage it – of cream; cheeses with a medium fat content, such as Chambourcy, Gervais and petits suisses, will require less. This is a matter of taste and texture and your own judgement.

Pack into small pots or plastic cartons and leave in a cool place overnight. If you're lucky enough to be able to make your own cream cheese from unpasteurized milk, pierce a few holes in the cartons so that the whey continues to drain from the cheese. This is not necessary with commercially produced cream cheeses, as a rule.

Sauce à la crème

A marvellous sauce, simple to make, expensive, and quite delicious. Happily one encounters it frequently in Normandy and north-western France, served with boiled chicken or fish (try it with poached salmon, bass or John Dory).

> about half the quantity of *fines herbes*
>   above
> 5 oz. unsalted butter
> ½ pint double cream
> lemon juice, salt, pepper to taste

A warning, this sauce takes a few minutes to make and must be served immediately, so have everything else dished up and ready.

Melt the butter in an enamelled or non-stick frying pan. When it bubbles, pour in the double cream. Stir over a gentle heat until they are well amalgamated and thick. Add the parsley and herb mixture, season to taste with lemon juice, salt and pepper.

Omelette aux fines herbes

Add the *fines herbes* above to 6 or 8 beaten eggs, according to taste. Season and cook in the usual way.

Crempog Las

The Welsh, living in a less prosperous land, make pancakes with herbs, rather than omelettes. I increase the quantities of herbs:

> ½ lb. plain flour

fines herbes mixture above, without
    garlic and lemon peel
2 beaten eggs
milk, salt and pepper

Mix to a pancake consistency. Cook in the usual way. Eat buttered
and hot. They are sometimes served with sausages and bacon.
Very good.

Quiche au persil

shortcrust pastry:

4 oz. flour
2 oz. butter
teaspoon icing sugar
beaten egg to mix

filling:

fines herbes mixture above
½ lb. chopped onion
3 oz. butter
½ pint cream
2 beaten eggs
salt and pepper

Line a fluted flan ring, about 9½ inches in diameter, and with a
removable base, with shortcrust pastry. Melt the butter in a heavy
pan, and sweat the onions in it until they're golden and transparent. Put into the pastry case. Beat cream, eggs and herb mixture together, season well and pour over the onions. Bake about
40 minutes in a moderate oven, about Mark 4–5, 350–375°F. Like
all other quiches, this one may be eaten hot, warm or cold, but
best of all warm I think.

Jambon persillé de Bourgogne

A famous Easter dish from Burgundy, which makes a splendid centre-piece for a cold table at any time of the year. It is often left to set in thick white china bowls or terrines, and served in slices from them. It can, alternatively, be turned out on to a large dish like any other jellied food. Whichever you decide to do, remember that a simple white background will show off the magnificent pink and green of parsley and ham much better than the ancestral Worcester or Sèvres.

> 3–4 lb. piece of gammon
> 1 calf's foot, or 3 pig's trotters
> veal knuckle
> 8 peppercorns
> bouquet garni
> 1 bottle dry white wine
> 1 tablespoon white wine vinegar
> plenty of chopped parsley, at least
>   6 heaped tablespoons
> salt, pepper

Cover the gammon generously with water, bring to the boil and simmer for 45 minutes. Cut the meat into chunks, put into a large pan with the calf's foot or trotters, the veal knuckle, peppercorns and herbs. Pour in the white wine until it covers the contents of the pan. Simmer gently until the gammon is well cooked.

Drain off the liquid through a muslin-lined sieve. Taste and adjust seasoning. Add the vinegar and leave to set slightly in a cool place.

Crush the ham into a roomy bowl. Keep the rest of the meat to make a separate dish of brawn.

Add the parsley to the setting liquor, pour it over the ham in the bowl and mix well. If you are intending to turn out the *jambon persillé* later on, keep back some of the parsley jelly to melt slightly and brush over it in a green layer.

When the *jambon* is cut, it has a beautifully marbled appearance. Very fresh and appetizing. Serve with good bread and unsalted or lightly salted butter.

Charter pie (for 8–10)

Parson Woodforde, the Norfolk clerical glutton, enjoyed a sociable day on 13 July 1785. 'We had for Dinner some Pyke and fryed Soals, a nice Piece of boiled Beef, Ham and a Couple of Fowls, Peas and Beans, a green Goose roasted, Gooseberry Pies, Currant Tarts, the Charter, hung Beef scraped and ...' All straightforward English food (he despised French cookery), things we might eat today if not all together at one meal, except for 'the Charter'. Was it sweet or savoury? Savoury, I think (on another occasion the dog ate the Charter which had been put to cool in the cellar). It bothered me for a couple of years until I found this *Charter Pie* (*Cornish Recipe*) in a Victorian recipe book compiled by Lady Sarah Lindsay. It's a winner of a dish, well worth the expensive ingredients, and quite up to Parson Woodforde's exacting standards:

shortcrust pastry:

8 oz. flour
2 oz. each butter and lard
dessertspoon icing sugar
1 egg
pinch salt
top of milk or beaten egg to glaze

filling:

2 chickens, about 3 lb. dressed weight
1 large onion, chopped
3 oz. butter
seasoned flour
2 bunches parsley
$\frac{1}{4}$ pint milk
$\frac{3}{4}$ pint double cream
salt, pepper

Make the pastry and leave it to rest. Sweat the onion in 1½ oz. of butter until transparent, and put into the pie dish (a large shallow one is best). Add the rest of the butter to the pan and fry the chicken in it, which should first be jointed and rolled in seasoned flour. When the pieces are lightly browned, lay them on top of the onion in the dish. Chop the parsley (excluding the tougher stalks) and simmer for 3 minutes in the milk. Pour over the chicken, with half the cream. Season well.

Put a pastry rim round the pie dish, moisten it and lay on the lid (see the chicken bones don't pierce it). Decorate and make a central hole, which should be kept open with a small roll of white card. Brush over with top of the milk or beaten egg, and put into a hot oven for 15 minutes. Mark 7, 425°F. Protect the top with paper and lower heat to about Mark 4, 350°F. Leave for an hour. Just before serving heat the rest of the cream and pour it into the pie by way of the central hole – remove the roll of card first.

Charter pie is very good cold – the sauce sets to an excellent jelly.

Note: Mary Norwak of the Farmers Weekly says that she makes a similar chicken pie, from a recipe given her by an American. Instead of onion, she includes peeled, diced potatoes, which do not need to be fried in butter like the onions above.

Parsnips

Parsnips should not at all be dismissed because only the Americans and the British seem to eat them in any quantity. They're an ingredient in French *pot-au-feu*, but otherwise few inventive cooks in Europe have troubled to make use of the parsnip's individual flavouring and sweetness.

I suspect that, like sea kale, it was one of the few vegetables of British origin (it's the cultivated form of the wild parsnip of chalk and limestone country), so it's been rejected in fine cooking with a degree of quite unjustified snobbery. Or perhaps the reputation of the parsnip was due to its once common and unholy alliance with salt cod in Lent. Certainly the English have been eating parsnips from the Middle Ages or earlier. A raw parsnip round your neck kept off adders or reduced swelling in the testicles. Cooked parsnip gave men an 'appetyt for wymen'.

Many of the old, rather humble and homely recipes for parsnips survive in American cookery, such as farmer's pie and parsnip pie. Not, I think, the best of parsnip dishes, which are perhaps parsnip and walnut fritters (but they are American, too) and curried parsnip soup. Cubes of parsnip, blanched in boiling salted water for 10 minutes, are good when dipped in batter and deep-fried.

The most striking use of parsnips I can recall was a resourceful wartime recipe. Boiled parsnip was sieved, and flavoured with banana essence. The vegetable provided enough sweetness and the right texture to make quite a convincing substitute, say, in banana sandwiches. Or at least it seemed convincing at the time – I would not vouch for it now with real bananas around to set the standard.

The thing to remember with parsnips is that both by themselves and in combination they require plenty of butter or some form of richness, such as oil or cream – and plenty of seasoning. They have a wonderful affinity with beef, and, more surprisingly, white fish, provided they are crisply presented. The cubes of parsnip in batter, for instance, are an excellent accompaniment to baked plaice or sole.

Parsnip salad

I've heard this salad called *poor man's lobster* which is stretching things a bit. The texture of cold parsnips may be a little like lobster – a very little – but the flavour is not. Anyway, parsnips are perfectly good as parsnips: they don't need apologetic (or pretentious) names:

>2–3 nice parsnips

>*mayonnaise:*
>1 egg yolk
>1 teaspoon mustard
>¼ pint olive oil
>lemon juice, salt, pepper

>*plus:*
>some lettuce leaves

Trim and scrub the parsnips and boil in salted water until tender.

Remove the skin and slice them. Leave to cool. Make the mayonnaise with the ingredients above, in the usual way.

Arrange the parsnip slices on the lettuce leaves, on a serving plate. Put some of the mayonnaise over them and serve the rest separately.

Roast parsnips with beef

Parsnips make a delicious accompaniment to beef, if treated with respect. One good way is to boil, then slice them, and finish in butter, lemon juice and parsley. Another favourite way is to roast them. Allow one medium-sized parsnip per person. Trim, peel, cut into slices about half an inch thick. Blanch in salted boiling water for five minutes, then drain in a colander.

Now there are two choices. You can either arrange the slices in the meat roasting tin, under the rack on which the beef sits, or cook them in a separate pan of fat at the top of the oven, just as if you were roasting potatoes (the two can of course be cooked together). The latter method will give you crisply coated parsnips, but the slices set under the beef will catch all its wonderful flavour.

The best solution is to use both methods, perhaps.

Parsnip and walnut fritters (for 6)

One would not think that parsnips and walnuts would go well together. But they do. So do parsnips and almonds, or parsnips and hazelnuts. My preference, though, is for walnuts. Try these fritters, and see if you agree that they make a very special dish.

> 2 lb. parsnips
> 4 oz. shelled walnuts
> 2 large eggs
> 3 oz. melted butter

2 heaped teaspoons flour
generous ¼ pint milk
salt, black pepper

Trim, clean and boil parsnips in the usual way. When they are
tender, put them through the *mouli-légumes*, discarding tough
bits of core. Mix to a smooth paste with the eggs, flour, butter and
milk. Season with salt and pepper and stir in the walnuts.

Bring a deep pan of oil to between 350° and 375°F (I use a
thermometer to make sure the temperature is right and is not too
reduced by the fritter mixture). Slip in spoonfuls of the mixture,
including a piece of walnut with each spoonful. Remove with a
draining spoon when they are deep golden brown. Serve as a
course on their own, or with white fish baked with butter and a
little white wine.

Pot-au-feu, or boiled beef

Many Frenchmen, it seems, have a button labelled *pot-au-feu*.
Press it, and you'll be swamped with nostalgia – cosy kitchen, fire
on the hearth, pot bubbling as it hangs from the pot crane,
mother flinging in vegetables, the pervading smell, the wonderful
beef, wonderful mother, those were the days. I suppose in fact
that *pot-au-feu* is the Gallic equivalent, emotionally, of our
mother's apple pie, it can certainly be just as boring and resist-
ible. Properly made, though, it's an excellently convenient dish.
You will end up with beef for hot and cold meals, possibly a
boiling fowl as well. And with several pints of beautiful broth for
sauces and soups, its rich sweetness depending on the combination of onions, carrots and parsnips, particularly parsnips.
(I read in a French flora the rather tart remark that parsnips
are cultivated in Brittany and Belgium to feed horses – it might
have been added that the pigs at Parma are fed on parsnips to give
the hams a specially good flavour – but at any rate the *pot-au-feu*,
classic of French bourgeois cooking, cannot be imagined without
them.)

3–4 lb. boiling beef (topside, silverside,
    neck, chuck)
veal knucklebone
1 boiling fowl (optional)
8 pints water
12 peppercorns
small bayleaf
several parsley stalks
2 sprigs thyme
large clove garlic
3 medium onions
3 cloves
4 medium carrots
2 medium parsnips
6 leeks
2 stalks celery
1 level tablespoon salt

Put the beef and veal knuckle into a huge pot, and cover with the water. Bring slowly to the boil (this takes about an hour), and skim off the rising clouds of scummy bubbles. Pour in a large cupful of cold water, and skim again. This is important, if you want to end up with a good clear stock. Meanwhile prepare the vegetables. Top and tail the onions, wash them, but leave the skins, which will add a golden colour to the stock. In the past pea pods, dried out in the baker's oven after the bread was finished, used also to be added to improve the colour and give a little sweetness: if you have a solid fuel stove with a plate-warming oven, you could dry your own pea pods, and store them when dry in an airtight tin.

Clean and slice carrots and parsnips. Wash and tie leeks and celery into a bundle.

When the water is scum free, and simmering, add vegetables, herbs, cloves and seasonings, and the boiling fowl if used. The combination of fowl and beef may sound odd, but it works well – think of cock-a-leekie, p. 196, the famous Scottish soup which at its best combines beef or beef stock with chicken.

The bundle of leeks and celery may be removed after about 20 minutes' simmering, to be eaten when cold with vinaigrette, as an hors d'œuvre sometimes known as *poor man's asparagus* (p. 193).

Watch the boiling fowl: it may be cooked after 2 hours, depending on its antiquity. After three hours the beef will be done, after three hours' simmering that is. Remove beef and chicken from the pot, and strain the broth into a large bowl through a cloth-lined colander.

Now the beef can be eaten hot with a little of the stock as sauce, plenty of French mustard, and freshly cooked glazed vegetables (the pot vegetables have given up their goodness to the broth and meat, and should be thrown away). Or it can be left to cool in the stock, and served later on, with potato or parsnip salad, lettuce and gherkins.

The boiling fowl is best eaten hot, accompanied by well-buttered rice, and a cream sauce made with some of the stock, single cream and a flour and butter *roux*.

Note: if you normally rely on stock cubes for soups and sauces, you will be surprised at the difference this broth makes to your usual recipes.

Curried parsnip soup (for 6–8)

This is a wonderful soup, delicately flavoured yet satisfying. One doesn't immediately recognize the parsnip taste, but no other root vegetable can produce such an excellent result.

> 3 oz. butter
> large parsnip
> 4 oz. chopped onion
> 1 clove garlic, crushed
> tablespoon flour
> rounded teaspoon curry powder
> 2 pints hot beef stock
> ¼ pint cream
> chives

Peel and slice the parsnip. Put the onion, parsnip and garlic into a heavy pan with the butter and cook for 10 minutes slowly with the lid on the pan. The vegetables must not brown, but gently absorb the butter. Add flour and curry powder to take up the fat, and gradually incorporate the hot beef stock (from the *pot-au-feu*, p. 221, for preference). Simmer until the parsnip is cooked. Liquidize or push through the *mouli-légumes*. Return to the pan, correct seasoning with salt, pepper and a little more curry powder if liked (but be cautious: keep the flavour mild). Add the cream and a sprinkling of chopped chives. Serve with croûtons of bread fried in butter and oil.

Note: liquidized soup may need the further dilution of some extra stock, or some creamy milk.

Glazed parsnips (for 6–8)

If you like the occasional dish of sweet potatoes with pork, veal or poultry, you will find this American recipe for glazed parsnips a much cheaper (and less fattening) substitute. It emphasizes the sweetness of parsnips – in fact, I've often thought it would make an excellent pudding, if served with cream.

> 3 lb. parsnips
> 4 oz. brown sugar
> 2 oz. melted butter, plus extra butter
> Juice of half a lemon
> ¼ pint orange juice or good cider
> teaspoon salt

Wash, boil and peel parsnips in the usual way. Slice them and leave to drain well. Choose a shallow baking dish, butter it and arrange half the parsnip slices in a single layer. Mix the salt, sugar, melted butter, lemon juice and orange juice or cider together. Pour half of it over the parsnips. Arrange the rest of the slices on top and pour over the rest of the sugar mixture. Dot with small knobs of extra butter and bake at Mark 5, 375°F, for about 20 minutes, or until the top is nicely glazed.

Parsnip and mushroom soufflé (for 6)

1½ lb. parsnips
4 oz. butter
4 oz. mushrooms, sliced
1 clove garlic, crushed
2 tablespoons double cream
4 egg yolks
4 egg whites

Wash and boil the parsnips in the usual way. Meanwhile cook sliced mushrooms and garlic together gently in the butter. Peel the parsnips when cooked, and put through the *mouli-légumes*. Add the mushroom mixture, the cream and egg yolks. Beat the whites until stiff. Season the parsnip purée well, and fold into the whites gently with a metal spoon.

Pour into a 1½ or 2 pint soufflé dish, collared and buttered in the usual way, and bake at Mark 7, 425°F, until risen and brown on top (about 20 minutes). Serve immediately.

Peas

Everybody loves peas. East and west, it's the world's favourite vegetable. Peas were the first vegetable to be canned, the first to be frozen. They are the gourmet's delight – and the only green vegetable that most children will eat. As far away as Peking, boys and girls listen for the pea vendor's bell in early summer. They rush out with their bowls when he trundles his car into the street, watch their ladle of peas being cooked, then run home picking at them as they go.

The peas of long antiquity were prized as an important part of winter's diet, not as summer's delight. Dried and grey, they could not be compared, even in their youth, with our modern garden peas, green, sweet, succulent.

For this we have to thank Italian gardeners of the late Renaissance, who developed better varieties of pea. No longer a case of cottager's pease pudding, lenten fare, but the courtier's pleasure. At Versailles the new *piselli*, or *petits pois*, the little peas from Italy, became an object of secret gluttony. Ladies who had

eaten with Louis XIV – and eaten some of the best food in Europe
– might be found gobbling peas last thing at night in the seclusion
of their bedrooms.

No such orgies are recorded at the English court, when mar-
rowfat peas were first developed at the beginning of the nineteenth century (the name describes the tenderness of these peas,
which are wrinkled with sweetness). But they had their little
drama. Do you remember the conflict between peas and politesse
at Mr Holbrooke's party, in Cranford? Mary, the young narrator,
recalls that 'when the duck and green peas came, we looked at
each other in dismay; we had only two-pronged, black-handled
forks . . . Miss Matty picked up her peas one by one, on the point
of the prongs . . . Miss Pole sighed over her delicate young peas as
she left them on one side of her plate untasted, for they *would*
drop between the prongs. I looked at my host; the peas were
going wholesale into his capacious mouth, shovelled up by his
large, round-ended knife. I saw, I imitated, I survived!'

Would she, I wonder, have imitated Mr Holbrooke if he'd
chosen another way –

> I eat my peas with honey,
> I've done it all my life.
> It may taste kind of funny,
> But it keeps them on my knife.

In these more relaxed days, our problem is not how to eat but
how to find good peas in the first place. People with gardens are
able to pick them at just the right moment, and cook them within
a couple of hours. This is perfection. The rest of us have to chase
round greengrocers' shops, trying to find peas which haven't been
picked too large, or kept too long.

Often one is driven back ineluctably to frozen peas, even in
June. Professional eaters-out may scoff, but if they lived in the
country and had to endure their neighbours' podded bullets, they
would conclude that frozen peas are sometimes the only honest
choice. They can be delicious, particularly the *petits pois*, if
cooked with care. I reflect that we have been trying to beat winter
starvation for centuries and centuries. I think we should be grateful, and not guilty, when we buy frozen peas – particularly in
December – reflecting that a hundred years ago one subsisted for
six or seven months of the year on root and dried vegetables.

I refuse, though, to feel any gratitude for canned peas, British style. Why can't our manufacturers lose their dye-bags, and study the methods of European firms? The tiny French peas stewed with onion and carrot are a vegetable no one need be ashamed of putting on the table.

Peas in cream (for 6)

Do you ever try cooking peas with any other flavouring than mint? With savory, for instance, or young green fennel leaves? Or with spices? This old recipe using nutmeg and mace is a good starting point for experiment.

> 1 lb. shelled peas
> 2 oz. butter
> scant ¼ pint water
> 1 teaspoon sugar
> salt, black pepper
> ¼ teaspoon each nutmeg and mace
> dessertspoon chopped parsley
> 1 heaped teaspoon flour
> 4–6 oz. double cream
> lemon juice

Bring water and butter to the boil. Put in peas, parsley, sugar, salt and spices. Simmer until the peas are nearly tender. Put the flour into a basin and stir in some of the cooking liquor, until you have a smooth paste. Stir in the cream and return to the pan. Cook gently until the liquor thickens and the peas are done. Taste and add more nutmeg and mace if necessary. Sharpen with a little lemon juice.

Serve as a separate course, with a dozen triangles of bread, fried in butter, tucked round the peas at the last moment before serving.

As a variation, cook a bunch of tiny young carrots separately, and add them to the peas before turning them into the serving dish.

Peas Stroganoff (for 6)

Every cook hopes, perhaps against reason, to find dishes which are particularly good to eat, quick to prepare, and if not cheap, at least not outrageously expensive. There aren't many. An obvious one is bœuf Stroganoff (rapidly becoming our national dish, to judge by reports in the *Good Food Guide*). It's a recipe which is easily adapted to other lean, i.e. expensive, cuts of meat – veal, for instance, or lamb chops:

> peas in cream, as above
> 4 inch-thick lamb chops
> 4 oz. butter
> salt, pepper, lemon juice

Strip the lean meat from the chops, discarding fat and bone. Cut into small slices about ⅛ inch thick; season them well with salt and pepper. Next prepare the peas in cream, and keep them hot. Also prepare 6 slices of toast (better with lamb than fried bread), cut the crusts off, and divide each piece into two triangles. Last of all, when everything else is ready, fry the lamb quickly in foaming butter for 4 or 5 minutes. Mix meat and pan juices with the peas. Correct the seasoning with more salt, pepper and lemon juice if necessary. The flavour should be both rich and piquant. Serve immediately, not giving the lamb a chance to become tough, with the toast round the edge of the dish.

The Amah's Peas (for 6)

When a friend of mine was a little girl in Peking, her *amah* used to cook peas this way as a special treat. It's a messy dish, but not as messy as asparagus. There are people who might think it a little noisy (the Chinese are less inhibited than we are over good food), so choose your guests with care. Be sure to provide them with large cloth napkins; paper ones disintegrate.

3 lb. peas
salted water

Peas of early middle age benefit most from this method of cooking. Pick them over, discarding leaves, stalks, and any pods which
are broken or blemished. Rinse and then cook them in a large pan
of boiling salted water. Drain them well and serve in individual
bowls as a first course (or a separate vegetable course). The idea is
to put a pod into your mouth, and suck out the steamed peas and
the small amount of delicious juice inside the pod. The outer
green part of the pod tastes good too (see pea pod soup, p. 231).

You may have noticed that the cook does not shell the peas.

Egg and peas in the Jewish style (for 4)

I've slightly adapted this recipe from the 1758 edition of Hannah
Glasse's *Art of Cookery*. It sounds very simple, even ordinary, but
in fact the combination of peas, eggs and spices tastes delicious.
An excellent first course for a dinner party. Be sure that the peas
are young and sweet, the eggs very fresh.

2 lbs. peas, or 1 pint shelled peas
½ gill water
½ gill olive oil (or butter, melted)
¼ teaspoon each nutmeg, mace, black
    pepper
sugar, salt
5 eggs
3 oz. single cream

Cook the peas with spices, water, oil and ¼ teaspoon salt, in a
covered frying pan (use an enamelled cast iron pan, or a paella
dish – something attractive enough to be put on the table). When
they are half-cooked, season with more salt and a little sugar if
necessary. With the back of a spoon, make four depressions in the
peas and slip an egg into each one. Replace the cover of the pan,
and continue to simmer for 5–10 minutes, until the peas are done
and the eggs set, but not hard. Meanwhile break the fifth egg into
a cup, beating it up with the cream. Pour over the eggs and peas,

and put under a hot grill for a moment or two to set. Serve immediately.

Pea and ham soup

Peas and ham, smoked ham especially, are a wonderful combination, either as a main course, or cooked together in soup. This recipe solves the familiar summer problem of how to use up peas which looked fine in the shop, but turn out to be older and drier than one thought:

> 8 oz. shelled peas
> 2 oz. butter
> 3 oz. chopped onion
> 3 oz. smoked gammon rashers and 2 pints
>   water, *or* 3 oz. diced potato and 2 pints
>   smoked ham stock
> 1 egg yolk
> 3 tablespoons double cream
> nutmeg, salt, black pepper

Melt the onion and gammon, or onion and potato, in the butter for 10 minutes over a low heat. Add water, or stock, and peas and seasoning. Simmer until the peas are cooked, then liquidize or put through the *mouli-légumes*. Return to the cooking pan through a strainer and reheat. When the soup is just under the boil, pour a ladleful on the egg yolk and cream, beaten together in a basin. Put back into the pan and stir over a low heat. without boiling, for 5 minutes until the soup thickens a little more. Correct the seasoning.

Pea pod soup

A recipe for people who grow their own peas, and can't bear to waste the least result of their hard work. Only fresh, juicy pods should be used.

pea pods from 2 lb. peas
1 bunch spring onions, chopped
2 oz. butter
1 good sprig savory
1 small bunch chives
3 tablespoons double cream
1 egg yolk
salt, pepper

Put pea pods into a large pan, and cover them generously with at least 2 pints of water. Boil until the green part of the pods is soft. Put through the *mouli-légumes* (the tough white parts will be left behind). Meanwhile in another pan, melt the spring onions in the butter without browning them. Add the pea pod liquid, and the savory; season well and simmer until the onions are cooked. Liquidize or sieve the soup and return to the pan to reheat. Pour a little of the hot, almost boiling soup into a bowl, in which you have beaten together the cream and egg yolk. Whisk well and return to the pan. Stir over a low heat until the soup thickens a little, but don't let it boil or the egg will curdle. Correct the seasoning. Serve with the chives snipped over the soup.

Note: if a few peas can be spared, add them when the strained pea pod liquor is amalgamated with onions and savory. The flavour will be even more delicious.

Peas in the French style (for 6)

A marvellous way of cooking, or rather stewing peas, whether they are young or not quite so young. It's surprising what a smooth texture the lettuce gives to the sauce, and how well the peas taste after their slow simmering with onion and carrot. (Incidentally, it's the use of this type of recipe which makes French tinned peas so superior to any other kind.)

Quantities and timing are for middling peas. Small (or frozen) ones will need less time to cook, and half the amount of water.

Keep an eye on the peas to see how things are going; it's a mistake to overcook them.

> 1 lb. shelled peas
> 6 spring onions, roughly chopped
> 8 large lettuce leaves
> tablespoon chopped parsley
> ½ teaspoon salt
> 3 tablespoons butter
> 4 tablespoons water
> 2 very young carrots, finely chopped
> sugar

Cut the lettuce into strips, and put with all the other ingredients, except the sugar, into a heavy pan. Cover tightly and simmer for about 20 minutes, or until the peas are cooked. There should not be much juice left in the pan. Taste and season with extra salt, and sugar if necessary (don't make the dish too sweet).

Artichokes Clamart (for 6)

By a happy arrangement of nature, since their flavours go so well together, artichokes and peas are in season at the same time. This is a special dish, for a special meal.

The name Clamart is a souvenir of the days when Paris, like London, was ringed with market gardens. Different areas specialized in different vegetables, Clamart, to the south-west of Paris, being famous for peas. Every morning before sunrise carts from the suburbs would clatter into Paris with produce for the central markets, until in the nineteenth century the monstrous belly of the capital was no longer satisfied with young vegetables, and swallowed the gardens as well. It was the same with London – have you ever seen asparagus growing in twentieth-century Battersea? Most of the *petits pois* in Clamart these days are, I am sure, to be found in tins. But the name survives piously on menus and in cookery books; it still means 'garnished with the best young peas'.

> 6 large artichokes
> 2 tablespoons wine vinegar

> 1 lb. shelled peas cooked in the French
>   style, above
> 4 oz. butter
> heaped tablespoon chopped parsley
> lemon juice

Cut the artichoke stalks off close to their heads, and put them into a large pan of boiling salted water. Add the vinegar, cover the pan and cook for about 40 minutes, until a skewer goes easily into the base of the artichokes. Rinse them quickly under the cold tap, so that the leaves can be stripped off (keep them for another meal, to eat with vinaigrette sauce), and the hairy 'choke' removed. You will be left with 6 saucer-shapes of greyish-green artichoke – best part, the *fond* or heart.

Cook the peas in the French style, adding the artichokes for a few moments at the end to reheat. Mash the parsley and butter together, seasoning with lemon juice. Arrange the vegetables in a hot serving dish, with a knob of parsley butter in the hollow of each artichoke heart.

If you grow your own artichokes, you may find it more convenient to use 18 of the very young ones. Slice ¼ inch from the pointed leafy end of the artichokes, and boil them quickly in salted water until tender. Drain, and mix into the cooked peas. Stir the parsley butter into the pan before turning out onto a serving dish.

Risi e bisi, or rice and peas

Driving along between the arcaded, de Chirico towns of Cuneo and Turin, one may round a corner to find that life has shifted suddenly to the Far East. Rows of girls, with skirts kilted up and low conical straw hats on the back of their necks, paddle along pushing rice plants into flooded fields. The extra large grains that these paddy fields produce give the rice dishes of Northern Italy special succulence. For this dish of *risi e piselli*, or *risi e bisi* to Venetians, who make it a great deal, try to buy some of this delicious rice from an Italian delicatessen.

3–4 oz. chopped onion
3 tablespoons olive oil
8 oz. Italian rice
1 lb. shelled peas
¾ pint water
sugar, salt, black pepper
grated Parmesan cheese

Brown the onion lightly in the oil. Add the rice and stir it over the heat until transparent – about 5 minutes. Add ¾ pint water, and leave to simmer with the lid on the pan, until the rice is tender and the water absorbed. You may need to add more water, so watch the rice as it cooks. Meanwhile cook the peas in boiling water, seasoned with salt, pepper and a little sugar. Drain and mix with the cooked rice. Stir in 2 tablespoons Parmesan cheese, serve extra grated cheese in a separate bowl.

By adding hot chicken stock at the end, this dish can be turned into a hearty soup.

A last thought on peas

> Not only does earth grow bread enough
> To feed mankind with ease,
> But roses and myrtles, beauty and joy,
> And (in the season) peas.
>
> Yes, sweet green peas for everyone
> As soon as the pods will burst.
> Heaven we'll leave to the angels, and
> The sparrows, who had it first.

Heine. *Germany: A Winter's Tale.*
Translated by T. J. Reed

Spinach

Don't be put off by either of two thoughts about spinach. First that it's baby food, and good for you. Second, that it's so often turned into a green slick, without taste or joy.

Perhaps when you stuff its unhairy plain leaves into your string-bag, or saucepan, you might reflect that spinach has a long and most respectable history. It has an Arab name (spinach: isfināj according to my dictionary), though it only came to Europe by way of the Arab world. They had eaten spinach in Greece and Rome, and earlier still. It is one of those plants of ancient cultivation whose wild forms and place of origin are unknown. Over the centuries it has driven out less worthy competitors in the line of a soft-leaved vegetable, annual, easy and quick to grow, easy and quick to prepare.

A soothing veg. There was a Frenchman who once said (according to the gardener and epicure Edward Bunyard) that you have only to eat a few spoonfuls of spinach to increase in gentleness, benevolence and amiability. 'You will be loving to your children and your wife: your home will be ruled by peace and harmony.'

Perhaps so. But only if your spinach has been allowed to absorb plenty of butter or plenty of cream – not to say, salt, pepper and nutmeg.

Our dampish climate certainly gives us some of the most succulent spinach in the world. Our subsidizing government certainly gives us some of the cheapest butter in the world. Put the two together. (If you've never cooked, let's say in France, where butter costs between 45p and 50p a lb., you don't know how lucky you are in this country.)

Spinach has its own flavour, but the point is that it marries so well – with eggs, fish, ham, cheese, carrots, lemon juice, orange juice. And as a rule it's improved by the opposite accompaniment of something crisp. It always strikes me that, in cooking, far too many people fail to see how appetizing it is to provide contrasts in texture. A few triangles of fried bread, fried in butter or olive oil, can turn spinach into a course on its own, instead of spoonfuls on the side of a plate.

Basic spinach

For six people allow about 3 lb. of spinach. Pick off the tougher bits of stalk; discard brown, and alien, leaves. Wash in two or three changes of water, turning the spinach over and over to free it of earth – spinach can be very dirty. Drain in a colander.

Take a large, heavy saucepan and stuff in the spinach – or as much of it as you can. *Do not add any water*. Put the lid on, with a weight if necessary, and set over a low heat. There will soon be a bubbling noise, as the spinach exudes its moisture. Prod with a wooden spoon, adding the rest of the spinach in the colander as soon as the spinach in the pan begins to cook down. Raise the heat and cook with the lid off, stirring from time to time to make sure that the underneath leaves aren't sticking to the pan.

This sounds a long business, but the total cooking time will be about 10 minutes. Put the cooked spinach into a large sieve to drain, cutting it gently with the edge of a fish slice to help the liquid run away.

Just before the meal, melt a large knob of butter (4 oz.) in a clean pan, and put the drained spinach back to absorb the butter. Season with salt, pepper and nutmeg. If the spinach still seems wet, it will need a little while longer to drain.

This is the minimum of effort required to produce edible spinach. You may think I've been pedantic, and made the recipe – really very simple – sound complicated. But it's important that three principles about cooking spinach should be absolutely clear – it must be well washed, well dried out in the cooking, and well buttered.

Now you can have some fun with this delicious vegetable.

Creamed spinach with orange (for 6)

---

    3 lb. spinach, cooked as above
    ¼ pint double cream
    1½ large oranges quartered
    3 large slices of bread
    3 oz. butter

Remove crusts from the bread, cut into triangles and fry in the butter. Meanwhile add the cream to the cooked spinach instead of the knob of butter mentioned in the basic preparation, and cook until the cream is absorbed. Serve in a shallow oval or round dish, with the orange quarters in the middle, peel-side up (to be squeezed over the spinach), and the croûtons of bread tucked round the edge. If it's the right time of year, the flavour of the spinach is improved by squeezing the juice of a large Seville orange into it before arranging on the dish: include the quarters of sweet orange as well.

The unusual idea of orange with spinach comes from an eighteenth-century cookery book. It's an excellent combination of flavours – and colours.

Spinach and carrots (for 6)

Another dish which is beautiful to look at. Like the creamed spinach and orange above, it should be served as a course on its own.

> 3 lb. spinach, cooked as above
> 1 lb. young carrots
> 6 oz. butter
> 3 large slices of bread, fried in butter
> lemon juice, salt, pepper, sugar

Wash and scrape the carrots. Melt 3 oz. butter in a heavy pan, remove from the heat and grate the carrots into it, using a fine shredder. Cover and simmer gently until the carrots are cooked, but not overcooked – about 5–10 minutes. Season with salt, pepper and lemon juice, and with a little sugar if the carrots are not as full of flavour as they should be. Keep warm.

Add the other 3 oz. of butter to the well-drained spinach. Stir over a good heat until it's been absorbed.

Arrange the carrots in a border round the edge of a hot serving dish, put the spinach in the middle with the croûtons stuck into it. Serve immediately.

Four-day spinach (for 6–8)

This recipe of unusual deliciousness shows the ability of spinach to absorb butter. I believe one can go on adding butter to it for seven days, but by the end of four days it looks and tastes so good that it has to be eaten.

> 3–4 lb. spinach
> 1 lb. unsalted butter
> salt, pepper, nutmeg, lemon juice

Day 1: cook the spinach and drain it in the usual way. Chop it roughly before adding 4 oz. of butter; keep the pan over a good heat until the butter's absorbed. Leave to cool in a clean pudding basin. Store in the refrigerator.

Day 2: reheat the spinach with another 4 oz. of butter. Leave to cool.

Days 3 and 4: repeat day two, except that on the 4th day the spinach will be served hot and not be left to cool.

You will have a rich, dark green purée, a cream or sauce rather than a vegetable. Spinach for adults, decidedly. Serve with boiled gammon, or a roast joint of beef, or with grilled steak or grilled salmon.

Should there be any spinach left over, use it to stuff an omelette. Or to make individual eggs Florentine.

Terrine aux herbes

A reader living in the department of Essonne in northern France has sent me this delicious recipe for a herb pâté. As with all the other pâtés – game, hare, lark, chicken, duck – the basis and background is pork.

> 2 lb. pork throat meat
> ½ lb. pig's liver
> 6 oz. gammon, or smoked lean bacon
> 6 oz. green streaky bacon
> 1½ lb. spinach (include some sorrel if possible)
> 2 medium onions, chopped very finely
> 2 large cloves garlic, chopped
> 2 beaten eggs
>
> *seasonings:*
> rosemary, thyme, basil, marjoram, nutmeg, salt and freshly ground black pepper

Mince the meat (or, preferably, chop it – a Moulinette automatic chopper is a great convenience). Cook the spinach, drain it well and chop it up. Mix everything together, adding the seasonings to taste: if you are not prepared to chop onions very finely, they must be sweated in some butter, without browning them, until soft and golden – they should disappear into the pâté.

Put into a well-greased terrine (or more conveniently into two) and bake for about an hour at a very moderate heat, Mark 2–3, 300–325°F. Cover with a lid of foil, which should be removed about 15 minutes before the end of cooking time to allow the top to brown.

Although this pâté is best made with fresh green herbs and spinach, dried herbs and frozen leaf spinach may be substituted. The inclusion of sorrel is to be recommended, for its sharp pungency.

Serve it with wholemeal bread (in lieu of *pain de campagne*) and anchovy butter.

Eggs Florentine (for 6)

The Italians love spinach, and make more use of it than we do. All those green pasta, the pasta verde, are not coloured and flavoured by drops from a bottle, but by the addition of spinach and spinach juice. Sometimes ravioli and tortellini are filled with a mixture of spinach and cream cheese and Parmesan (a variation of the delicious little Middle-Eastern spinach pasties on p. 243). When eggs, fish and ham are cooked and served with spinach and cheese sauce, we describe them as 'Florentine', in the style of Florence.

> 3–4 lb. spinach, cooked as before
> 6 medium eggs
> 1 oz. butter
> 1 oz. flour
> ½ pint hot milk
> ¼ pint single cream
> heaped tablespoon Parmesan cheese,
>   or Cheddar to taste
> 2 crumbled rusks or biscottes
> salt, pepper, nutmeg

As the spinach cooks, make the sauce. Melt the butter in a heavy pan, stir in the flour with a wooden spoon. Cook gently for 2 minutes, then incorporate the hot milk gradually, to avoid lumps, and the single cream. Season with half the cheese or a little more to taste, with salt, pepper and nutmeg, and leave to simmer over a low heat for at least 15 minutes.

Meanwhile, having drained the spinach, put it into a buttered ovenproof dish, and prepare the eggs. They can be poached, but, if like me you're not an admirer of poached eggs, try cooking them this way – put them into a pan of fast-boiling water *for exactly 5 minutes.* Then plunge them into a pan of cold water, set under a gently running cold tap. The moment they're cool enough to handle, tap them all over carefully and peel them (remember that the yolks will not be hard-boiled, so do this gently).

Make six depressions in the spinach with the back of a tablespoon, and set the eggs well down, Strain the hot sauce over the dish. Mix the rest of the cheese with the rusk crumbs, and sprinkle over the top. Bake in a hot oven for about 10 minutes, until the sauce bubbles and the top turns golden brown.

For sole or plaice fillets Florentine: roll up the fillets and secure them with a toothpick. Put them on the spinach instead of the eggs. Finish the dish as above, but bake for 30 minutes in a moderate oven to cook the sole or plaice. The top can be browned under the grill, if necessary.

For ham Florentine: roll up slices of cooked ham, spear with a toothpick, and lay on the spinach. Pour over the sauce and finish as for eggs Florentine. If uncooked gammon is used pour boiling water over the slices and leave for 5 minutes to remove excess saltiness. Lay them, overlapping each other, on top of the spinach, and finish as for eggs Florentine.

For individual eggs Florentine: put a spoonful of spinach (4-day spinach is ideal for this dish) into a buttered ramekin. Break an egg and slide it on top of the spinach. Bake in an oven (or in a pan of simmering water) until the white just starts to look opaque. Pour in a tablespoon of double cream; sprinkle with cheese, salt, pepper, and rusk crumbs; brown quickly under the grill. Don't overcook. Serve with toast fingers.

Middle-Eastern spinach pasties

A Lebanese reader sent me this recipe for some delicious tiny pasties, of a kind which are popular all over the Middle East. Variety of filling and of dough is enormous, depending on the resources and ingenuity of the cook. Bread dough may be used, or flaky pastry, or shortcrust pastry, or that papery-fine pastry called *fila* which is sold in Greek delicatessen shops.

dough made with 1 lb. flour

filling:
2 lb. spinach
1 very large onion, chopped
3 tablespoons olive oil or butter
salt, pepper
either 3 oz. pine kernels or other nuts
or 6–8 oz. Gruyère, or crumbly cheese

plus:
1 egg yolk beaten with 1 tablespoon
   water

Cook the onion gently in the oil or butter until it's golden and transparent. Cook and drain the spinach very well. Mix with the onion, and season. Fry the chopped nuts, if used, in the liquid remaining from the onion cooking. Stir into the spinach. Alternatively grate the cheese and stir that in instead.

Roll out the dough as thinly as possible. Cut into squares and circles about 3 inches wide. Put a knob of filling in the middle, moisten the pastry edges and fold the pastry to enclose the spinach mixture. Press the edges firmly together.

Brush with egg and water (leave to prove, if bread dough is used), and bake at the appropriate temperature until the pasties are light and golden. Puff pastry needs a very high temperature, the other ones need something between Mark 5–6, 375–400°F.

An alternative method, a very good one, is to deep-fry the pasties. They will puff up to golden brown lightness very much more quickly than they will in the oven.

But whichever method of cooking you choose, they should be eaten very hot as a first course. Or as part of a buffet at a party. Meat can also be included in the filling; spices can be used as flavouring too. The main thing is to make a really piquant filling, otherwise these tiny mouthfuls are not worth the bother of making – or eating.

Tomatoes

Millions of us eat tomatoes; few of us ever eat a good one; and few of our great-great-grandparents ever ate a tomato at all.

Odd? Well perhaps not. The tomato needs sun. It's a native of the hot lands of Central and Southern America ('tomato' from the Mexican *tomatl*). Early sixteenth-century travellers brought it to Europe, where it soon flourished in the warmth of Spain and Italy. Can you imagine Italian cooking without the tomato?

Italians called the new fruit *pomo d'oro*, Golden Apple. They still do. The name refers to its shining brilliance; it was not intended as a prognostic of our 'Moneymaker', the variety most of us have to endure if we are to eat tomatoes at all. Another early name, *Pomo dei Mori*, Moors' Apple, is reputed to be the origin of the French *pomme d'amour*. And so of our British 'Love Apple'. But 'its supposed power of exciting tender feelings' did not weaken English suspicions of the tomato. Tomatoes were still regarded as medicine in the eighteenth century. Even the most advanced gardeners were shocked at Italians and Spaniards who 'eat these Apples as we do Cucumbers, with Pepper, Oil and Salt; and some eat them stewed in Sauces, etc., but considering their great Moisture and Coldness, the Nourishment they afford must be bad.'

It was not until after the 1850s that the Love Apple commonly became the tomato. Its popularity increased, but slowly. People still needed reassurance that it didn't cause gout or cancer. Perhaps the tale that Fijians enjoyed tomatoes as a side-dish to Cold Missionary had some effect on its slow progress in the national diet.

Now we know that tomatoes are a valuable source of vitamin C. Twice as valuable if grown out of doors. Hybrids have been developed for northern industrial conditions and climate. We buy nice-looking, glossy, even-sized tomatoes all the year round; they are the growers' and grocers' delight, 'moneymakers' to the last pip. In *Guides to the Grades No. 4 Tomatoes*, the Ministry of Agriculture describes this perfectly desirable object, classifying it elaborately down to the last millimetre, into Extra Class, Class 1, 2 and 3. Advice is handed out on packing and labelling. The only word missing is 'flavour'. In the twenty-four pages there is little indication of the fact that tomatoes are for eating; they're just for buying and selling, like the tins of sardines in a favourite Jewish story.

The ideal tomato is firm to the knife all through, sun-ripened out of doors to a rich but refreshing flavour, often a 'large, irregularly-shaped furrowed fruit', as a nineteenth-century botanical dictionary described it, a glorious red, not only furrowed but scarred and split in a way that would horrify a supermarket manager ('unattractive in appearance', Min. of Ag. *op. cit.*). You'll have to grow tomatoes yourself, choosing a variety recommended for its flavour by a good nurseryman, unless you can afford to day-trip to France once a week. So the problem is, how to make the best of the poor commercial tomato we're left with.

Sugar first, then freshly ground black pepper and unadulterated sea salt. These are the three great flavour-enhancers; our tomato needs them all. Essential accompaniments are parsley, and the onion family from garlic to shallots, onions and chives.

In Italy the two great herbs for tomato dishes are sweet basil and sweet marjoram (*origano*). Both need sun. We can grow them (they are both annuals), but out of doors they are chancy, needing a warm summer. On the windowsill, or in a greenhouse, they have a better chance of success. Origano dries quite successfully, but to my mind basil loses its essential freshness, its magical flavour of the sun, and becomes too strong when dried.

Tomato salad

The simplest and best way of serving good tomatoes. But don't make the salad too long before eating it, or it will lose freshness and become nasty.

Pour boiling water over 1 lb. tomatoes and leave for 15–20 seconds. Run the tomatoes under a cold tap. The skin will peel off easily. Slice into a serving dish. Sprinkle evenly with about a dessertspoon of sugar (depending on the tomatoes), a few turns of the black pepper mill, and a mean teaspoon of sea-salt crystals. Drip a teaspoon of vinegar, wine vinegar, over the salad – malt vinegar is too brutish – and a tablespoon of olive oil. Just before serving, scatter with finely chopped garlic, or chives, or raw onion, and parsley. Sweet basil alone, if you have it. For vinegar and oil, you could substitute three tablespoons of thick cream and lemon juice to taste.

A salad which goes well with hot or cold roast duck and pork, if you add two peeled, sliced oranges.

Egg and tomato salad

A build-up of egg and tomato slices and chopped chives or shallots, dressed with oil, vinegar, salt and pepper, is a favourite French hors d'œuvre. Bowls of it provide a refreshing start to midday picnics during the grape harvest in Touraine. You must use first-class fresh eggs, and season each layer of the salad as you build it up, using a little sugar on the tomatoes only. Serve immediately.

In French middle-class homes and small hotels, presentation is a little more elegant. And in the wonderful cooked-food shops to be found in every French community above a village. Slice the tomatoes almost, but not quite through. They will fan out, so that you can slip a slice, or half a slice of hard-boiled egg and a sliver of anchovy fillet into each cut. Garnish with chopped parsley and the chopped whites from the ends of the hard-boiled eggs. Serve with a bowl of mayonnaise (p. 163). Add black olives, salami, crisp green salad (p. 210), some unsalted butter and a good loaf of bread, and you have a fine lunch for a hot day.

Stuffed tomatoes

I am no believer in tomato water-lilies and tomato baskets: there are better uses for one's time. But there is no denying that stuffed tomatoes are a useful way of stretching delicious and expensive mixtures, such as crab or lobster mayonnaise. A small tin of tunny fish (preferably canned *without oil*), broken up and mixed with chopped anchovies, parsley, 2 or 3 hard-boiled eggs, and mayonnaise, makes a cheaper but excellent filling. Peel the tomatoes first, cut off a lid, scoop out the inside and leave upside down to drain. Season with salt, pepper and a little sugar before filling.

For baked stuffed tomatoes, there are many simple fillings, with variations depending on what you may happen to have in larder or store cupboard. I think that garlic in fair quantity is a good idea: crush a couple of large cloves and fry them gently in butter with a chopped medium to large onion, then mix in breadcrumbs and parsley, the chopped firm inside part of the tomatoes, salt, pepper and perhaps some nutmeg. A rasher of lean smoked bacon can be chopped up and fried with onions and garlic. Remember not to peel the tomatoes, or they will collapse as they cook. Bake in a buttered dish, at Mark 5, 375°F, for 20–30 minutes (the temperature may be altered to suit your convenience of course, when other things are being cooked at the same time). With large tomatoes, an egg may be baked in the centre instead of stuffing.

Basic tomato sauce

When we return from staying in France or Italy, I spend a despairing fortnight trying to recreate hot and vivid noonday flavours. A hopeless pastime. It's bound to be. But I persevere with this tomato sauce, made from canned tomatoes, which produce a better flavoured result than fresh ones sold in shops. As you will see, this sauce has many uses:

> 1 tablespoon each butter and olive oil
> 8 oz. chopped onion
> 1 outer stalk celery, chopped
> 3 oz. chopped carrot
> 2 rashers bacon, diced (optional)
> 2 large cloves garlic, finely chopped
> 1 lb. 14 oz. can Italian tomatoes
> 1 heaped tablespoon sugar
> dessertspoon wine vinegar
> ¼ pint red wine
> good teaspoon sea salt
> black pepper, dried origano, basil, fresh
>   parsley

Sweat the onion, celery, carrot, bacon if used, and garlic in the butter and oil for 10 minutes, then turn the heat up so that they brown lightly. Add the rest of the ingredients, and bring to the boil. Don't cover the pan, but keep the sauce bubbling and busy for at least 15 minutes. It will reduce to a rich stew. No need to stir.

This sauce can be stored in the fridge for a day or two, and used in the following ways:

Pizzaiola sauce

Sieve or put through the coarse plate of a *mouli-légumes*. Don't liquidize. Serve with steak or spaghetti.

Tomato soup

Liquidize half a pint of the sauce with half a pint of beef or veal stock. Add a pinch of bicarbonate of soda and reheat, adding more stock if you like a thinner consistency. When the soup is just under the boil, add ¼ pint of boiling single cream and serve immediately, sprinkled with parsley, without allowing it to come to the boil. Small cubes of bread fried in olive oil or butter are a good accompaniment.

Peperonata and ratatouille

Italian and French vegetable stew, eaten hot or cold. The main English fault when making them is wateriness, but this can be avoided if you use about ½ pint of the tomato sauce and cook the other vegetables in it. For peperonata take two or three red and yellow peppers. Cut them into strips – remove stalks and seeds first – and simmer in the sauce for half an hour. For ratatouille, slice one or two aubergines, and half a pound of courgettes, and cook in the same way. Don't peel the vegetables. Quantities depend on taste, supply and pocket.

If you feel that these mixtures (particularly ratatouille) are becoming too liquid, turn up the heat and boil hard without a lid on the pan.

Cod, fresh or dried, in tomato sauce

With fresh cod, cut it into cubes of 1 inch, discarding skin and bones. Add to the tomato sauce and simmer for 15 minutes (never overcook fish – remember that it will continue to cook a little in the hot sauce as it's dished up and brought to table). Add 16 black, stoned (for preference) olives to the stew for the last 5 minutes.

With dried salt cod, soak it for 24 hours first, changing the water several times. Drain and put into a pan of cold water and bring slowly to the boil. The moment the water bubbles, remove the cod and cut it into pieces. Discard skin and bones. Add it to the tomato sauce and cook for about 10 minutes, or until cooked but not disintegrating. Olives to be put in as above.

Roasting chicken with tomato sauce

Joint, roll in seasoned flour and brown in olive oil, add to the tomato sauce and simmer until cooked (40–60 minutes). A good recipe for battery chicken.

Soufflé aux tomates

Prepare a soufflé dish with a greased collar of foil. Liquidize ½ pint of the sauce, or sieve it finely. Melt 1 oz. butter in a heavy pan, stir in 1 oz. plain flour, then ¼ pint warmed milk. Cook to a thick sauce, which will leave the sides of the pan. Add sieved tomato sauce, then 3 egg yolks one by one, off the heat. Beat 4 egg whites to a stiff foam, fold into tomato mixture gently with a metal spoon. Add 3 oz. Gruyère, diced. Pour into buttered soufflé dish, sprinkle 2 tablespoons of grated Parmesan cheese on top. Lay a butter paper across the collar, and bake for 20 minutes at Mark 5–6, 375–400°F. Timing is always a little difficult with soufflés, as it can be altered by the size of dish used, and naturally the amount of mixture. When the top is risen and browned nicely, it's usually a good indication that the soufflé is done. Serve immediately, having first removed the foil collar. The centre will be creamy as the serving spoon dips into it; the outside will be a deliciously crusty brown.

Veal with tomato sauce (ossi buchi)

Find an intelligent butcher who will cut 1½ inch thick veal slices for you, across the shin of the animal. These are *ossi buchi*, hollow (marrow) bones, a favourite Milanese food. Season and brown these bones carefully, so that the marrow doesn't fall out, in olive oil. Pour over a large glass of dry white wine. Boil hard to reduce, for about 5 minutes. Transfer the bones to a casserole, where they can lie flat in a single layer. Add a good pint of tomato sauce to the pan juices, bring to the boil and pour over the veal. Simmer gently in a low oven until tender. This can be done in advance, and the dish reheated just before the meal.

Serve sprinkled with 2 tablespoons chopped parsley, mixed with the grated rind of half a large lemon, and 1 chopped clove of garlic. Boiled rice is the usual accompaniment to this excellent dish.

Fruit

Apple and Quince

We have rather betrayed the apple. It's the most important fruit
in our eating and cooking. It's the foundation fruit of our Western
culture. It's the fruit of Aphrodite and the Virgin, of earthly and
heavenly love, and so on. What a pity, and what a betrayal, that
commercial growers have now concentrated on look, at the expense of flavour and texture (and scent).

Apple history or prehistory provides a clue for cooking. The
sour crab in the copse or hedge may descend from orchard apples
but orchard apples don't descend from the crab: if botanists are
right, they descend from an apple tree native of south-west Asia
and the Balkans, with fruit sizeable and often sweet.

Sweetness is the clue, or the cue. In the kitchen avoid most of
the cookers (unless you have space to keep them until they are
mellow) and cook with eaters. Experiment with the eaters you can
buy or the ones in your orchard. Don't use just any apple, or the
ones which happen to have fallen most and soonest, for apple

sauce, to give an example. Among the best for that purpose – and for apple dishes in general – sweet but not too sweet and not needing so much sugar, are Cox's Orange Pippin (which Mr Cox, a retired brewer, raised in his garden near Slough, about 1830), and the Reinette d'Orléans, favourite apple of the French, which was first recorded in 1776.

No difficulty with the Coxes. Grocers may sometimes have Reinettes (a Reinette tree is easily bought for the garden). Get them if you can. They last well into the summer, and in apple sauce their clear, concentrated flavour goes especially well with summer veal, and with chicken.

In apple dishes the rule is: avoid water. For flavour the apple's best allies are butter and cream. Expensive, but I prefer eating a little of something delicious to eating quantities of acid-mush-cum-sugar.

The apple has another cooking ally, its relative the quince, altogether more oriental, original home Central Asia: apple tart with quince, baked quince, quince and apple jelly, etc. And the scent and the look of a bowl of ripe quinces in the house in the autumn are enough to make you believe that the golden fruit Earth gave to Hera and Zeus when they were married was quince and not apple. Quinces seem to be coming back. Good greengrocers have them in a good quince year, and a quince tree in a damp corner doesn't have to be very big before it bears. You will have the bonus, too, of the most beautiful of the blossoms of spring, the quince's soft pink globes, with their falling ruff of silver green leaves.

Bircher muesli

This raw fruit porridge, more appetizingly known as Bircher muesli, makes a luxurious breakfast dish. It was invented by Dr Bircher-Benner, the pioneer of food reform, for patients at his Zürich clinic.

He explained that he felt muesli 'corresponds with the laws of the human organism', its composition – i.e. its proportions of protein, fat and carbohydrate calories – being identical with mother's milk. This may be so (but is mother's milk a suitable food for mature adults, one wonders). The fact is that Bircher muesli tastes delicious: it's the one great contribution of the vegetarian movement to the pleasures of European eating.

Raisins, blackberries and peaches make fine additions to the basic recipe given below. Soaked, dried fruit such as apricots and peaches may also be added, but I think that a proportion at least of grated apple is essential to the texture of the dish. I think, too, that the dish is better made immediately before breakfast, even if the coarsest oatmeal is used, as this gives a drier, more appetizing mixture. Soaking the oats overnight makes muesli uncomfortably close to cold porridge.

Here, though, is the true original recipe:

ingredients per person
1 level tablespoon coarse oatmeal, or
   rolled oats
3 tablespoons water
1 tablespoon Nestlé's condensed,
   sweetened milk (or honey and single
   cream)
juice of half a lemon
5¼ oz. apple, or apple and other fruit
   mixed
1 tablespoon chopped nuts

Put oats and water into a pudding basin and soak for 12 hours (overnight). Just before eating, stir in the sweetened condensed milk (or honey and cream), and the lemon juice, which sharpens the flavour agreeably and helps to keep the apple from turning brown. Put a flat grater over the basin and grate in the apple, peel, core and all, but no stalk. Stir the apple into the oatmeal mixture every so often, to stop it discolouring. Add the nuts and serve.

Blackberries are surprisingly good with muesli, and peaches and strawberries make it into a luxurious dish. More of a pudding than a breakfast food.

Pheasant à la Normande

Pork with apple sauce and duck with apple sauce are often eaten in England. The apple tartness is used to cut the richness of the meat. Apples however can be combined with cream to make very successful sauces for drier things such as pheasants or veal or chicken; and this and the following recipe show how it's done with both large and small pieces of meat. The apples should be eating apples of Reinette or Cox type, which provide a slightly acid flavour and enough natural sweetness to need no sugar.

> 1 large pheasant
> 6 medium-sized Reinettes or Coxes
> 3 oz. butter
> 4 oz. double cream
> salt, pepper, cinnamon

Brown the pheasant all over in half the butter. Peel, core and slice the apples; fry them lightly in the rest of the butter, sprinkling them with cinnamon as they cook. Put a thin layer of apple into a deep casserole, arrange the pheasant on top, breast down. Tuck the rest of the apples round the sides so that the bird is embedded in them. Pour in half the cream. Cover and cook in the oven, Mark 4, 350°F, for about an hour. Turn the bird breast side up at half time, seasoning it with salt and pepper. Cover again and complete the cooking. Stir the rest of the cream into the apples when the pheasant is cooked, giving it a few moments to heat through.

Serve in the casserole, or carve the pheasant and put it on a bed of apple and cream sauce on a clean serving dish. The pheasant juices make the sauce particularly good. (Chicken can be cooked in the same way.)

Note: Calvados as a final addition, makes the sauce even better.

Apple sauce (for 4)

Reinettes, Coxes or Sturmers are best for this useful sauce. Try it with veal escalopes, or thin slices of pork tenderloin, dipped in egg and breadcrumbs and fried in butter. Or with boiled chicken, or sweetbreads. Apart from some boiled potatoes accompanying vegetables are unnecessary, indeed undesirable.

> 3 good-sized apples
> 2 oz. butter
> ¼ pint dry white wine, cider or light
>   stock
> 3–4 oz. thick cream
> 1 tablespoon Calvados, or brandy
> sugar, lemon juice, salt, pepper to
>   taste

Peel, core and cut the apples into ¼ inch dice. Cook gently in the butter in a covered frying pan, stirring from time to time. When they are golden, remove to a serving dish and keep warm. Add wine to pan juices, boiling down by half to a rich sauce. Pour in the cream. When the sauce is amalgamated, flavour with Calvados or brandy and seasonings, and pour over the apples.

Arrange the meat on top. As with all cream sauces, make sure that serving plate and dinner plates are really hot.

Apple meringue pudding (for 6)

A delicious Sunday pudding.

> 2 oz. butter
> 2 lb. eating apples
>   or 1¾ lb. cookers and ¼ lb. quinces
> apricot jam, or cinnamon, or cloves
> sugar to taste

> *meringue:*
> 3 egg whites
> 6 oz. sugar
> 1 heaped teaspoon cornflour
> 1 teaspoon vinegar
> 2 oz. blanched and split almonds

Melt the butter in a large pan, and add the apples (and quinces) washed and cut into rough quarters. Cover and simmer gently until there is about an inch of juice in the pan, then turn up the heat until the apples are cooked. They won't burn if the heat is low enough to start with: water is to be avoided. Push the fruit through a sieve and season with sugar and apricot jam (Golden Delicious), or cinnamon or cloves (cookers). Cox's Orange Pippins have a good enough flavour to be left alone usually. With cookers, quince provides the best flavouring of all. Spread the purée into a shallow serving dish, ovenproof, and leave to cool.

To make the meringue, beat the egg whites stiff. Fold in sugar and cornflour, sifted together, and last of all the vinegar. Pile up on top of the apple, keeping the meringue thin at the edges as it will spread a little while cooking. Stick the almonds all over the meringue. Bake at Mark $\frac{1}{2}$, 250°F, for 1–1$\frac{1}{4}$ hours. If the meringue could be browner at the end of this time, turn the heat up a little. Remove from the oven, and serve warm or cold with single cream.

Evreux apple tarts

At the Vieille Gabelle restaurant in Evreux, 55 miles to the west of Paris, they serve these tarts made with Golden Delicious apples. Do not be tempted to cook the tarts before the meal, or the juices will soak away into the pastry. Put them into a hot oven as you serve the first course, and baste once or twice with the apricot mixture.

shortcrust:

8 oz. flour
5 oz. butter and lard mixed
2 level tablespoons icing sugar
1 egg

crème pâtissière:

1 oz. flour
2 egg yolks
1 egg
2 oz. sugar
$\frac{1}{2}$ pt. milk

apricot mixture:

6 tablespoons apricot jam
2 tablespoons water

plus:

1¼ lb. Golden Delicious apples

Make the pastry and use it to line four straight-sided patty pans, of about 4¼ inches diameter (from Woolworth's). Make the *crème pâtissière* next: mix in a bowl the flour, egg yolks, egg and sugar, and stir in the milk, which should first be brought to just under boiling point. Cook over a low heat until the custard is thick. Cool, then pour a ¼ inch layer of it into the pastry cases.

Peel, core and cut the apples into ⅛ inch slices. Halve the slices and arrange curved side up in the *crème pâtissière,* so that they resemble records nicely graded in a rack.

Melt the apricot jam and water together and sieve. Pour a little over the tarts. Cook in a hot oven, Mark 6–7, 400–425°F, basting from time to time with the rest of the apricot mixture. The top edges of the apple slices should catch the heat and turn dark brown. Golden Delicious apples will not lose their shape, or disintegrate to white fluff as cookers do. When you cut into the tarts, a delicious aromatic juice bursts out. Serve plenty of cream with them.

This recipe sounds like a lot of trouble, but it's worth it for the blend and contrast of flavours.

Moroccan meat stews with quince

One of the interesting things about Middle-Eastern and Arab cooking from an Englishman's point of view, is its similarity to our own medieval food. The abundant use of sweet substances with meat, the strong seasonings of ginger and various peppers, remind us that once dishes and courses were not so separately conceived as they are now (the well defined three or four-course dinner is really a nineteenth-century institution soup, fish, meat, dessert and so on). To jump from reading a modern Middle-Eastern cookery book to a fifteenth-century English one is much less of a change than going from the fifteenth-century one to Mrs Beeton. It may seem obvious to say 'Crusaders!', but I'm reluctant to believe such romantic notions, remembering that Marco Polo didn't bring back from Cathay half the things he's credited with. Let's be cautious, and say that such dishes, whatever their origin, came to us via France and our medieval French court (like the recipe following, for quince pies).

> 1 large chicken, jointed, plus
>   2 tablespoons butter (or 2½ lb. cubed
>   mutton or lamb)
> 2 large finely chopped onions
> bunch parsley, chopped
> about ½ teaspoon ground ginger
> salt, black Cayenne and Paprika pepper
> 3 oz. butter
> 1 lb. quinces (or more to taste)

Put meat (and, in the case of the chicken, its butter) into a large pan with onions and parsley. Just cover with cold water and season with ginger, salt and peppers. Bring to the boil and simmer for about an hour, until cooked. Slice and core the quinces (leave peel on), brown them very lightly in butter, and add to the stew half an hour before the end of cooking time.

Note: the meat is not browned before cooking, and lamb has enough fat of its own to do without the butter.

Quinces in paste

This fifteenth-century recipe for a corporate quince dumpling is delicious. It should be made with the usual shortcrust paste in a deep pie dish or cake tin, according to the size of the quinces.

'Take and make fair round coffins of fair paste; then take fair raw quinces and pare them with a knife, and take fair out the core thereof; then take enough sugar and a little powdered ginger, and stop the hole full; and couch two or three quinces in a coffin and cover them and let them bake; and for default of sugar, take honey; but then put powdered pepper thereon and ginger, in the manner aforesaid.'

Cover the coffins of quinces over with a lid of pastry, brush over with beaten egg, and bake for 20 minutes at Mark 6, 400°F, then for about an hour at Mark 4, 350°F, until the quinces are cooked.

Quince pie

Here's a pie from three centuries later, this time with a flavouring of orange, or of mulberries. First make:

Mulberry syrup: put ripe mulberries into a large jar, and stand in a pan of boiling water. As the fruit gives up its juice, pour it off into a measuring jug. To each pint, add 1 lb. sugar and boil to the consistency of cream. Skim well and bottle when cold. (To make a preserve, boil the juice with 1½ lb. sugar to 1 pint. Add 2 lb. ripe mulberries, ripe but not soft, and simmer for ¼ hour. Leave until next day. Strain the juice into a pan and boil again until thick, add the mulberries and simmer for a further ¼ hour. Good with cream cheese, junket and so on.)

Quince pie: Line a pie dish with shortcrust pastry, then fill it with peeled, cored and sliced quinces; add sugar, cinnamon and strips of candied orange peel to the layers of fruit. Pour over ¼ pint of orange juice or mulberry syrup. Put on a pastry lid and bake as above, first in a hot, then in a moderate oven.

Pears with quinces (for 6)

Apples and quinces are a famous – and ancient – combination. Pears too are enhanced by the flavour of quinces, which one does not quite expect.

3 medium quinces
6 large pears
1 vanilla pod
½ pint water
4–6 oz. sugar

Peel and quarter the quinces, removing their cores, then put them quickly into a bowl of cold water to prevent them turning brown. Peel, quarter and core the pears. Split the vanilla pod (vanilla essence won't do at all) and put it in a large pan with the water and 4 oz. of sugar. Bring to the boil, stirring to dissolve the sugar, then add pears and quinces. Simmer, covered, for an hour – or until the fruit is tender. Taste the syrupy juice at half time, and add more sugar if necessary, but be careful not to oversweeten the dish. Leave to cool, and serve well chilled with cream.

Pears and juice take on a deep coral red colour from the quinces, which is accented by the black vanilla pod. A most beautiful dish in every way.

Sir Isaac Newton's baked quinces

This favourite pudding of Newton's is a recipe for the fortunate with a supply of good quinces. If three or four are likely to be your annual total, it's better to distribute them among apple pies and puddings, apple sauce and apple jelly as a spicing ingredient.

Choose one fine quince for each person. Gently rub off the whitish-grey fluff, wash and core them. Stand in a baking dish respectable enough for the table (oval yellow and brown *gratin* dishes are ideal for baked fruit). Add ¼ inch of water. Stuff caster sugar into the cavities and top with a good lump of butter. Bake in a moderately hot oven, Mark 4–5, 350–375°F, for about an hour (timing depends on the size and state of the fruit – they're done when a skewer easily pierces the fruit round the centre cavity). Serve hot or warm with cream.

Note: when baking apples by this method, sprinkle them generously with sesame seeds, and a little caster sugar, about half an hour before the end of cooking time.

An eighteenth-century quince pudding

Make a quince purée by cooking the fruit whole in water and then cutting it in quarters and pushing it through a sieve. Sweeten with sugar and add some ginger to taste. Beat ½ pint of cream, double, single or the two mixed, with 2 egg yolks; then add to it a generous ¼ pint of quince purée. Adjust the seasoning of sugar and ginger to taste. Cut 2 oz. of butter into little pieces and stir into the mixture.

Butter a baking dish, pour in the quince mixture and bake at about Mark 5, 375°F, or less, until set. Eat hot. As this pudding is a kind of fruit custard, it's important not to cook it so fast that the mixture boils – this will curdle the eggs. The proportion of fruit purée to custard may be varied to taste. It's important that the purée should be on the dry side, not in the least sloppy.

Membrilo, or quince paste

This deep red Spanish quince paste is delicious eaten with cream cheese and sugar as dessert. Some people like slices of it with grilled pork and lamb. It could also be used – but discreetly, on account of the sugar – to flavour a chicken or lamb stew, when quinces are not in season (see recipe, p. 261).

Wash 4 lb. of quinces. The weight can be made up with apples, but too many will spoil the flavour; in the Orléanais, where a more elaborate quince paste is made, oranges are used sometimes in the proportion of 1 to 3 by weight.

Quarter the quinces and stew them with ½ pint of water until they're soft. Sieve, weigh and put into a clean pan with an equal amount of sugar. Boil slowly until the mixture leaves the sides of the pan. *Don't burn the mixture, keep stirring* (wrap your hand in a tea towel and use a wooden spoon). Pour into greaseproof-lined metal trays, for instance a jam roll or other oblong tin. Dry for 3–4 days in an airing cupboard, or on top of a solid fuel stove – protect it from dust with a light muslin cloth. Cut into small pieces or oblong slabs, roll in caster sugar and store in airtight boxes between sheets of greaseproof paper. The caster sugar can be spiced with ginger and cinnamon.

Quince paste was once thought to be particularly good for the stomach.

Pickled Siberian crab apples

In our village Siberian crab apples go to waste. The tiny perfect yellow and red fruit fall to the ground, and are crushed by cars and passers-by. Even the children don't bother with their sharp sweetness. But just as the tree is a great embellishment to any garden, so jars of pickled Siberian crabs (or of Siberian crab apple jelly) are a great embellishment to winter supplies.

> 3–4 lb. crab apples
> 2 pints wine or spirit vinegar
> 1 lb. white sugar
> 1 inch stick of cinnamon
> 15 cloves
> 15 allspice berries

Tie the spices in a little bag. Put them into a pan with the vinegar and sugar and bring to the boil, stirring so that the sugar dissolves. The crab apples should be washed and their stalks trimmed to $\frac{1}{4}$ inch with scissors. Put them into something such as a chip basket and lower them into the boiling vinegar. Leave for 5 minutes: they should be removed before the skins start to crack. Put the apples into small bottling jars or jam pots. Meanwhile boil down the vinegar and sugar until it's syrupy, then cover the apples with it, and seal immediately. Leave for 2 months.

In time the apples lose more and more of their red colour to the liquid, which makes a beautiful-looking pickle. Serve with pork or ham.

Soft fruit, e.g. peaches, may be dealt with in the same way, but use 1 lb. sugar to $\frac{1}{2}$ pint vinegar, and vary the spices according to the fruit.

Apple or quince or medlar jelly

A simple method which can be used for windfall apples, for Siberian and wild crab apples, for quinces on their own or mixed with apples. For medlars too. Ordinary windfalls may be flavoured with cloves or cinnamon stick (don't use powdered cinnamon, it's inferior in quality and will make a sediment in the jelly), or just a few quinces. Crab apples are best left alone with their wonderful flavour.

Such jellies may be eaten with pork instead of apple sauce, or with bread and butter, or as a dessert with the cream cheese hearts and mousse described on pp. 304 and 305. A versatile addition to the store cupboard.

Cut the fruit into rough pieces. Put into a large pan: cover with water. Bring to the boil and simmer until the fruit is soft. Lay a large white cloth over a colander, set the colander across a large bowl and pour into it the fruit pulp. Make a bag of the cloth, and leave to drip overnight.

Measure the juice next day (don't squeeze the jelly bag, or the final results will be cloudy). Allow a pound of sugar to a pint of juice and boil until settling point is reached; spices such as cinnamon or cloves should be tied in a little bag and removed when the flavour is not too strong. Bottle in sterilized jars and cover immediately in the usual way.

Note: medlars should be firm, and not bletted.

Gooseberries

Gooseberries which are northern and condescend to grow up to the Arctic Circle provide the first fruit of the year. Unless you count strawberries flown in from Kenya. I don't.

Edward Bunyard, the fruit gourmet and grower, wrote in the 1920s very nicely of gooseberries as 'the fruit *par excellence* for ambulant consumption. The freedom of the bush should be given to all visitors . . . and the exercise of gathering, too, is beneficial to the middle-aged and also stimulates their absorptive capacity;'* i.e. for lunch, he was describing that sociable summer hour which ambles along – or used to – between Matins and Sunday lunch.

From the cook's point of view the best gooseberries aren't entirely the fattest, sweetest, ripest, and yellowest. Gooseberries small, green, primitive and hairy – early gooseberries – make the best pies, jams, jellies and fools. And the best sauce for mackerel. That's a habit we seem to have lost, gooseberries with mackerel, let alone with pork, veal, lamb, goose or duck. We've forgotten

*Edward Bunyard: *The Anatomy of Dessert*, Chatto & Windus, 1933.

how well the sweet-sour astringency of young gooseberry purée goes with such rich flavours.

A word about picking gooseberries. A blacksmith in our village years ago – so the legend goes – used to pull his hand firmly down the gooseberry branches, when he wanted his Whitsun pie. Off sprang the fruit (and leaves) at high speed without that carapaced hand receiving one scratch. This method is said to be painless, even if you haven't spent a lifetime at the anvil. It may be true. I've never had the nerve to find out, preferring to shield hands and wrists with solid leather gloves.

Incidentally it's quicker to top and tail gooseberries with a pair of scissors, rather than a knife.

Gooseberry sauce for mackerel

By tradition, gooseberry sauce is the Maytime companion of boiled or grilled mackerel. The French honour this antique alliance by naming the gooseberry *groseille à maquereau*: in practice they usually serve a purée of sorrel instead – the two acidities have a similar taste – as gooseberries are not widely grown in France. Make the most of the early green fruit (the later, mellow gooseberries will not do at all) and serve one or other variation of this sweet-sour sauce with roast duck, pork, goose or lamb, or with roast and grilled veal.

Here are four recipes for a sauce which has been eaten for centuries in Germany, France, Holland and Great Britain:

1. Top and tail 1 lb. gooseberries. Put into a heavy pan with a walnut of butter, and cook gently, with the lid on the pan, until the fruit is soft enough to put through a sieve. Add either an egg or 3 tablespoonfuls of béchamel sauce. Season with a teaspoon of sugar, and ginger or nutmeg to taste.

2. Top and tail 1 lb. gooseberries. Cover with cold water and bring gently to the boil. By this time or very soon after, a gooseberry taken from the pan will give a little between the fingers,

without collapsing to a mush. Drain and mix into a béchamel sauce made with 1 oz. butter, 1 oz. flour and a generous half pint of hot milk (the gooseberries can either be sieved or left whole). Reheat and season with a heaped dessertspoon of chopped new fennel leaves, a little nutmeg and some salt, pepper and lemon juice. A teaspoon of sugar may also be an improvement if the gooseberries are very young.

3. Prepare and blanch 1 lb. gooseberries as in recipe No. 2. Drain them well. Put 2 tablespoons water and 4 oz. sugar into a frying pan and bring to a spanking boil. Turn the gooseberries over in the syrup, shaking the pan very gently. Pour round the meat or fish as a garnish. This recipe, which depends for seasoning solely on the sharpness of the gooseberries, and the sweetness of the sugar, was very popular with Germans at the beginning of the nineteenth century.

4. Put 8 oz. gooseberries in a pan with 1 oz. butter. Cover and cook gently until they are soft enough to go through a sieve. Add ¼ pint boiled cream and 2 tablespoons of fish or meat juices from the dish the sauce is intended for. I like sauces of this kind, which are linked in flavour with the food they accompany. They give a rightness and succulence that are more agreeable, and they are never quite the same twice running. This gooseberry sauce comes from *French Provincial Cooking* by Elizabeth David (Penguin); it's a very good one.

Robert Southey's Gooseberry pie (for 6–8)

Do you follow the country tradition of eating the first gooseberry pie of the season at Whitsunday lunch? If you do, here's a nice proposition of Robert Southey's to stimulate some quiet post-prandial reflection: 'Two gooseberry pies being supposed, their paste made at the same time, had indeed of one mass, the gooseberries gathered from the same bushes and of equal age, the sugar in just proportion, and clotted cream to eat with both, it follows that the largest is preferable. I love gooseberry pie ... and I think the case is plain.'

> 2 lb. gooseberries, young and green
> 6–8 oz. sugar
> 1 oz. butter
> 8 oz. shortcrust pastry
> 1 egg white
> extra sugar

Grease a 2-pint pie dish with the butter. Roll out the pastry; moisten the edges of the pie dish and fasten a strip of pastry round it. Top and tail the gooseberries, put them into the pie dish with sugar between the layers (very sharp gooseberries will need 8 oz.) and mound them up in the centre above the rim of the dish. Brush the pastry edge with egg white before laying on the pastry lid; knock up the edges, brush the pastry with egg white and sprinkle it with an even layer of caster sugar. Bake at Mark 6, 400°F, for 30–40 minutes. Serve with plenty of cream.

Raised gooseberry pie (for 6)

In some parts of England, from Gloucestershire up to the Midlands, a raised gooseberry pie is made around Whitsun. It looks just like a pork pie:

> *hot water crust:*
>
> 1 lb. plain flour
> 7 oz. water
> 6 oz. lard
> ½ teaspoon salt
> 3 tablespoons icing sugar
>
> *filling:*
>
> gooseberries
> sugar (4 oz. to each lb. of fruit)

Sift flour, salt and sugar into a bowl. Make a well in the middle.

Bring water and lard to the boil and pour immediately into the well, mixing the flour in gradually with a wooden spoon, until a smooth ball of dough is formed. Leave in a warm place until the paste is just cool enough to handle and keep its shape.

Using greased jam jars, upside down, make the bases of the pies, tying a piece of brown paper outside the pastry to hold it in shape when the jar is removed. Cool and chill in the refrigerator until the pastry is set, then remove the jars and turn the cases right way up. Fill with gooseberries and sugar, moisten the rims and fix on a lid. Brush with beaten egg. Bake for 1–1¼ hours at Mark 3, 325°F. Let the pies cool before removing the paper.

One can occasionally buy wooden pie moulds to shape the pastry round. The easy way out is to use a cake tin with a removable base, and bake the pie inside it. For raised meat pies, see p. 59.

Gooseberry tart (for 6)

As gooseberries become larger and sweeter, tarts like this are a better way of using them:

> *shortcrust pastry:*
> 8 oz. flour
> 4 oz. butter
> 2 tablespoons icing sugar
> 1 egg or water
>
> *filling:*
> 1½ lb. prepared gooseberries
> ½ pint single cream
> 2 egg yolks
> 3 oz. sugar

Line small tart tins (or one large flan tin with a removable base) with the pastry. Arrange the gooseberries close together in a single layer, tail-end down, on the pastry. Mix cream and egg yolks and sugar and pour over them. Bake in a moderately hot oven, Mark 5, 375°F, for 15 minutes (30 minutes for one large tart). Serve warm or cold.

Gooseberries, Frontignan and elderflowers

'I was very well brought up,' wrote Colette. 'As a first proof of so categorical a statement, I shall simply say that I was no more than three years old when my father poured out my first full liqueur glass of an amber-coloured wine which was sent up to him from the Midi, where he was born; the muscat of Frontignan.' This lovely dessert wine, made from muscat grapes grown on the slopes outside the small town of Frontignan on the Languedoc coast, was drunk in quantity in Britain during the eighteenth and early nineteenth centuries – one of the great periods of gooseberry enjoyment and cultivation. It was so popular that home-made elderflower wine, which does have a muscat flavour, became known as 'English Frontignan'. It was perhaps when drinking such wines with summer fruit and puddings that people discovered how perfectly the fragrance of muscat goes with gooseberries.

Gooseberry and elderflower jelly

4 lb. gooseberries, young and green
sugar
2 large elderflower heads

Put the gooseberries in a large pan and barely cover with water. Simmer until they are soft and mushy. Strain through a jelly bag without squeezing the pulp. Measure the juice and put into a clean pan with ¾ lb. sugar to every pint of juice. Boil until setting point is reached. Tie the elderflowers in muslin and stir them round in the hot jelly, until the right balance of flavours is achieved. The muscat flavour should not be too dominant. Pour into sterilized jars and cover.

Gooseberry salad

A wonderfully fresh dessert:

> 1½ lb. large sweet gooseberries
> 4 oz. sugar
> ½ pint *muscat de Frontignan*

Three hours before the meal top and tail the gooseberries. Put them into a deep bowl with sugar and wine, and leave in a cool place (but not the refrigerator, which is too cold). Serve in individual glasses.

Gooseberry fool (for 4–6)

Everybody knows that gooseberry fool, like steak and kidney pudding or junket, is a truly national dish. What many people don't know is that 'fool' comes from the French verb *fouler*, to crush; it's not a description of someone prepared to pay the price of half a pint of cream. In France grapes, not gooseberries, are *foulés*, crushed, or rather mangled, quite literally, on their way to the winepress. This, I think, gives a good idea of how a gooseberry fool should be made. Too often gooseberries are overcooked, then sieved or liquidized to a smooth slop. Ideally, they should be very lightly cooked, then crushed with a fork, before being folded into whipped cream. Egg custard is an honourable, and an ancient alternative to cream; commercial powder custard is not. Don't spoil this springtime luxury. It's better to halve the quantities, than to serve a great floury bowlful.

> ¾ lb. young gooseberries, topped and
>   tailed
> 2 oz. butter
> sugar
> ½ pint double cream, whipped, *or*
>   ¼ pint each double and single cream *or*
>   ¼ pint single cream and 3 egg yolks

Stew the gooseberries slowly in a covered pan, with the butter, until they are yellow and just cooked. Crush with a fork, sweeten to taste and mix them carefully and lightly into the whipped cream.

To make the custard, bring single cream (or rich milk) to the boil, and pour on to the egg yolks, whisking all the time. Set the bowl over a pan of hot water and stir steadily until the custard thickens to double cream consistency. Strain into a bowl, and leave to cool before folding in the gooseberries.

Serve in custard glasses or plain white cups, with some home-made almond biscuits or macaroons. It's said (and reported in *Kettner's Book of the Table*, Centaur Press reprint) that the young folk of Northamptonshire, 'after eating as much as they possibly can of this gooseberry fool,' used frequently to roll down a hill and begin eating again. Cream must have been cheaper in those days.

Gooseberry fools can be frozen and served as cream ice: in this case, sieve the fruit as the pieces of gooseberry produced by mashing would spoil the texture of the ice. Later in the year other fruit may be substituted for gooseberries, uncooked raspberries and strawberries and peaches for instance, and in the autumn cooked purées of apple flavoured with apricot jam, and of quinces. Use just over half a pint of purée to half a pint of cream or custard.

Gooseberry cream (for 6–8)

Here is a gooseberry dish – not so rich as gooseberry fool – which was popular during the eighteenth century. One person who enjoyed it was that Norfolk glutton, Parson Woodforde, who left his rectory at Weston Longeville one summer day of 1784 to visit a friend at Mattishall. The small party of nine ate for dinner: boiled beef, roast and boiled chicken, part of a fine ham, a couple of ducks roasted and peas, puddings, tarts and cheesecakes. In the evening there was a 'cold collation' of lamb steaks, green peas, and – finally – gooseberry cream, etc. No doubt the etc. included wine, which would have helped the company to clear the last dish of the day, and to keep merry until four in the morning.

That gooseberry cream was very likely made from Hannah Glasse's best-selling *Art of Cookery*; there was a big reprint that year, 1784, backed by 26 publishers.

> 1¼ lb. gooseberries, topped and tailed
> ¼ pint water
> 2 oz. unsalted butter
> sugar
> 3 eggs, beaten
> orange-flower water, Malaga, or
>   Frontignan

Put the gooseberries in a pan with the water and cook slowly until they can be put through a sieve. Measure the purée – a pint is required. Sweeten to taste and reheat. Stir in butter and eggs, and keep stirring over a low heat until the gooseberry cream is thick. *Don't let it boil*, or the eggs will curdle. Leave to cool and flavour with orange-flower water, Malaga or Frontignan. Alternatively put a head of elderflowers, tied in muslin, into the cream after adding eggs and butter; remove as soon as the flavour is right – it should not be too strong.

Lemons

I think it's just worth remembering that lemons don't originate in boxes or grocers' shops, but on trees – trees which filtered through from the Far East to Spain and Italy.

Italy is our lemon land (smaller supplies reach us from Cyprus, Israel, the United States and Spain) and I suppose the nearest place where you can taste lemon juice, fresh, real ripe lemon juice, in its purest form, from freshly picked lemons, is at Limone on Lake Garda, where you are hardly clear of the Alps – *limone spremuta*, lemon juice squeezed into a glass, and served with iced water and small packets of sugar; down below the blue of Garda, up above snow on the mountains – and a German sketching at an easel at every corner.

D. H. Lawrence, when he was on Garda after running off with his Frieda Weekley, was taken round the lemon gardens in November when they were under their winter roofs of wood. The *padrone's* wife told him lemons had been brought there by St

Francis of Assisi, and that one lemon from a Garda lemon-house was worth two from an entirely open-air tree in Sicily (which is the source of most of our Italian lemons). Lawrence, in turn, thought of St Francis wandering about with a lemon in his pocket, or making lemonade – *limone spremuta* – in the hot summer; and then remarking to himself that 'Bacchus had been before him in the drink trade.'

In the food trade, in cooking, lemons came into their own far north of the Alps before and especially after Mrs Beeton's day. Italian lemons poured into Britain (no longer possible to be '12 miles from a lemon' as Sydney Smith had once complained when he began living in a North Riding rectory). British cooks diversified and improved on old recipes for such things as 'lemoned honeycomb' (which was in Hannah Glasse's cookery book of 1767) or lemon cheesecake; they borrowed, they invented new lemon puddings, new lemon desserts, and ices, preserves and drinks.

What I think is about the tastiest of all northern lemony sweets I have taken from Mrs Beeton's first edition of 1861 – neatly reproduced in facsimile by Jonathan Cape in 1968. Snowdon pudding represents the solid tradition of British puds, and a cold lemon soufflé the modern American style of light but rich desserts. The most surprising recipe, surprising in its exquisite finality rather than in its ingredients, is for lemon rice, taken from the Portuguese. By the way, if a lemon is a bit green, don't reject it. It is artificial ripening with ethylene gas which gives trade lemons their smart uniformity of yellow.

Avgolemono soup (for 6)

The name means egg and lemon, which are the two important finishing ingredients of this soup. In Greek restaurants here, it's usually made with a basis of chicken stock – but try using fish stock as they often do in Greece. Most fishmongers are delighted to hand over free plaice bones, or cheap fish pieces, left over from filleting, which gives you a luxurious soup at a low price. Avgolemono has a light foamy texture, which tastes particularly agreeable on warm days.

For the stock

1½–2 lb. fish bones and pieces
3 pints water
¼ pint wine vinegar
medium onion, stuck with 4 cloves
medium carrot, sliced
8 peppercorns
½ bay leaf, sprig of thyme and parsley

Simmer together for 1 hour. Strain and reduce to about 2½ pints. Correct the seasoning.

To finish the soup:

2–3 oz. rice
3 eggs
1–2 lemons

Simmer the rice in the stock until cooked. Have ready in a bowl the eggs beaten up with the juice of 1 lemon. Add a ladleful of hot soup, whisking all the time. Return to the pan, and *without boiling*, cook until slightly thickened. Keep whisking. Add more lemon juice to taste. Serve at once.

Chicken with chervil sauce

The combination of lemon with meat does not come quite so naturally to us as it does to an Italian, a Viennese or a Frenchman. Parsley and lemon butter are often served with grilled steak, it's true, but very rarely with grilled lamb – which is a pity. Stews of chicken or veal, with tomato or pale sauces, could be much improved by the last-minute Italian addition of chopped parsley, lemon peel, garlic and an anchovy fillet. Mayonnaise and vinaigrette sauces often go better with cold meats, if lemon juice has been substituted for vinegar.

Here's a lemon and herb sauce for roast or boiled chicken, written down by the great Frenchman Carême. He prided himself on the *grosses pièces* he invented for the tables of Napoleon, the Prince Regent, Tallcyrand and the Rothschilds, yet he appreciated (and improved on) the recipes of homelier kitchens.

> 1 tablespoon flour
> 1 tablespoon unsalted butter
> good ½ pint chicken stock
> salt, pepper, nutmeg to taste
> juice of half a lemon
> 1 tablespoon chopped chervil
> extra tablespoon unsalted butter

Melt 1 tablespoon of butter in a heavy pan. Stir in the flour, and then, gradually, the hot chicken stock. This can be from the boiled-chicken pot, or made from giblets of a roasting chicken.

When the sauce is smooth and thick, season with salt, pepper and nutmeg. Simmer gently for at least 15 minutes, giving an occasional stir; the most trouble-free way of doing this is to place the pan over another pan of simmering water – the sauce can then be virtually ignored until dishing-up time.

Just before serving, add lemon juice, extra butter and chopped chervil (an equal quantity of parsley can be substituted, or half the quantity of tarragon). If the sauce has thickened too much, add more chicken stock or a little water.

Honeycomb mould (for 6)

This delicious pudding of childhood should not be relegated to the nursery. It clear, true flavour (not to be found in packet mix versions) is a luxury these days. The mixture plops into a jelly mould – choose one with an elaborate pattern – and several hours later it comes out as an elegant three layered pudding.

> juice and rind of 2 lemons
> 3 large eggs
> ½ oz. gelatine (one packet)
> 3 oz. sugar
> generous ¾ pint Channel Island milk
> 6 tablespoons cream

Separate the yolks and whites of the eggs. Put the yolks in a large basin. Add the thinly pared lemon rind, gelatine, sugar and cream. Heat the milk to just under boiling-point and whisk into the egg yolk mixture (creamy Channel Islands milk, gold top milk, gives the best results). Set the basin over a pan of simmering water, and stir until you have a custard the consistency of double cream more or less. Taste and add more sugar if you like, but this pudding should not be very sweet. Mix in the lemon juice and strain the custard into the whites, which should have been stiffly beaten; use a metal rather than a wooden spoon to fold it in. Pour into a 2 pint jelly mould. When it's firmly set, slip a knife round the edge of the pudding, which will then turn out easily (no need to dip the mould into hot water). It will have a cap of clear lemon jelly, then a thin band of opaque cream jelly, and a honeycombed spongey base which makes a slight crinkling noise as it's eaten.

Mrs Beeton's baked lemon pudding (for 6–8)

I've halved most of the quantities for this richest and best of lemon-curd tarts (or, as they often used to be called, lemon cheese cakes), in the interests of modern digestion. Double the amount was described by Mrs Beeton as being right for 6 to 7 people – the Victorians certainly ate with stamina and capacity. She used a puff pastry crust, but most of us these days would, I think, prefer a crisp, sweet shortcrust.

pastry:

6 oz. flour
3 oz. butter
1 heaped tablespoon icing sugar
1 egg
pinch of salt

filling:

juice of 2 lemons
grated rind of 1 lemon
¼ lb. caster sugar

6 tablespoons (about 3 oz.) double cream
4 egg yolks
2 oz. ground almonds
¼ lb. unsalted butter, melted

To make the pastry, cream together butter, sugar and salt. Add the egg and then the flour, until a dough is formed. Leave it to rest for 1 hour or so, then roll it out and line an 8½ or 9 inch tart tin with a removable base. Bake blind for 15 minutes.

Beat the filling ingredients together until smooth. Pour into the pastry case, and decorate with a lattice made from the pastry trimmings. Bake for 30–40 minutes in a slow oven, Mark 2–3, 300–325°F, until risen and nicely browned. Serve hot, warm or cold, with some single cream (on the whole, I think it's best warm).

Lemon soufflé (for 6–8)

As we're not Christmas pudding eaters, finding it too bulky, too unrefreshing after the turkey course, we've made our own tradition of this cold lemon soufflé. I've tried to vary the recipe by adding orange juice and peel, by altering the amount of eggs and cream, but it's no good. Everyone says, 'Yes, this is nice, but please next year may we have our proper lemon soufflé again?'

3 egg yolks and 3 egg whites
6 oz. caster sugar
2 large or 3 small lemons
½ pint double cream, or ¼ pint each
    double and single
packet of gelatine (½ oz.)
2 oz. hot water
2 oz. almonds, blanched and split

Put yolks, sugar, grated rind and juice of the lemons into a large pudding basin. Stand it over a pan of simmering water and whisk with a rotary beater until the mixture is a thick liquid, about 5 minutes. Take the pudding basin from the pan, stand it on a table and beat for another 5 minutes. By now it will be pale yellow, and thick and billowy. Dissolve the gelatine in the hot water, and add it to the lemon custard. Whisk the cream until it begins to hold its shape and fold that into the custard. Last of all whisk the egg whites until they are very stiff. Fold in the cream and custard mixture with light movements until everything is amalgamated. Pour into a collared soufflé dish, and leave in the refrigerator to set. Toast the split almonds in the oven until they're golden brown. When cool, use them to decorate the soufflé. Remove the paper collar before serving, so that the cold soufflé rising above its dish has the appearance of a well-risen hot soufflé. Single cream may be served with it.

Lemon rice pudding (for 6)

This beautiful lemon pudding is based on the Portuguese *Arroz Doce*, sweet rice. Guaranteed to convert the most ardent rice-pudding-hater.

> 1½ oz. rice
> ½ pint creamy milk ⎱ or 1 pint
> ½ pint single cream ⎰ single cream
> 1 oz. butter
> 1 oz. sugar
> 1 lemon
> cinnamon
> extra cream

Wash the rice, and peel the lemon thinly, taking off strips about ¼ inch wide and 1 to 2 inches long. Put rice, lemon peel, sugar, butter and single cream and milk into a pyrex or other ovenproof dish. Cook in a very slow oven, Mark ½, 250°F, for 2 to 3 hours until the rice is cooked. Stir it every ¾ hour. About ½ hour before the pudding is cooked, add about a teaspoon of cinnamon or less, depending on your taste. When the pudding is done, stir it up well adding the lemon juice and some more cream if it's too solid. Put a light sprinkling of cinnamon on top and place under a medium hot grill to brown the top lightly. Serve well chilled. You will find that the lemon peel has almost dissolved, and so has the rice although it still feels gently grainy to the tongue.

Snowdon Pudding (for 8)

'This pudding,' wrote Eliza Acton in *Modern Cookery*, published in 1845, 'is constantly served to travellers at the hotel at the foot of the mountain from which it derives its name.' I don't think that this is so any longer. I notice that the Wales Gas Board in their excellent booklet *Croeso Cymreig, A Welsh Welcome*, use her recipe.

First, though, you will need to make some lemon marmalade.

> 1½ lb. lemons
> 3 pints water
> 3 lb. sugar

Halve the lemons and squeeze out the juice. Cut the halves into half again, and remove with a sharp knife as much as you can of the ragged insides and pith. Put all this into a muslin bag and suspend it by string from the handle of a heavy pan. Add water, lemon juice and the peel shredded. Simmer until the peel is soft. Add the sugar and boil fast until setting point is reached.

> *For the pudding:*
> 8 oz. beef suet
> 6 eggs
> 8 oz. breadcrumbs
> 1½ oz. ground rice
> 6 oz. dark brown sugar
> 6 oz. lemon marmalade
> grated rind of 2 lemons
> pinch of salt
> 4 oz. seedless raisins
> butter

Butter a 2½ pint pudding basin liberally. Ornament it with some of the raisins, cut in half but not separated, placing the cut side to the buttered basin. Beat the eggs and mix with the other ingredients. Cover and boil for 1½ hours. Serve with this wine sauce of Miss Acton's:

> thinly pared rind of half a lemon
> 1½ oz. sugar
> wineglass of water (about ¼ pint)
> 1 oz. butter
> generous ½ teaspoon flour
> 1½ wineglasses of sherry, Madeira or
>   good white wine

TO COOK A STEAMED PUDDING

1. Fill the buttered basin

2. Cover with a cloth, tied with string

3. Place in a pan of water on a rack

4. Cover, and boil required time

Simmer lemon rind and sugar in the water for 15 minutes. Mash together butter and flour, and add to the strained lemon water over a gentle heat, until it thickens. Stir in the wine, reheat to just below boiling point and serve immediately.

Or with this:

Lemon and gin sauce (for 4)

This simply-made, aromatic sauce is an excellent complement to our robust steamed puddings. Try it, too, with bananas rolled in cinnamon and sugar, then baked, like apple dumplings, in a rich, sweet shortcrust pastry. The recipe comes from *Kettner's Book of The Table*, first published in 1877, and reprinted in 1968 by the Centaur Press. This lively and erudite dictionary was written by the journalist E. S. Dallas. Advice, recipes and free meals were provided by Auguste Kettner, the Soho restaurateur. It was a splendid partnership:

'Put the thin rind of a lemon with 3 tablespoonfuls of sugar to simmer for 20 minutes in a tumblerful of water. Some persons think it enough to grate the lemon with lumps of sugar – but this detracts from the clearness of the sauce. When the simmering is ended take out the lemon-peel and add the strained juice of the lemon. This is extremely simple, but it is nicer than many a much more laboured sauce. Perhaps it is not quite fair to add that it is sometimes supplemented with gin. To be used with sweet entremets.'

In other words, the gin is what matters. Add a measure – that is about half a miniature bottle – to the above quantity of sauce. Reheat gently, without boiling.

Lemonade and milk lemonade

In the early, dark months of the year it was the habit in South Shields (and no doubt in other places, too) to brew lemonade in quantity. My grandmother called it Spring Medicine. She felt that her children's blood needed a springclean just as much as her china from China, or the huge antipodean shells her husband had brought home from voyages in the Far East. Perhaps she shared his seaman's fear of scurvy.

Our winter diet today may not be as stodgy as it was then for struggling widows on crowded, coaly Tyne, but the sharp clarity of lemonade comes gratefully, all the same, in early spring and summer.

The method used was the one given for Kettner's lemon sauce above, adding more water and a pinch of cream of tartar, but stopping short at gin. Unless you're making lemonade for children (who tend, unflatteringly, to prefer squash and pop), don't follow her example in this respect: the flavour of juniper goes particularly well with lemon.

Milk lemonade belongs to the prosperous Tennysonian nineteenth century we prefer, not to the North of whitened doorsteps. Its light, interesting flavour was popular on vicarage lawns, under the cedar, on hot days of middle-class leisure. In our more strenuous lives, it makes an excellent long drink – very refreshing.

> 3 lemons
> 1 lb. caster sugar
> 1 pint dry white wine
> 3 pints milk

Peel the lemons thinly and put the peel into a large bowl. Pour over ¼ pint boiling water. Leave overnight. Next day add the juice of 2 of the lemons, the wine and the sugar. Bring the milk to boiling point – unpasteurized milk is best, if you can get it – and add quickly to the other ingredients. Leave to cool. As the milk will have turned to curds and whey, the lemonade must now be strained through muslin two or three times until it's perfectly clear.

Taste and add the juice from the third lemon, if required. Serve well chilled.

Some versions of this recipe substitute ¼ pint of sherry for the white wine, but I find the flavour of sherry too obtrusive.

Prunes

Many people dislike prunes. With good reason, as anyone who has done time in a boarding school, a boarding house or a prison knows. Such prune-haters should be converted, they should be purged of their stewed prune memories, the prune being an essential to some of the best meat and fish recipes ever devised.

The prune is a dried plum, full of sunshine and sweetness (for instance, when added to a bottle of rough *marc*, prunes soften the taste and make a classy drink out of a merely alcoholic one). The finest prunes have come for centuries from the plum orchards of the Agenais district of south-west France. Monks of the abbey of Clairac, between Agen and Bordeaux, are said to have had their prune industry well organized by the sixteenth century. And by the sixteenth century the prunes of Tours were famous, and on sale in Paris.

Owing I suppose to a less reliable sun, the prune industry of

Touraine has given way to Agenais producers. And the housewives no longer dry their own plums for the winter store cupboard. One may walk along a sunken lane in the harmonious land
between Loire and Loir, and come to a hamlet of old cave houses
warrening an exposed rock face. There will be a walnut tree or
two as a token of past living, a bay tree, some apples, a quince,
and a medlar, but the plum trees will have disappeared. Chimneys
poke through the slopes of the cliff-top above, but there's no
smoke. The only other sign of past existence, of life before the
first world war, is a blackened flare of rock above a gaping hole at
waist-height, beside one of the cave doors. A child could crawl
into this minuscule cave, this horseshoe shaped oven cut into the
rock and lined with bricks or wedge-shaped stones. One imagines
the wives of the hamlet baking their bread, then quickly laying
the wicker trays of plums in the drying heat. Next day the process
would be repeated, and the day after that. When the plums had
wrinkled from purple to black, they'd be stored away – with bay
leaves tucked sometimes between the layers.

Modern methods have regularized but not changed this old
process. Plums stay on the trees as long as possible to acquire as
much sweetness as they can from the sun. Then they are dried out
of doors, or in tunnels warmed by controlled blasts of hot air. In
California, where more prunes are produced than anywhere else
in the world, it's still a French plum, the *prune d'Agen*, that provides ninety per cent of the crop (the industry was started by a
Frenchman, Louis Pellier, in 1856). Now the Californians, particularly those of the Santa Clara valley, produce about 340
million pounds of prunes a year, far more than the Agenais
growers with their average of 11¼ million. No wonder the packages of prunes in the grocery shops of Tours itself are more often
than not marked 'Santa Clara' (in a discreet corner).

If these American prunes are not quite so rich, or so liqueur-
flavoured as the French ones, they are almost as good. It would I
think be unwise to claim to tell the difference between Agen
prunes from Agen and Agen prunes from California, when eating a
matelote of eel. Both yield their excellence with generosity.

One must ignore what modern puritans of the last century or
two have done to prunes, the dreadful alliances they have made
between prunes and rice, or prunes and custard powder. These
recipes I've chosen go back to a medieval tradition abandoned in

English cooking: the tradition of mixing sweet and savoury in such things as genuine mincemeat (ox-tongue, beef or mutton with suet and dried fruits); or plum (i.e. prune) porridge, the original of the plum pudding, which was made with tongue, raisins, prunes, spices, wine, meat stock and breadcrumbs. Prunes add a succulence to meat and fish, a blandness as well as an always welcome contrast – or anyway a slight change of texture. Moreover using prunes this way saves you the need of providing a green vegetable. A few boiled or mashed potatoes, or fried croûtons, are all that's required, though a green salad should follow, preferably chilled, as buffer and refreshment before you come to cheese or pudding.

When it comes to puddings or desserts made with prunes, re-member the Middle-Eastern origin of the cultivated plum, and concentrate on richness. Walnuts, almonds, rum, wine, cream – they are the key to success.

Giant prunes are the best (25–35 to the lb.). If your grocer doesn't have them, try a health food store. (Whole Food Ltd, 112 Baker Street, London W1 sell fine prunes from the Agenais.) They don't need long soaking: often an hour or two is all that's necess-ary to start them off – final plumpness comes with the cooking.

Matelote of eel in the Anjou style (for 6)

Fresh-water eels stewed in wine are very popular in France. Different regions make their own variations, and naturally along the Loire prunes are included to increase the richness of the sauce. Strangely enough the delicate flavour of the eel is en-hanced.

Some London fish shops sell eels. Out of London you may have to persuade an angler to catch, kill and skin one for you. This is worth some determination, as eels are luxuries. They can some-times even be acquired for nothing. Medium-sized ones are best. Very large, they become a little oily.

Ideally, eels should be killed immediately before cooking. To remove the skin, suspend the eel by a slip-knot just below the neck from a strong hook. Slit the skin round with a sharp (Stanley) knife – it's very tough and was used in the past to hold the two parts of a flail together, and by small boys for whipping their tops. Now pull the skin down as if you were pulling off a glove. Some people find this quite easy, but I resort to pliers in one hand and a cloth in the other. Wash and clean the eel, and cut into 3 inch pieces.

>2–3 lb. eel
>½–1 lb. prunes soaked in tea
>¼ lb. button mushrooms
>¾ pint white wine, preferably from
>   Saumur
>4 oz. butter
>1 glass brandy
>2 tablespoons double cream
>1 egg yolk
>1 lemon
>bunch parsley
>bay leaf
>salt, pepper to taste

Squeeze the lemon and soak the eel in the juice for 15 minutes. Drain the pieces, then brown them lightly in 2 oz. of butter. Pour in the brandy, warmed, and set alight. When the flames have gone out, add the mushrooms to the pan; cover and cook gently for 10 minutes.

Pour in the wine. Add prunes and bay leaf, and season. Boil hard until the eel begins to part from its bones – about 15 minutes. Arrange eel, prunes and mushrooms on a hot serving dish. Discard the bay leaf, and attend to the sauce.

Beat egg yolk and cream together. Stir into the cooking liquid with the heat very low, so that the sauce thickens *without boiling* or the egg yolk will curdle. Correct the seasoning. Add the rest of the butter in small knobs to the sauce, without any further cooking: this gives the sauce a specially good flavour and a shiny appearance. Pour over the eel, etc., sprinkle with parsley and serve immediately.

Variation: in Touraine red wine might be used, and there would be salt pork and onions instead of the mushrooms:

> ½ lb. salt pork or green streaky bacon
>   diced
> 15 pickling onions
> 1 tablespoon lard
> dessertspoon flour
> ½ pint red wine (or dry white)
> ¼ pint water
> bouquet garni, salt, pepper
> 2–3 lb. eel, cut into pieces
> ½ lb. prunes, soaked
> 3 tablespoons oil
> generous liqueur glass *marc* or brandy
> parsley
> triangles of fried bread

Brown pork and onions in lard. Stir in flour and brown lightly, incorporate wine and water to make a smooth sauce. Add herbs and seasoning. Cook for half an hour. Brown eel pieces in oil, flame them with *marc* or brandy, and add with prunes to the sauce. Simmer until eel is cooked. Serve with triangles of fried bread and a sprinkling of parsley.

Note: it is important to flame eel with brandy or spirits. It reduces its oiliness.

Beef (or hare) with prunes (for 6)

> 2 lb. chuck steak, or 1 hare, jointed
> ½ lb. green streaky bacon in a piece
> ¼ lb. button mushrooms
> 3 large onions, chopped
> 3 large carrots, sliced
> 24 pickling onions
> 1 dessertspoon sugar
> ¼–½ pint beef stock
> 4 oz. butter
> 1 heaped tablespoon flour
> bouquet garni
> 1 lb. giant prunes
> nutmeg, ginger, pepper, cinnamon, salt

marinade:

1 bottle red wine
1 liqueur glass brandy
2 onions sliced
1 large carrot, sliced
3 cloves
bay leaf
sprig thyme
sprig rosemary
12 peppercorns
½ teaspoon salt

Put the steak, cut into 2-inch pieces, or the hare into a bowl with the marinade ingredients, and leave overnight. An hour before cooking preparations are started add the prunes, with some cinnamon.

Cut the rind from the bacon and chop it into small cubes. Brown it, with the chopped onions and carrot, in 2 oz. of the butter. Transfer to a casserole, and add the drained meat to the frying pan. When it's lightly browned, stir in the flour and leave it to colour. Pour in the strained marinade gradually (keep the prunes to one side); when it thickens transfer meat and sauce to the casserole, season with spices, herbs and salt and simmer until nearly done. The hare may take 2 hours, whereas the beef will be cooked in just over an hour.

Meanwhile peel the pickling onions. Put them whole into a heavy pan with 1 oz. butter, a pinch of salt and the sugar. Put over a low heat until the butter's melted, then add enough stock barely to cover the onions. Boil steadily until the stock etc., reduces to a rich brown caramel, and the onions are cooked, and well glazed (shake them about from time to time). Use the last ounce of butter to cook the button mushrooms.

When the beef or hare is almost ready, add the prunes and finish the cooking (10–20 minutes). Arrange the onions and mushrooms on top of the casseroled meat, bring up a prune or two to make an appetizing contrast. Serve very hot.

If you have the hare's blood, mix it with 2 tablespoons of cream and a little of the hot sauce from the meat. Pour it into the casserole (before adding onions and mushrooms), which should be just off the boil. Stir over a very low heat for a few moments – if the sauce boils again the blood will curdle.

Turkey or capon stuffed with prunes and chestnuts

This Breton recipe adds a moist richness to turkey or capon. For a chicken of more moderate size reduce the quantity of prunes by one third, and of the other ingredients by half.

> 1½ lb. pork, ⅓ fat, ⅔ lean
> 3 rashers lean unsmoked bacon
> 2 heaped tablespoons parsley
> 3 heaped tablespoons breadcrumbs
> ½ teaspoon each nutmeg, cinnamon,
>   ground cloves
> salt, freshly ground black pepper to taste
> 40 chestnuts
> 30 prunes soaked overnight in tea
> *plus* butter for roasting the bird
> and a glass of port for the sauce

Slice the hard skin of the chestnuts round the middle on both sides. Boil for 20 minutes. Remove a few at a time from the pan, and take off the two skins. Chop half the chestnuts into nuggets, leave the rest whole. Stone the prunes. Chop half of them roughly, leave the rest whole.

Mince pork and bacon. Mix all the stuffing ingredients together, except the whole chestnuts and prunes. Make sure the seasoning is strong enough. Stuff the bird not too tightly.

To roast, butter the bird lavishly all over. Lay it on one side of the breast in a roasting tin. Put on a lid of double foil. Cook at Mark 5, 375°F, for 2–3 hours according to the weight of the bird, turning it onto the other side of the breast at half time. When the bird is almost done, remove the foil and pour off as much fat as you can, leaving the meat juices behind. Turn the bird onto its back. Sprinkle with salt and a little flour, then put back in the oven to brown surrounded by the whole chestnuts and whole prunes (about 20 minutes).

Transfer bird to warm serving dish. Arrange chestnuts and prunes round it. Skim surplus fat from the pan juices, then boil up with a glass of port to make the sauce. Correct the seasoning and pour over the chestnuts and prunes.

Tripe de Gourin aux pruneaux (for 4)

Gourin, a market town in the Breton Black Mountains, is the centre of an important stock-raising distr¦ct. So you would expect tripe (a favourite market-day dish in Brittany) to be a particular speciality.

> 1 lb. tripe cut into small squares
> 3 oz. butter
> 3 medium-sized carrots, sliced
> 10 shallots, chopped, or 9–10 oz. chopped
>   mild onion
> bouquet garni
> 3 cloves
> 15 large soaked prunes
> beef stock
> generous liqueur glass brandy

Fry the tripe to golden-brown quickly in the butter. Remove it to a casserole (or small *tripière*, if you have one), and fry the carrots and shallots. Add to the tripe with all the other ingredients, including enough beef stock just to cover. Fasten on the lid with a strip of flour and water paste, or a double layer of silver foil, and simmer for 2 hours.

Rabbit with prunes (for 6)

This excellent recipe adds flavour to the insipid domestic rabbit (or battery chicken). Made with wild rabbit, it's a recipe for a special occasion.

> 1 rabbit, jointed
> seasoned flour
> 3 oz. butter

4 medium-sized carrots, sliced
12 small onions (pickling)
½ pint beef stock
½ pint red or white wine
12 oz. prunes, soaked
bouquet garni
salt, pepper

and to finish:

1 glass of port
3 oz. each currants and sultanas
chopped parsley
triangles of bread fried in butter

Turn the rabbit pieces in the flour, and cook the stew as for *Tripe de Gourin* above. Adjust the cooking time to the age and tenderness of the rabbit. Finally add port, currants and sultanas, and keep just under the boil for 10 minutes. Before serving, sprinkle chopped parsley over the dish, and tuck the croûtons round the side of the casserole.

Noisettes de porc aux pruneaux de Tours (for 8)

This classic dish of French provincial cooking combined originally the prunes of Huismes, downstream from Tours, and the white wine of Vouvray, upstream from Tours on the opposite bank of the Loire. The prunes may nowadays come from California, but at least the Vouvray wine is still with us. The vineyards there are on the top slopes of the cliff, with the wine, as so often in Touraine, stored beneath them in caves. A neat arrangement. Above all the white wine producer needs nerve: he has to wait, before picking his grapes, through the red wine and rosé vendange of October, past All Saints Day and into November with its trickier weather. This is because the grapes need to be 'pourri', almost rotting, if they are to produce a good white wine.

This recipe comes from *Recettes des provinces de France*, chosen by Curnonsky.

50 giant prunes (about 1½ lb.)
½ bottle Vouvray
8 slices fillet of pork (or loin chops)
2 oz. butter
2 tablespoons seasoned flour
salt, pepper
1 tablespoon redcurrant jelly
¾ pint double cream

Soak the prunes 6 hours or overnight in the Vouvray. Turn the pork slices in the seasoned flour and fry in butter on both sides until golden. Cook gently with a lid on the pan until the meat is done. Meanwhile simmer the prunes for half an hour in the Vouvray. Drain them and arrange on a serving dish with the pork. Add the prune liquor to the meat juices, reduce, add the redcurrant jelly and bind with the cream. Pour over the pork and prunes, and serve very hot.

Prunes stewed in Vouvray

This combination of prunes and Vouvray produces almost as good a result as the more famous *porc aux pruneaux de Tours* above. Almost, but not quite – the pork recipe is one of the best I know; few dishes come up to it.

1 bottle Vouvray wine
3 oz. sugar
1 vanilla pod, split lengthways
grating of nutmeg
3 curls of lemon peel
1 lb. giant prunes

Put the prunes to soak for an hour. Simmer the rest of the ingredients for 20 minutes, strain into a clean pan and bring back to the boil when the prunes have finished soaking. Boil the prunes gently for *4 minutes only*. Pour the whole panful into a bowl and leave in the refrigerator for 3 days. The prunes will have absorbed a lot of the wine, and taste delicious. Serve with a separate bowl of whipped, slightly sweetened cream.

Prune tart

Another dish from Tours. For success, the prune purée must be rich and well-flavoured, not in the least watery.

> 8 oz. shortcrust pastry
> 1 lb. giant prunes, soaked
> sugar
> water
> rum
> beaten egg

Line a tart tin with a removable base with pastry (save the trimmings). Prick all over with a fork and bake blind until cooked, but not very brown.

Simmer the prunes in just enough water to cover them. Drain and sieve. Flavour the purée with sugar and rum, and put into the pastry case. Using the pastry trimmings, make a criss-cross lattice over it, with strips about ¼ inch wide. Brush the pastry with beaten egg, and bake until golden-brown. Serve with cream.

Note: mix the prune purée above with double its weight in home-made vanilla ice-cream. Refreeze. Serve with almond biscuits, p. 353. I know this sounds unpromising, but try it.

Pruneaux Fourrés de Tours

Walking along the main street of Tours, one's eye is caught again and again by the cake and confectionery shops. And of all these shops the finest is the Maison Sabat. There in the ravishing window display, among the other specialities of the Sabat family, are charming little baskets, miniature hampers, filled with rows of stuffed prunes. These *pruneaux fourrés* are one of the great specialities of Tours. Each house makes its own (no sweet factory to vulgarize the old recipes). What I like about them is that they are not too sweet, that their flavour is rich but subtle, with just a hint of kirsch or rum. Discerning natives of Tours prefer the original *pruneaux noirs* which go back I think to the eighteenth century – they are stuffed with a prune and rum purée. I find it difficult to choose between them and the ones filled with pale green almond paste or an orange apricot purée, flavoured in both cases with a little kirsch.

Mlle Madeleine Sabat finds it more and more difficult to get traditional baskets for the prunes. They are only made now by the old ladies of Vilaine, a village in Balzac country near Chinon which once relied on supplying baskets to local prune-packers at Huismes. (With the decline of the prune trade, the young people of Vilaine concentrate on fashionable and profitable wicker furniture.) Soon the *pruneaux fourrés* will all be packed in paper boxes. Soon, too, the prunes may come from California – at the moment they come from Agen.

> 2 lb. giant prunes, soaked, stoned
>   and dried
>
> *almond filling:*
>
> 8 oz. sugar
> ½ gill water
> 4 oz. ground almonds
> kirsch
> few drops green colouring
>
> *prune or apricot filling:*
>
> 4 oz. prunes or apricots, soaked
> about 4 oz. sugar
> rum or kirsch
>
> *coating syrup:*
>
> 8 oz. sugar
> ½ gill water

Leave the soaked and stoned prunes to dry on a rack in a warm kitchen.

To make the almond paste, bring sugar and water to the soft ball stage. Pour in the almonds, remove from heat and beat until cold (use an electric beater) adding kirsch to taste, and just enough green colouring to produce a delicate tone. Knead the paste on icing sugar spread over a formica or marble surface, until the marzipan is coherent and firm.

To make the fruit purées, stew apricots or prunes with a very little water until they begin to be soft. Drain and weigh (discard prune stones first). Add about half the weight of fruit in sugar and sieve, or blend in a liquidizer using a little of the cooking liquor if the fruit sticks. Put the purée into a heavy pan and cook slowly over a steady heat until it dries to a thick mass. Extra sugar may be added but these purées should not be over-sweet. Remove from heat, flavour with Kirsch (apricots) or rum (prunes) and leave to cool.

To fill the prunes, roll the paste into fat nuggets and slip them into the prunes. The filling should show an almond-shaped bulge through the split in the prune. Make two or three light indentations across the filling at a slant, for decoration (illustration, p. 288).

At the Maison Sabat, the fruit purées are piped into the Prunes with a forcing bag before they have set. I think it's easier to shape the mixtures with a teaspoon, rolling them in caster sugar if they are a little sticky.

Bring sugar and water to the hard ball stage to make the coating syrup, and have ready an oiled rack. Quickly dip the prunes into the syrup (use a larding needle or knitting needle), and transfer them to the draining rack. This makes them shiny. It also makes them sticky, so put them into tiny paper cases before handing them round, or packing them into a small basket.

More stuffed prunes

Prunes and haddock: pour boiling water over ½ lb. smoked haddock. Leave for 10 minutes, then drain and mash with 3 tablespoons of double cream. Season well with salt, black and Cayenne pepper. Stuff 1 lb. prunes soaked and stoned. Heat in the oven and serve on croûtons of bread fried in butter.

Devils on horseback: replace the stone in each soaked prune with a salted almond. Wrap the prunes in pieces of bacon, fastened in place by a cocktail stick, and grill.

Prunes for a goose: this delicious recipe of Louis P. de Gouy's demands 1½ lb. prunes soaked and simmered in half water, half red wine, plus a sliced lemon. Chop ¾ lb. pork (⅔ lean, ⅓ fat), and fry in 2 oz. butter with 2 oz. chopped onion, 18 small green olives (or 12 large), stoned and chopped. Season with salt, pepper, nutmeg, mace, marjoram and thyme. When the mixture is cooked, put into a basin and leave to cool. When it's just warm beat in 2 eggs. When it's cold, stuff the prunes. Leave in the refrigerator 24 hours, and put into the goose 2 hours before it is roasted.

Prunes and cheese: stuff soaked and stoned prunes with a knob of high fat cream cheese. Put a toasted almond down the middle.

Strawberries

A rich man whose teeth, constitution and heart were all stainless steel, might reasonably look back to life in the mid-eighteenth century with longing. But not if he liked strawberries. Strawberries are one of the fruits of modernity which are better as well as bigger.

The fruit our ancestors knew was one species or other of small European strawberry – fruit sacred to the Northern fertility goddess, Frigg, and then to the Virgin. Bulgy modern strawberries would hardly be recognized by a medieval miniature painter, who ran hautboys – or wood strawberries – round the margins of his Book of Hours.

The grand improvement came from a happy conjunction of the Virginian and Chilean strawberries in a French market garden at the end of the eighteenth century. The two species, one with good colour and flavour, one with size, had the same number of chromosomes, but had been separated by the expanse of the Americas.

Since then directed variation has never ceased. Experiments are now assailing the chief disability of the strawberry – that it will only grow low on the ground, out of doors, in summer rain and sun. This keeps up the price. Strawberries have to be picked by hand (fruits ripen on the same plant at different times).

In the strawberry field, women of the village pick along the rows of plants on their hands and knees. They have to be knowing to select the right strawberries, careful in handling the delicate fruit. It's a sweaty, muddy, skilful job, for women, not for unthinking girls. And not for the sort of people who joined that strawberry-picking party in Jane Austen's *Emma*: large bonnets, little baskets with pink ribbons, a gipsy party under the trees, a table in the shade, everything as 'natural' and 'simple' as a wealthy landowner and employer of labour could make it. Listen to the conversation: 'Morning decidedly the best time – never tired – every sort good – hautboy definitely superior – Chili preferred – white wood finest flavour of all . . . only objection . . . the stooping – glaring sun – tired to death – could bear it no longer must go and sit in the shade.'

After half an hour. How modern pickers would have laughed.

So did Jane Austen. She knew all about the realities of strawberry-picking. But it was a good scene for the central moments of a love story ('sweet to the eye and mind. English verdure, English culture, English comfort, seen under a bright sun, without being oppressive'). Against a background of strawberries, misunderstandings knot to an intricate tangle. And suddenly we are back four centuries with Hieronymus Bosch and his great painting of the 'Garden of Delights', which wheels round a naked man presenting a strawberry of delight to a naked girl – the theme of all love stories. 'You shall be Queen . . . and feast upon strawberries, sugar and cream.'

Strawberries, sugar, cream. The combination allows no improvement, you think? But certainly the cream can be improved, and occasionally the strawberries.

Strawberries and cream

When you find a greengrocer selling proper weights of strawberries in openwork punnets, stick to him. If you live near a
strawberry field, you'll be able to buy the best strawberries available, freshly picked at the best moment. Beware of roadside
strawberry sellers, unless they are unmistakably attached to a
nearby strawberry field. Don't neglect cheaper 'jam' strawberries:
they sometimes excel in flavour, with a sharper sweetness than
the more perfect-looking specimens.

Preparation: strawberries are easily bruised, do not keep well, and
*should always be washed quickly in the minimum of water, before
removing the stems.*
   If you have to keep them overnight, wash and stem them, then
leave in a dish in a cool place with a good sprinkling of sugar. If
the refrigerator is the only cool place, cover the dish closely (or
you will find the smell difficult to get rid of) and leave in the
crisper salad drawer. If your strawberries are not as ripe as they
should be, leave the dish 2 or 3 hours in the sunshine, if you can,
with a good sprinkling of sugar.

Serve straightaway, washed but not stemmed, in individual bowls,
with individual bowls of sugar and cream. Each person dips his
strawberries by their leaves first into sugar and then into cream.
Flavour the cream with a few drops of lemon juice. Or beat equal
quantities of soured and double cream together, until they are
thick, not stiff. Modern pasteurized cream is too bland. It lacks
the sourish tang of French cream, which brings out so well the
flavour of fruit.

Cœur à la crème

Cream is cheap in France, compared with the price of other food,
but frugal housewives stretch it most successfully by the addition

of fresh cheese (*fromage frais, fromage blanc*) and beaten egg-white. Usually it's served in a large bowl, but for special occasions heart shapes of this delectable mixture appear surrounded by strawberries. Few of us are able to buy drippingly fresh cheese, but cottage cheese, petit suisse or Gervais will do. And it's no good making your own in a muslin drip bag, from our pasteurized milk; the result is a rubbery, bitter curd. If you can buy un-pasteurized milk, it's another matter.

One used to buy heart-shaped metal moulds, pierced with draining holes, from Madame Cadec at her Soho shop. Now Elizabeth David Ltd, 46 Bourne Street, London SW1, sells little white china hearts, and so do some of the better kitchen suppliers. They make a good summer birthday present.

> ¼ pint double cream, whipped
> ½ lb. cottage chese, or cream cheese,
>   sieved
> 1 egg white, whipped stiff
> sugar to taste

Mix the cream into the cheese, fold in the egg white with a metal spoon. Add sugar – don't overdo it. Line the moulds with butter muslin and pile in the cheese mixture, smoothing the top. Leave to drain overnight in a cool place, or the refrigerator.

To serve, turn out and surround with strawberries. Additional sugar, single cream and thin home-made almond biscuits (p.353) are good accompaniments.

In France, this cheese mixture is often served with apricot jam, the kind with large pieces of fruit in it, or strawberry jam from Plougastel in Brittany. Quince jelly or crab apple jelly go well with it too. An ideal way of using up runny jams.

Cream cheese mousse

A simple delicious mousse, one of the delights of summer when served with strawberries (or other soft fruit, but particularly strawberries). It's really a more elaborate form of *cœur à la crème*, made with the low-fat cheese on sale in most grocers' shops.

> ½ lb. low fat cottage cheese
> 2 egg yolks
> 2 oz. sugar, vanilla sugar for preference
> ½ oz. gelatine
> 6 tablespoons very hot water
> 4 oz. each double and single cream

Sieve the cottage cheese to get rid of the large-grained texture (if homemade cheese is used, make sure it's well drained before weighing). Beat in egg yolks and sugar – for quick vanilla sugar see p. 347. Dissolve the gelatine in the hot water, add the two creams and whisk until stiff. Fold in the cheese carefully, so that the mixture is well blended, but still light and fluffy. Brush a 1½ pint mould (or little heart-shaped moulds) with a thin film of non-tasting oil and sprinkle with caster sugar. Pour in the mousse and leave to set. Serve chilled, with unchilled strawberries dressed with a little orange juice or orange liqueur.

Strawberry brûlée

Adapted from an American recipe, strawberry brûlée sounds complicated, but it's really worth the trouble. You need a round, sightly, ovenproof dish (pyrex is ideal) at least 1 inch deep and about 8½ inches across.

> *sweet shortcrust:*
>
> 8 oz. flour
> 2 tablespoons icing sugar
> 4 oz. butter
> 1 egg
>
> *filling:*
>
> ½ pint single cream
> ¼ pint double cream
> 4 egg yolks

15–20 large strawberries
1 tablespoon each orange liqueur and
    sugar
extra caster sugar

Make the pastry in the usual way and line the pyrex dish (keep what is left over for the next recipe). Prick all over with a fork, and bake blind until light brown and cooked. A sheet of foil and haricot beans may be used as well to keep the pastry from rising, but the fork treatment is usually enough.

Boil the cream, both kinds together, for one minute exactly. Stir into the egg yolks, beating with a fork. Set over a pan of simmering water for five minutes, stirring all the time to avoid lumps. Pour through a sieve into a clean basin and leave to cool.

Meanwhile halve the strawberries. Sprinkle with sugar and liqueur and set aside for an hour.

Assemble the tart about 2½ hours before the meal. Arrange the strawberries in a single close layer, flat side down on the pastry case. Mix their juice into the custard and pour over the fruit. Chill for 2 hours. Sprinkle the top with a bare ¼ inch layer of caster sugar. Set under a hot grill, turning from time to time, so that the sugar melts into an even golden-brown marbled sheet of caramel. Chill for half an hour (while serving and eating the first course or courses).

Barquettes aux fraises

Use boat-shaped tartlet tins, though, of course, round ones will do. Line with pastry, the sweet shortcrust left over from strawberry brûlée, rolled thinly. Bake blind. Cool, then store for a day or two until required in an airtight tin.

Arrange a nicely graded line of ripe, firm red strawberries in each *barquette*. Melt 2 tablespoons each redcurrant jelly and raspberry (or apricot) jam together in a pan, and sieve. Spoon carefully over the strawberries while just warm and still runny.

Large strawberry tarts can be made in the same way, but they are most successful if the strawberries are arranged on a bed of *crème pâtissière*, as the apples are in the Evreux tart on p. 260. Pour the jam over just before serving.

Strawberries and sharpness

In Venice, in the season of Alpine strawberries, they are served with lemon juice, or red or white wine, and sugar. No cream. In France, in the Vendômois, one friend sprinkles large *Quatre Saisons* from his garden with a few drops of red wine vinegar to bring out the juice. This really works very well, though it may require an act of faith to try it the first time. They are then eaten with cream and sugar in the usual way, or with his own red wine.

In England, we've eaten strawberries in claret for centuries. Try orange juice and orange liqueurs, fortified wines, or champagne, or Asti Spumante. Purées of fresh ripe raspberries and blackcurrants bring out the sharpness and sweetness of the strawberry.

These seasonings must be added at the last possible moment, mostly at table, but never more than half an hour before eating.

Walnuts

After the grape harvest comes the harvest of walnuts, in such districts as the Corrèze in France and the Vaucluse (where the nuts for Fuller's layer cake come from), and the peninsula of Sorrento below Naples. Poles move along sunken lanes like lances in Velazquez's 'Surrender of Breda', heads appear, like Green Men in church carving, above the tops of the trees or right in the middle of the high foliage, walnuts patter to the dry ground, the new season's supply, much of which will end up in our shops and on our sideboards.

In cooking with walnuts, it's a good idea to use them early in the season before the kernels shrink and lose their finest flavour. In October and November, early November, one may see in greengrocers' shops netted sacks labelled 'fresh walnuts from France'. They are very juicy, the ones to go for if you want to make walnut and onion bread from Burgundy, or a walnut cake, or soup.

A little later on, the kiln-dried Sorrento walnuts come in, from the same place as the ones which were found under the dust of Pompeii, lying in their bowl beside eggs and cereal, still waiting for the priests of Isis. One year I was tempted by the perfect appearance of some enormous walnuts from Turkey, walnuts the size of golf balls, but they were tasteless compared with the smaller French and Italian nuts in neighbouring boxes.

English walnut trees produce good fruit, but they are not very certain croppers, as you might expect of an introduced tree whose native home stretches from south-eastern Europe to the Far East. In walnut you have the same word as in Wales and the Welsh – the country of foreigners, the foreign nut. Further south, in France, Italy, Spain, Portugal, where it's found a second home and been thriving for centuries, the walnut is called simply 'the nut'.

Perhaps it is this uncertain status of walnuts in our island that explains why traditional uses of them are almost confined to walnut ketchup, to pickled walnuts, and to walnuts as dessert, walnuts with wine, walnuts with raisins. The last is an old medieval combination (like the four mendicants or friars – dried figs, raisins, hazelnuts and blanched almonds, whose colours resembled the habits of the Dominicans, the Franciscans, the Austin friars and the Carmelites) from the time when fresh fruit was hard to come by in winter. Walnut layer cakes, tea breads and salads, now so familiar to us, arrived in Britain from America at the beginning of this century. It's to that country and to France, to the Middle East and to China, that we must turn for recipes which show the walnut to be as versatile in cookery as the more popular almond.

Walnuts can replace or augment almonds in mincemeat, or in biscuits. If you use an American cookery book, you will find them a good – and cheaper – substitute for pecans.

Walnut Soup (for 6)

This French soup – which I first came across in Elizabeth David's *Summer Cooking* (Penguins) – is one of the most delicious and unusual ones I know. Particularly when made with fresh walnuts. The garlic is not optional, but essential to the flavour (without being identifiable by people who may think they don't like it).

> 6 oz. shelled walnuts
> up to 2 pints light stock (see recipe)

large clove garlic
¼ pint cream
salt, freshly ground black pepper

Crush walnuts and garlic to a paste with a little of the stock (use a liquidizer, a pestle and mortar, or the end of a wooden rolling pin and a pudding basin). Incorporate the rest of the stock slowly until the mixture is the consistency of single cream. If the walnuts have been liquidized, they will probably take up most of the 2 pints; if they've been pounded by hand, they'll take about 1½ pints. Pour the soup through a sieve into a saucepan, and bring to the boil. Add the cream and correct the seasoning with salt and pepper. Serve straightaway.

Walnut bread from southern Burgundy

John Evelyn, in exile, seems to have loved especially the walnut trees of France. 'Burgundy abounds with them,' he wrote in his *Sylva* of 1658, 'where they stand in the midst of goodly wheatlands, at sixty and an 100 feet distance, and so far are they from hurting the crop, that they are looked upon as great preservers by keeping the ground warm, nor do the roots hinder the plow'. I expect this bread was made then, real farmer's food, filling but tasty. (Further north, where walnut trees begin to thin out, in Touraine for instance, fresh walnuts are eaten with bread hot from the baker's oven, salt, and a glass of white wine.)

1½ lb. strong bread flour
¼ oz. salt
1 oz. sugar
generous oz. yeast
¾ pint warm milk
4 oz. roughly chopped walnuts
6 oz. finely chopped onion
¼ pint walnut oil or 4 oz. melted but
   cool butter

Sift flour, salt and sugar into a warm bowl. Cream the yeast with ¼ pint of the milk, and pour it into the middle of the flour, together with the walnut oil (or butter), and the rest of the milk. Knead well until the dough is firm and blended into a smooth, springy ball (about 10 minutes). Leave in a warm place to rise for 2 hours (or in a cool place overnight). Knock down the dough, mix in the walnuts and onion, shape into four rounds and leave on a greased baking tray to prove for 45 minutes. Bake at Mark 5, 375°F for 45 minutes, or until the loaves sound hollow when tapped underneath.

Cerneaux, or walnuts pickled in the French style

John Evelyn again, this time on green walnuts: 'In France they eat them blanched and fresh, with wine and salt, having first cut them out of their shells before they are hardened, with a short brass knife, because iron rusts; and these they call Cernois, from their manner of scooping them out.' *Cerner* means to cut away or cut round.

Three hundred and eleven years later, the same recipe given in more detail in *La vraie cuisine de l'Anjou et de la Touraine*, by Roger Lallemand.

'Take walnuts which are not ripe. Halve them and remove the soft kernels from the shells without breaking them. Blanch in water acidulated with a little vinegar. Leave them for several days to soak in good white wine vinegar, with tarragon and tiny onions. Drain and serve them as an hors d'œuvre, dressed with oil and other seasonings, preferably verjuice.' For the verjuice, the acid juice of unripe grapes, we must substitute lemon juice or vinegar.

Eliza Acton records a simpler version of this salad. She had spent a year in France as a girl, a century and a half after Evelyn wrote his *Sylva*, and had become engaged briefly to a Frenchman. Her memories of dishes eaten there are gently coloured with romantic *gourmandise*, an unembittered nostalgia.

She writes that 'this is a common summer salad in France, where the growth of walnuts is generally abundant, but is not much served in England; though the sweet flavour of the just-formed nut is very agreeable. Take the walnuts when a pin will pierce them *easily*, pare them down to the kernels, and toss them gently, just before they are served, in a French or English salad-dressing (the former would generally be preferred we think), and turn them into the salad-bowl for table.'

Pickled walnuts in the English style

This wonderful black pickle, a favourite in England, has changed as little over the centuries as the *Cerneaux* recipe above. Hannah Glasse, Eliza Acton, and the flock of lesser cookery writers disagree only about the blend of aromatics. The method has never changed. For clarity, I've chosen Mrs Beeton's instructions:

> 100 walnuts
> salt and water
> to each quart of vinegar:
> > 2 oz. whole black peppercorns
> > 1 oz. allspice
> > 1 oz. bruised ginger

'Procure the walnuts while young' – from the beginning to the middle of July, before they harden – 'be careful they are not woody, and prick them well with a fork; prepare a strong brine of salt and water (4 lb. salt to each gallon of water), into which put the walnuts, letting them remain 9 days, and changing the brine every third day; drain them off, put them on a dish, place it in the sun until they become perfectly black, which will be in 2 or 3 days; have ready dry jars, into which place the walnuts, and do not quite fill the jars. Boil sufficient vinegar to cover them for 10 minutes, with spices in the above proportion, and pour it hot over the walnuts, which must be quite covered with the pickle; tie down with bladder,' – use small bottling jars, which fasten tight with a rubber ring – 'and keep in a dry place. They will be fit for use in a month, and will keep good 2 or 3 years.'

Note: For best results use sea salt and wine vinegar. You could also insert an onion or two, stuck with cloves, in the middle of the nuts, as Hannah Glasse and Eliza Acton did, and augment the spices with mustard seed and mace. Eat with cheese and salads; add 10 or 12 to a beef stew as a cheap piquant substitute for oysters.

Pheasant in the Georgian style (for 4–5)

This lovely and unusual dish takes time to prepare, but it's worth the trouble. Make it above all in autumn, in November, when walnuts are still fresh and juicy and the first good grapes and oranges arrive. The version here is French, coming by way of Escoffier from *La gastronomie en Russie*, by A. Petit, published in 1860. Georgia sounds like paradise: walnuts, oranges, grapes, tea and pheasants all flourish there.

Keep any vegetables you may think of serving as a separate course. This is a dish on its own.

> 1 pheasant
> 30 walnuts, or 8 oz. shelled walnuts
> 2 lb. grapes
> 4 oranges, preferably blood oranges
> ¼ pint sweet muscatel wine, e.g.
>   Frontignan
> 1 tea bag preferably containing green
>   tea
> 3 oz. butter
> salt, pepper
> 1 oz. flour

Pour boiling water over the shelled walnuts, leave for three or four minutes and then remove the skin surrounding the nuts themselves (a pointed knife helps). This removes the bitter part of the walnuts. Put the grapes through a *mouli-légumes* (or liquidize and sieve) to obtain a thick juice. Squeeze the oranges. Pour ¼ pint boiling water over the tea bag, brew for 5 minutes, then strain off the tea. Put all these ingredients, with the pheasant, the wine and half the butter, into a casserole; ideally, it should be of a size only a little larger than the bird, so that the other ingredients almost cover it. Season with salt and pepper, and cover. Bake in a moderate oven, Mark 4–5, 350–375°F, for 50 minutes or until the pheasant is just cooked. Cut it into four, or carve it as appropriate; arrange the pieces on a hot serving dish, and put the strained walnuts around them. Measure the cooking juices (there will be about 1½–2 pints) and reduce to half the quantity by boiling hard. Meanwhile keep the pheasant warm in the oven (protect with buttered paper), and fork the flour into the remaining butter. When the reducing is completed, add the flour and butter to the sauce in little pieces, stirring them in well. The sauce will thicken, and acquire an appetizing glaze. Pour a little of it over the pheasant, and serve the rest in a sauceboat.

Two walnut stuffings

For boned loin, breast or shoulder of lamb

> 4 oz. breadcrumbs
> 1 tablespoon chopped parsley
> 4 oz. dried apricots, soaked overnight
> 2 oz. melted butter
> 2 oz. walnuts, roughly chopped
> 1 large egg
> salt, pepper

Chop the apricots, and mix all the ingredients together.

For duck or goose (half the quantities for duck)

> 2 large eating apples, peeled, cored
> and diced
> 4 oz. breadcrumbs
> ¾ lb. belly of pork, minced
> 2 oz. walnuts, chopped
> 4 oz. chopped onion
> 1 large clove garlic, crushed
> 2 oz. butter

.1 dessertspoon honey
1 large egg
1 tablespoon chopped parsley
salt and pepper

Fry onion, garlic, apples and pork in the butter gently for about 15 minutes. Mix with the other ingredients. The chopped liver of the bird may also be added.

Prunes stuffed with walnuts

A *Book of Middle Eastern Food*, by Claudia Roden (Penguins), is the kind of cookery book I like, and use frequently. It's not just a collection of recipes, but recipes explained, recipes plus information – poems, stories about that holy wit and gourmet, the Hodja, bits of social and religious history – which help one to understand this cookery so basic to our own in western Europe. I was interested to find a walnut sweetmeat identical to one made in Perigord (a nugget of almond paste sandwiched between walnut halves, topped with a blob of brittle caramel), and this rich-tasting but light confection of prunes and walnuts and cream.

1 lb. prunes
freshly made tea
as many shelled walnut halves as
  there are prunes
2–3 tablespoons sugar
1 tablespoon lemon juice
½ pint water
¼ pint each double and single cream,
  mixed
2 tablespoons caster sugar (optional)

'Wash the prunes if necessary. Pour strained boiling hot tea over them and let them soak overnight. Drain. Remove the stones, replacing them with half a shelled walnut. If you find this difficult, boil the prunes in the tea until nearly tender, then cool, remove their stones and stuff them.

'Bring the water, sugar and lemon juice to the boil and simmer for a few minutes. Drop in the stuffed prunes and simmer gently, covered, for ½ hour, adding more water if necessary. The walnuts will become impregnated with the rich syrup. Allow to cool and serve chilled with cream, whipped and sweetened with caster sugar if you wish; or allow to cool, smother with the whipped cream and chill together for a few hours. This last method is particularly delicious.

'Modern variations which add to the aroma of the prunes include cooking them in sweet red wine (in this case using less sugar or none at all) or in the tea in which they have been soaked, flavoured with a few drops of vanilla or a packet of vanilla sugar.'

Note: hesitating to drop the prunes into the syrup for fear the walnuts came out, I arranged them in a single layer in a large pan, fitting them closely together, and poured the boiling syrup over them.

Lavardin cakes

A year or two ago a new pastrycook arrived in Montoire, a small market town in the department of Loir-et-Cher. Everyone watched his window – Montoire is careful of its gastronomic reputation – to see what sort of show he'd put on (and how he'd compare with his two rivals). Very soon, among the evanescent stars of the usual repertoire, the éclairs, the *barquettes aux fraises*, the *amandines*, the *présidents*, rows of plain, white-iced discs appeared. They were labelled *Lavardins, notre specialité*. Now Lavardin castle, or its remains, on one side of Montoire, together with Trôo church on the other, dominates our valley landscape of the Bas-Vendômois. Could these cakes be a local speciality we'd all missed? We bought some – feeling a little piqued – and they were so delectable that I asked for the recipe.

I learnt, in the simple, beautiful kitchen behind the shop, that lavardin cakes had nothing to do with Lavardin at all, that they came from the south-west of France, via an old pastrycook in Normandy who had specialized, against the dominant French tradition, in cakes which keep. And these do. They are also very much to the English taste. In fact of all the recipes in this section, I think that lavardins show off best the flavour and texture of walnuts.

sweet pastry:

1 lb flour
8 oz. butter
8 oz. caster sugar
3 standard eggs

filling:

10 oz. sugar
3 tablespoons water (2 oz.)
6 oz. tin evaporated milk
scant 2 oz. unsalted butter
generous 2 oz. double cream
pinch bicarbonate of soda
10 oz. walnuts, roughly chopped

icing:

2 egg whites
4 oz. icing sugar

First make the filling: bring sugar and water to the hard crack stage over a brisk heat, stirring with a wooden spoon from time to time. Remove from heat and quickly stir in the evaporated milk, butter, cream and bicarbonate of soda. Stir until the mixture reaches firm soft-ball stage, add the walnuts and pour out onto a marble slab or a sheet of greased paper. It will cool to a soft nut toffee.

While the filling cools, make the pastry in the usual way. Roll it out thinly and line 3- to 4-inch flan rings laid on a greased baking sheet (or smooth-sided tart tins) leaving a little frill of pastry overlapping the edge. Fill slightly over half-full with the walnut mixture. Brush the pastry edges with water and fit in lids of pastry, which have been pricked half a dozen times with a fork. Take off the surplus pastry by running a rolling pin across the tins.

Bake at Mark 3, 350°F, or a little less, until the pastry is cooked but not brown – about 15 minutes. As with mince pies, the point is to bake these little cakes so that the pastry cooks without the filling bursting through. Remove the lavardins from their rings or tins, and cool upside down on a wire rack.

Set a pudding basin over a pan of boiling water, put in the egg whites and icing sugar, and whisk until they blow up to a fairly stiff meringue, which feels hot but not uncomfortably so. Spread thinly over the top and sides of the cooled and inverted cakes with a palette knife, leaving the pricked surface exposed. Dry overnight in a cool-place, or in the refrigerator, and store in an airtight tin.

If time is short, there is no reason why you shouldn't make 2 or 3 large lavardins, instead of the 20–30 small ones. Use a French flan ring, a tart tin with a removable base, or a straight-sided tart tin.

Chinese walnut brittle

I sometimes think that the charm of a country's cookery lies not so much in its classic dishes as in its quirks and fancies. Take this recipe, for instance – the universal (and boring) nut brittle, transformed by a little salt and a lot of freshly-ground black pepper into a delicacy entirely Chinese. The surprising thing is that it tastes spicy rather than peppery. It leaves one's mouth feeling fresh and clear.

> 6 oz. sugar (see recipe)
> level teaspoon salt
> 4 oz. shelled walnuts
> black pepper in a pepper mill

The shelled walnuts may be left as halves, or split again into quarters. Put sugar and 2 oz. water (the Chinese use brown sugar, but white burns less easily) into a heavy pan. Stir over a good heat until it reaches the soft-ball stage – a saucepan thermometer for measuring the heat of sugar, jam or fat is a good investment, which I recommend to any cook. Add salt and walnuts. Bring the mixture to the hard-crack stage, turning the pepper mill about 20 to 25 times over the pan between stirs. The nuts will take up the sugar until they are lightly coated and sticking together in a cluster. Pour out onto a greased baking tray. As the mixture cools, which it does quite rapidly, pull it apart into pieces with a couple of forks. Eat the same day.

Note: don't use ready-milled black pepper, or any kind of white pepper which is less aromatic than the black, and more fiercely hot.

Walnut biscuits

Almonds are so often used to make biscuits, and so successfully, that walnuts are overlooked. They produce a stronger flavour than almonds which goes well with coffee, and a delightfully chewy texture. A good accompaniment, too, to coffee, walnut or chocolate ice-cream (see p. 348).

>4 egg whites
>4 oz. grated walnuts
>2 oz. chopped walnuts
>4 oz. brown sugar
>2 heaped teaspoons plain flour
>4 sheets rice paper

Whisk the egg whites until they are stiff. Fold in the other ingredients carefully. Arrange the rice paper on two baking trays and spread spoonfuls of the walnut mixture on it (it does not run much in the baking, so the spoonfuls can be set fairly close together).

Bake at Mark 2, 300°F for about 20 minutes, until lightly browned and firm. Tear away from the uncovered rice paper, and cool the biscuits on a wire rack.

Walnut pie

Anyone who has a weakness for English treacle tart will like this version of North American pecan pie. In fact they'll probably prefer it: the nuts cut the sweetness of the filling much more deliciously than the breadcrumbs in our traditional recipe.

shortcrust pastry:

8 oz. flour
4 oz. butter
2 tablespoons icing sugar
1 large egg
about 1 tablespoon water

filling:

4 oz. soft brown sugar
4 oz. unsalted butter
3 eggs
juice and rind 1 lemon
6 oz. golden syrup
8 oz. shelled walnuts
pinch salt

Make the pastry in the usual way, and line an 8½ or 9½ inch tart tin. Bake blind for 10 minutes. For the filling, cream together butter and sugar until light and smooth. Beat in the eggs one at a time. Warm the syrup very slightly until it's runny (to weigh syrup, put a small saucepan on the scales, then pour in the syrup to give you the weight of the pan plus 6 oz.) and mix into the butter and sugar, etc., with the walnuts, lemon juice and rind and salt. Turn into the pastry case. Bake for about ¾ hour at Mark 4, 350°F, until the filling is lightly browned and risen. Eat warm or cold, and serve with single cream.

Cheese and walnuts

A walnut cheese from France is on sale in many grocers these days. The walnuts are fine, but the cheese is soapy, processed and unrewarding. This recipe, from *Pottery*, a pamphlet by Cyril Connolly's father, is a great improvement.

> 8 oz. Cheddar cheese
> 3 oz. fresh butter
> 1 mustardspoon made mustard
> 1 tablespoon Chili vinegar
> 12 chopped walnuts (24 halves)

Rub the cheese through a wire sieve, mix in butter smoothly, stir mustard with vinegar and mix again; add walnuts chopped very finely. Press mixture into small jars and cover very thinly with butter.

For variety a little paprika may be mixed in.

Walnut oil

Walnut oil may once have been popular all over Europe with painters, for mixing 'white and other delicate colours, also for gold size and varnish', but its use in cookery has been confined to kitchens of the walnut districts of France. In other words one will not find it mentioned in manuals of bourgeoise and haute cuisine. Turn instead to the regional cookery books of Perigord, Burgundy and Touraine.

It may be that there has never been a great deal of walnut oil to spare – certainly it holds no place in the fat-consumption statistics of France – but we are able to buy it in one or two places in this country (Louis Roche, 14 Old Compton Street, Soho, London W1; Elizabeth David Ltd, 46 Bourne Street, London SW1). It's worth making an effort to find some, as the delicious flavour adds variety to many salads we take for granted.

Dressing: 1 dessertspoon wine vinegar, 4 dessertspoons walnut oil; season with salt, freshly ground black pepper, French mustard, sugar and garlic to taste.

'Chapon': a good addition to green salads and soups – cut a slice of white bread per person. Rub it over lightly with crushed garlic, and cut into cubes or triangles. Fry to golden brown in walnut oil.

Green salads: lettuce, batavia, lambs' tongues, endive, chicory, with walnut oil dressing and *chapons*. Garnish with hard-boiled egg, or a few shelled walnuts.

Touraine salad: diced cooked potatoes, cooked green beans sliced, and small haricot beans soaked and cooked. Bind with mayonnaise made with walnut oil. Sprinkle with chopped tarragon and parsley.

Anjou salad: vegetables as for Touraine salad, with walnut oil dressing.

Potato salad: slice boiled waxy potatoes while hot. Put into the salad bowl with 2 or 3 tablespoons white wine. Leave for half an hour, turning over after 10 and 20 minutes. Add walnut oil dressing, plus a dessertspoon chopped mild onion or shallots. Garnish with slices of hard-boiled egg and pickled gherkins.

Tomato salad: peel and slice 1 lb. tomatoes. Leave for several hours with salt, pepper, a dusting of sugar and a generous teaspoon brandy. Drain and dress with walnut oil dressing. Garnish with thinly cut rings of mild onion. (Brandy and sugar are great improvers of our tasteless, commercially grown tomatoes.)

Leek salad: in other words Poor Man's Asparagus, and asparagus itself, are delicious with walnut oil dressing, and chopped hard-boiled egg mixed with some chopped parsley.

Cress and walnut salad: 1 bunch watercress, 2 oz. Gruyère diced, 1 eating apple, cored and diced, 4 oz. shelled walnuts, 1 tablespoon chopped onion, 3–4 hard-boiled eggs quartered. Walnut oil dressing.

Dessert and Fruit Liqueurs

Five French Cakes

Pâtisserie need not be left to professional pastrycooks. One's first attempt at a *Villesalem* or a *gâteau St-Honoré* may lack style, but there is no reason, given the right ingredients, why it should not be extremely edible. Slimmers may call such things the works of the devil: the particular devil was in fact the great chef Carême, who turned his intellect and incorruptible skill to reviving French cookery after the Revolution.

He began with *pâtisserie*; he considered it a branch of architecture, making up the designs from rococo and neo-classical engravings (later nineteenth-century elaborate plaster ceilings are referred to, slightly disparagingly, as *pâtisserie*). His masters were the masters of Europe. Europe's diplomacy in fact revolved round his original *pièces montées*. As for the content of his confections, rather more important, Carême improved old recipes and invented new ones; and so inspired a magnificent century of inventive pastrycooks. If I go into English cake shops, home-made genteel ones, alongside cathedrals, I reflect sadly that

Carême *might* have reformed our confectionery too (how about a Dec. or Perp. *pièce montée?*). He did come to England to work for the Prince Regent, but went home when the Prince became concerned about the weight of the Royal Belly. 'My job,' he remarked, 'is to stimulate Your Highness's appetite, not to curb it.'

It is Carême's spirit which survives in the *pâtisseries* of most small towns in France, working for the Sunday lunch, the First Communion and weddings. And for the discerning French appetite.

The main essential in French cake-making is not so much cream as unsalted butter, liqueurs, almonds (don't buy ready-blanched, ready-flaked packages – with half the flavour gone), farm eggs, finely flavoured plain chocolate (Velma Suchard, I am sorry to say at 10p the 100 gramme block), and caster sugar which has been imbibing flavour in its screw-top jar from a vanilla pod. It helps if you have an electric mixer and a sugar thermometer.

The following five cakes, and many other recipes, in the French repertoire, involve the simple making of six subsidiaries: three containers, two fillers and a flavouring. The containers are puff pastry, choux pastry and sweet shortcrust pastry. For the first two kinds, follow any good general cookery manual. For the sweet shortcrust, follow the usual method but with these ingredients: 8 oz. plain flour sifted with 1 oz. each caster and icing sugar, a pinch of salt, 4 oz. unsalted butter, and 1 medium egg to bind the mixture together.

The two fillers are *crème pâtissière* and French butter cream, the flavouring is praline powder:

Crème pâtissière, or confectioner's custard, is widely used in France where we might use cream. Bring to the boil 1 pint milk containing a short piece of vanilla pod. Pour on to 4 egg yolks and 1 whole egg, beaten together in a large basin. Whisk in ½ lb. vanilla sugar and 2 oz. flour. Set the basin over a pan of simmering water and stir until custard is thick and cooked (about 25 minutes). Keep testing, and remove the vanilla pod when the flavour is strong enough. Strain into a clean bowl, fold in ½ oz. gelatine dissolved in 2 tablespoons hot water. For *gâteau St-Honoré*, to lighten the cream, 4 stiffly beaten egg whites are added to the mixture: this is called *crème Chiboust*, in honour of the pastrycook, who invented the cake about 1879. His shop was in the rue St Honoré in Paris, at that time the street of pastry-cooks and bakers.

Butter cream. Put 4 oz. caster sugar and 1 tablespoon of water into a heavy pan and heat to the small-crack stage (280°F on the sugar thermometer). But as a rough guide, a little of the melted sugar syrup dropped into cold water should form fine, hard threads – chill the water with ice-cubes first). Pour quickly on to 2 egg yolks, stirring with a fork. When this mixture is nearly cold, mix in 4 oz. unsalted butter. This is much more satisfactory and subtle in flavour than the slap-happy English system of beating icing sugar and ordinary salted butter together.

Butter cream à l'anglaise. A very super French recipe – in spite of the name. Bring 1½ gills of milk to the boil. Meanwhile put the yolks of 6 eggs into a bowl with 7 oz. of sugar and beat them to a thick foam. Pour on the boiling milk, stirring well. Return to the fire (over a pan of simmering water, if you want to be safe) and stir with a wooden spoon until the custard thickly coats the spoon. Strain it into a clean bowl and leave this custard – *crème anglaise* – to cool. Put 14 oz. of unsalted butter into a bowl over a pan of hot water. Beat with a wooden spoon until it turns to a cream; don't let it melt. Stir in the cooled custard (take the butter off its pan of hot water first).

These creams can be flavoured in various ways. With 4 oz. of plain chocolate, melted, to 8 oz. of butter cream. Or with 1 table-spoon of Nescafé, mixed to a paste with a teaspoon of boiling water. Or with 1 dessertspoon of liqueur. Or with:

Praline powder – the best flavouring in confectionery apart from the liqueurs. Take ½ lb. blanched, split almonds, and roast them to pale golden brown in the oven. Melt ½ lb. sugar in a heavy pan with 4 tablespoons of water. As it becomes a thick syrup, add the almonds, cooking until the whole thing is toffee-coloured. Pour out onto a sheet of buttered greaseproof paper. Break into pieces when cold, store in an airtight jar and powder in an electric coffee mill, or with a wooden rolling pin, as required. Use about 4 oz. of this praline powder to 8 oz. of butter cream.

And now the five cake recipes:

Paris-Brest

> choux pastry made with 4 oz. flour
> 2 oz. blanched almonds
> ½ pint cream, whipped
>   or ½ lb. butter cream
> 4 oz. praline powder
> icing sugar

Pipe the choux paste into a circle on a greased baking tray, a circle about the size of a dinner plate. Sprinkle the top with split and slivered almonds. Invert a biscuit tin over the paste. Bake for 20 minutes in a hot oven (Mark 7, 425°F), 10 minutes at Mark 4, 350°F. Slice across into two while hot, and leave to cool. Just before the meal, sandwich the two pieces together with plenty of whipped cream or butter cream, flavoured with praline powder. Dredge with icing sugar. Like all choux pastry, this cake will not appreciate standing around, or being kept until next day, with the filling in it.

Gâteau St-Honoré

'One day when Honorius, Bishop of Amiens, was celebrating mass, a divine hand sent down a loaf of bread. Thereupon the bakers adopted him as their patron saint.'

> 4 oz. sweet shortcrust pastry
> 4 oz. choux pastry
> ½ lb. sugar
> ½ pint water
> *crème Chiboust,* p. 328
>   or whipped and sweetened cream
> glacé fruits and toasted almonds
> (optional)

Use a dinner plate to cut a circle of sweet shortcrust pastry. Lay it on a greased baking sheet and prick with a fork all over. Pipe a smooth ring of choux pastry just inside the edge of the circle, then pipe 8 or 10 small balls of choux paste on a separate baking tray. Bake the circle in a hot oven (Mark 7, 425°F) for 25 minutes, without opening the oven door. Then bake the tray of puffs at the same temperature for 15–20 minutes.

Bring sugar and water to the crack stage in a thick pan (280°F, turns to threads in cold water). Dip each small puff into the syrup, so that it acquires a transparent toffee cap. Dip the opposite end into the syrup and stick it on to the choux wall of the pastry circle. (The final effect of this cake is rather like Old King Cole's

crown.) When the cake is cool, not too long before serving it, fill the centre with *crème Chiboust*, or with whipped cream. If you like, decorate with glacé fruits and toasted almonds.

Villesalem

The Villesalem monastery is a beautiful ruin of a place, a mile or two outside the Vienne town of Montmorillon, where the owner and master-cook, Monsieur Mercier, of the Hôtel de France produces this exquisite delicacy at the end of a fine meal. He has sent me his recipe:

For 10 Villesalem:

500 grammes of Velma Suchard
    chocolate
butter cream, 1st recipe on p. 329
10 boudoir biscuits
2 tablespoons each Grand Marnier,
    cognac and *marc*
crystallized fruit

You will also need 10 bucket-shaped paper cases about 2¾ inches high and 1½ inches across the top. Or any other paper case for cakes that you can buy – the bucket shape is difficult to find.

Melt the chocolate in a basin at the side of the stove or over hot water. Fill a paper case using a small ladle. Immediately pour the chocolate back into the basin. A layer of chocolate will have adhered to the paper. Turn it upside down on to a baking sheet and continue with the other 9 cases. Refrigerate. Keep the remaining chocolate to one side.

Make the butter cream. Soak the biscuits in the three alcohols (use extra brandy if you have no *marc*) until they are impregnated but not mushy. Chop the crystallized fruit. Warm the baking sheet very gently and remove the chocolate cases. Fill each one with a layer of butter cream, some fruit, a layer of biscuits and a final layer of butter cream. Refrigerate. Cover each cake with a lid of chocolate, re-melted and smeared on with a palette knife. Refrigerate again, peel off the paper cases (a damp cloth makes this easier) and there are your ten *Villesalem.*

Note: it's sometimes difficult finding the right-shaped paper cases. One has to improvise. Buy some small fluted cake cases, the kind stocked by any grocer or stationer. Stand one in each hole of a small tartlet tin, preferably of the smooth-sided kind. This is essential, as the melted chocolate will flatten out the fluted paper if it's not supported. Put a good spoonful of melted chocolate into each paper case, and as it cools mould it up the sides to the top. Not a quick job, but a peaceful one. It doesn't matter if the inside looks a bit rugged, as it won't show when the cakes are filled, but try and get the chocolate as even as you can. Put into the refrigerator to set, and then follow the recipe as usual.

Naturally these chocolate cases can be made well in advance, and stored in airtight tins. Their shape will not be so *soigné* as the Villesalem, but they are still impressive by comparison with the cakes one can buy in this country.

Gâteau de Pithiviers Feuilleté

Having adapted this recipe from Carême, who published it a century and a half ago, I was delighted to find that an exactly similar almond mixture is still being used in the *Peché Mignon* restaurant, set among chestnut trees in the Beauce town of Pithiviers. When you have made the cake a few times, vary it by the addition of a roasted, minced pig's kidney. The filling will taste interestingly granular – nobody will be able to guess why. Incidentally, they no longer make this addition at Pithiviers, which is, I think, a pity.

Puff pastry made with 8 oz. flour and 8 oz. butter.

> *filling:*
> 4 oz. each ground almonds and caster
>   sugar
> 1½ oz. melted butter
> 2 egg yolks
> 2 tablespoons double cream
> 1 roasted, minced kidney (optional)
>
> *glaze:*
> 1 beaten egg
> icing sugar

Roll out the pastry. Use half to line a greased enamel or tin plate (9½ inches diameter). Mix the filling ingredients together, preferably in a blender, until smooth. Put into the pastry-lined plate, leaving the flat rim free. Brush the rim with the beaten egg (glaze ingredients), fasten on the lid of puff pastry, pressing it down round the edges. Make a small central hole, brush over with beaten egg and leave for five minutes in a cool place.

Using a knife, nick the edge of the pastry twelve times at

regular intervals. Push up the pastry on either side of each nick to form a scalloped, rose petal edge. Score light inner scallops, and then long curving lines from the central hole outwards to designate formal petals. Be careful not to cut through the pastry.

Bake for 10 minutes in a very hot oven (Mark 8, 450°F), then lower the heat to Mark 6, 400°F and bake for 30 minutes. Dredge with icing sugar and return to a very hot oven – the sugar will turn to a dark brown glaze. Serve warm with single cream.

Gâteau de Pithiviers Fondant

The other Pithiviers cake is also an almond mixture, but this time without the pastry. It has a rich, moist texture inside and a crisp outer crust. I bake it as a fairly thin cake to serve with coffee and dessert. For more than six people the quantities should be doubled.

> 4 oz. each ground almonds, icing sugar
>   and melted butter
> 3 egg yolks
> 3 oz. flour
>
> *icing:*
>
> 6 oz. icing sugar
> 1½ tablespoons hot water
> glacé cherries and angelica

Mix the cake ingredients together. Line a shallow sponge tin or a flan tin with removable base, about 7–9½ inches diameter, with kitchen foil. Brush it lightly with corn oil, or melted butter. Put in the cake mixture and spread it out; it will need a little space to rise, but not much. Bake for 40 minutes, or until cooked, at Mark 4, 350°F. (Should you be doubling the quantities and making a thicker cake, it would be prudent to bake it at Mark 3, 325°F for about an hour. At a higher temperature the outside will become too crusty before the inside is cooked.)

Let the cake stand for 5 minutes when you take it out of the oven, then raise it gently by means of the foil lining. Lay it on a wire rack to cool. Then turn the cake over carefully, remove the foil and ice it, using a knife blade dipped in hot water and dried to push the icing evenly about. Decorate with glacé cherries and angelica and leave to harden. This cake keeps well in an airtight tin.

Water and Cream Ices

Home-made water and cream ices can be delicious. And they are easy to make as long as you have an ordinary refrigerator with a freezing compartment. In their simplicity they seem entirely the product of modern technology, serving our modern desire for convenience.

Most people, I think, would credit the first ices to the Italians (they do, after all, make the best in the world, and many of our refrigerators come from Italian factories these days), or to the Americans, who designed and manufactured the first household fridges at the beginning of the twentieth century.

Both guesses would be wrong. Water ices in particular have a much longer history. The business of refrigeration started with the Chinese. As early as the third century B.C., someone worked out that blocks of river ice could be stored underground, in a dry place, until the hot weather arrived. The miracle of ice in summer to cool food and drink.

By the T'ang dynasty, in the eighth century, magistrates in cold corners of the empire were well organized in supplying ice for the

icepits and ice-houses of the great palace at Changan. Royal refreshment included water-melons brought up from cold storage,
and served in jade bowls on beds of ice (the nearest thing in
nature to a water ice is the crisp, chill flesh of water-melon).
There was iced tea, and, for one young emperor, milk mixed with
snow-like flakes of camphor and frozen in an ice-box – the first
dairy ice cream?

A description of the ices of those times by a lady of the
eleventh-century Japanese court, Sei Shonagon, makes one think
of an Italian granita: 'chips of ice mixed with fruit juice and served
in a new silver bowl'.* How refreshing, how elegant that ice must
have been, semi-liquid, a little grainy to the tongue.

Ices did not arrive in Britain until centuries later. They had a
long journey to make along the silk road to the Middle East – our
words sorbet and sherbet derive from *shariba*, Arabic for a drink,
a cool drink naturally – then to Renaissance Italy, and then to
seventeenth-century France. It was Charles II who built the first
ice-house in Britain in 1660, soon after his Restoration (no doubt
he licked his first ice at the French court, in exile). He included it
in his improvements to St James's park –

> Yonder the harvest of cold months laid up,
> Gives a fresh coolness to the royal cup,
> There ice, like crystals, firm and never lost,
> Tempers hot July with December's frost.

No doubt the ice came from there to make the first ice cream
known to have been eaten in England, at Windsor Castle in
1677.

Those who could afford this royal innovation soon followed
suit and in time most estates acquired an ice-house. A few of
them have survived the invention of refrigerators – the ice-house
at Rufford Abbey was in use still in the 1930s – but shabbily by
comparison with more decorative souvenirs of China such as
orangeries and grottoes.

Nowadays the water ices of the Jade Kingdom, and the cream
ices of the Stuarts, are within everyone's reach. This we owe to
the development of commercial, then domestic refrigeration in
the nineteenth and early twentieth centuries. One thing, though, I

*The Pillow Book of Sei Shonagon, Oxford University Press, 1967. Trans-
lated and edited by Ivan Morris.

do not understand. More and more people buy refrigerators. Ices, granite and sorbets in particular are easy to make. Yet the sales of brand ice creams are still enormous (would they be affected, I wonder, if ingredients and their quantities were clearly printed on the wrappers?). This is such a pity. I've never bought an ice in this country to match the ones made with so little trouble at home.

Lemon granita and lemon sorbet

Two warnings first of all. Lemon ices must have a pure, direct flavour so do not be tempted to use bottled lemon juice, and do not squeeze the lemons so thriftily that the juice is embittered by the pith of the fruit – a point to watch if you use an electric juicer.

> ½ pint lemon juice
> 10 oz. sugar
> 1 pint water
> 2 egg whites (for the sorbet)

Simmer sugar and water in a pan for 5 minutes. Cool, then flavour with the lemon juice: the full half pint may not be necessary if the lemons were particularly good. Strain into ice-trays and cover with silver foil (or use a plastic box with a lid). Set the refrigerator to the lowest possible temperature, and leave it half an hour before putting the ice into the freezing compartment. If you are using a *sorbetière*, follow its freezing instructions.

It's most important to stir the frozen sides of the mixture into the more liquid middle part every so often. With shallow trays this needs to be done every half hour; deep boxes can be left for much longer.

In 2 to 3 hours – the time depends on the depth of the mixture – you will have a thick mush of iced granules. This is what the Italians call a granita. Serve it in tall glasses, with almond biscuits (see page 353). I don't think that whipped cream goes well with citrus water ices, but this is a matter of personal taste.

In 3 to 4 hours you will have a firm but not impenetrable block of water ice ready to be turned into a sorbet. Beat the egg whites in a large bowl until they're stiff (use an electric beater if possible), then add spoonfuls of the ice gradually. If this is done too fast, sploshes of ice fly about the kitchen. Properly done the mixture blows up to a mass of white foam. Refreeze in a larger container until the sorbet has the consistency of firm snow: it is not necessary to stir this egg white mixture. Serve in biscuit flowers (page 352), or in wide glasses.

Lime sorbet

Occasionally limes are on sale in Sainsbury's and the better greengrocers' shops. They may seem expensive, but they are very juicy and make an exquisite ice. If you can only afford a couple of limes, add the cool syrup to their juice until it tastes very fresh and not too sweet.

> 5 limes
> 10 oz. sugar
> 1 pint water
> 2 egg whites (optional)

Follow the recipe for lemon sorbet (or granita).

Grape water ice

Most fruit can be turned into a good sorbet or granita, but black grapes provide a flavour which is rich and subtle compared with the simpler flavours of orange or peach. Particularly when they are reinforced with a muscatel dessert wine, or brandy. White grapes produce a lighter-tasting ice of golden transparency – it will be improved by a white wine which has a pronounced grapey flavour.

1 lb. grapes
¼ lb. sugar
¼–½ pint water
3 tablespoons of dessert wine, or a
      glass of white wine, or a liqueur glass
      of brandy
Juice of 1 lemon
1 or 2 egg whites (optional)

The method is similar to the recipe for lemon ice, but one has first to produce a fruit purée. Cut the grapes in half and mangle them through a *mouli-légumes*, or liquidize for a few seconds. Make a syrup of the sugar and ¼ pint water. When it is cool add the grape purée and strain. Flavour to taste with lemon juice. Dilute with the extra water if required.

Freeze in the usual way, adding the wine or brandy at the end. For instance with a granita, pour the wine in gradually at the last stirring; with a sorbet, add the wine when ice and beaten egg white are mixed together.

Serve with slightly sweetened whipped cream, and almond biscuits.

Strawberry or raspberry water ice

1 lb. strawberries or raspberries
10 oz. sugar
½–1 pint water
juice of 1 lemon
juice of 1 orange
4 tablespoons orange liqueur, or kirsch
2 egg whites (optional)

These two excellent ices can be made with frozen fruit, very successfully. Add the syrup gradually to the purée and stop before the mixture is too sweet – fruit varies so much in flavour that this is always a wise precaution. Follow the method for grape water ice above.

Blackcurrant sorbet

> 1 lb. blackcurrants
> 10 oz. sugar
> ¾–1 pint water
> dessertspoon lemon juice
> 4 tablespoons *crème de cassis* (optional)
> 2 egg whites (optional)

Follow the method for grape water ice. There is no doubt that water ices particularly are improved by alcoholic additions. If you cannot buy *crème de cassis*, use kirsch instead.

Cherry water ice

This Victorian recipe takes time and patience, but if you grow your own cherries you will find it worth while.

> 1 lb. morello cherries
> 6 blanched and bruised almonds
> 10 oz. sugar
> 1 pint water
> juice of 1 lemon
> 4 tablespoons kirsch (optional)
> 2 egg whites (optional)

Stone the cherries and crush them. Extract kernels from cherry stones and bruise them. Add to the syrup, with the almonds, while it's still hot. Strain into the cherry pulp when cold, and freeze in the usual way.

Iced orange

Ice-filled oranges, arranged in a plain white dish with sprigs of bay leaves, make a refreshing and beautiful end to rich dinners. The orange containers can be prepared in advance, like the water ice, and are not too difficult to deal with.

Choose large brilliant oranges, one for each person. Slice a neat cap from the stem end, and just enough from the opposite end to stop the orange keeling over on the serving dish. With a sharp knife cut a little way down the cap end, between segments and pith. Then slide in a dessertspoon, pressing the flesh inwards so that it separates from the pith neatly and can be removed. This works well so long as the spoon moves outside the skin of the segments. Press the pulp in a sieve over a bain – the juice can be used in one of the following recipes, or for drinks.

(Lemons and good-sized eating apples can be scooped out and filled with ice in the same way as oranges.)

> ¾ pint orange juice
> 1 pint water
> 6 oz. sugar
> juice of 1 lemon
> 3 tablespoons orange liqueur, or
>   orange flower water
> 2 egg whites (optional)

Follow the grape ice recipe above. Chill the oranges before filling them with water ice. To store, wrap them in foil and leave in the ice-making compartment of the refrigerator (or in a deep-freeze).

> 6 oz. can concentrated orange juice
> 2 heaped tablespoons sugar
> 2 heaped tablespoons maraschino or brandy
>   (optional)
> 1 egg white (optional)

Make a syrup of the sugar and 1 pint of water, as for lemon sorbet on page 338, by boiling them together for 5 minutes. Pour into a

2-pint measuring jug and leave to cool. Stir in the orange juice and enough water to bring the mixture up to 1¼ pints. Freeze in the usual way, adding liqueur and beaten egg white if required.

Peach and orange ice

Don't despise this American recipe because the fruit is canned – the combination of flavours is most successful. Use white peaches if you can, they are more finely piquant than the yellow ones.

> ½ pint sieved canned peaches
> ½ pint orange juice
> 4 oz. sugar
> dessertspoon lemon juice

Mix together until the sugar is dissolved. Freeze to a granita, stirring every half hour. Fresh strawberry pulp, or canned apricot pulp may be substituted for peaches – they all combine well with orange juice.

Granita al caffè con panna

On holiday in Italy in the heat, one rapidly discovers two surprising things – that *caffè espresso* is far more refreshing than water, or even a pink slice of water-melon, and that bought ices can taste deliciously clear and subtle. (The second discovery can be quite a shock after experiences of raspberry ripple, choc bars and iced lollies.) These two bits of wisdom soon lead one to the finest of all water ices, *granita al caffè*, which combines the stimulus of black coffee with the refreshment of intense cold. And do not forget the important words *'con panna'* – with cream – because whipped cream sets off perfectly the bitter-sweet granules of blackish-brown ice.

Use finely ground espresso coffee if you can buy it, otherwise a continental, after-dinner roast;

12 slightly rounded tablespoons coffee
2–3 oz. sugar
2 pints water

Warm a stoneware jug, put in the coffee and then the water which should be boiling. Stir well and leave in a warm place for 10 minutes to brew. Strain off and sweeten with 2 oz. sugar. When cold, pour twice through apiece of sheeting or doubled muslin. Add more sugar if required. Freeze in the usual way, stirring every half hour until the mixture is a mush of granules. Serve in tall glasses with a generous swirl of whipped cream on top.

Wine sherbet

Here is another superb water ice. To me it's the judgement of Paris, trying to decide between *granita al caffè*, this sherbet made with *muscat de Frontignan*, or the black grape water ice above.

Champagne or sweet sparkling wine can be used as the flavouring for the syrup, but Frontignan, or a similar muscatel dessert wine, is a more economical choice as such wines do not spoil with a little keeping, once the bottle has been opened.

½ pint wine
4 oz. sugar
½ pint water
juice of 1 lemon
juice of 1 orange

Make a syrup of sugar and water by simmering for 5 minutes. Cool, then add the other ingredients and freeze to a granita. Serve in champagne flutes, with a topping of slightly sweetened whipped cream, and some almond or vanilla biscuits (see page 353).

Grand Marnier water ice

Orange liqueurs make a very successful water ice, so does *crème de cassis*. Here are the proportions for liqueur ice:

> 12 oz. sugar
> scant 1¼ pints water
> juice of 1 lemon
> generous ¼ pint Grand Marnier

Make a syrup of the sugar and water. Cool and add the lemon juice. Freeze in the usual way, and when almost at the granita stage stir in the liqueur. Freeze until almost solid. Serve in glasses, with whipped cream flavoured with Grand Marnier.

Cream Ices

Although I like eating water ices better than cream ices, it's the latter I prefer to make. Their flavouring can be a most delicious exercise in ingenuity. The one thing not to forget is the word 'cream' – milk is no substitute as it turns to watery granules when frozen (unless it's combined with so many egg yolks that you might as well have bought cream in the first place).

There are four basic ways of making a good cream ice: one can add cream to a water ice mixture, or to a sweetened fruit purée, one can use cream alone with various flavourings, or – most successfully of all – one can mix a rich custard with cream.

Water ice method

> Ingredients for a water ice, minus egg whites
> ¼ pint each double and single cream

Follow the water ice methods (pp. 338–45), but fold in beaten cream instead of beaten egg white.

This produces a light cream ice which is very refreshing in hot weather. The following recipes are all very much richer in texture and flavour. This sounds expensive, and indeed it's not cheap, but heavier ices are eaten in much smaller quantities.

Ices made with cream only

This is the simplest, quickest way of making good ice cream. For perfect texture and flavour, it's true that you need a cream and custard mixture (see pp. 348–50), but this is a useful second best when unexpected visitors arrive for a meal. And on hot days when you don't want to spend time over a stove.

The flavouring can be nuggets of candied fruit or ginger, grated chocolate, toasted nuts, or a glass of orange, chocolate or coffee liqueur. Or more homely ingredients such as wholemeal bread and oatmeal – the results do not taste homely at all:

> ½ pint each double and single cream
> 6 oz. vanilla sugar (see below)
> 6 oz. wholemeal breadcrumbs, or
>   3 oz. oatmeal
> 2 oz. granulated sugar
> 4 tablespoons water

Whip creams and vanilla sugar to a light thick mass. Freeze (in shallow trays for extra speed) at the lowest possible temperature, turning sides to middle when they begin to harden. Toast the breadcrumbs in the oven to a crisp golden-brown (for Brown Bread ice cream); or dry rather than toast the oatmeal until it's hard and crunchy and slightly brown (Caledonian ice cream). Boil the granulated sugar and water together for a few minutes and leave to cool: syrup from preserved ginger, chow-chow or fruit in brandy can be substituted when these flavourings are being used.

When the cream is solid, but not rocklike, transfer it to a basin. Mix the breadcrumbs or oatmeal with the syrup and immediately stir into the ice cream, beating the mixture well. Refreeze. Serve with thin biscuits or oatcakes. A stiffly beaten egg white may also be folded in after the crumbs or oatmeal. This makes the mixture lighter (and bulkier).

To make vanilla sugar: Put a vanilla pod and plenty of caster sugar into a large screw-top jar. Leave for a week or two, and always keep the jar filled up, as the vanilla pod will impart its wonderful flavour for many months.

For quick vanilla sugar, pulverize a 3-inch piece of vanilla pod with 4 oz. sugar. This produces a fine, black-speckled powder which should be mixed with caster sugar until the flavour is insistent but not overpowering.

Biscuit Tortoni

Tortoni's was an Italian establishment which opened in Paris at the very beginning of the nineteenth century. Victor Hugo, Dumas and de Musset all came to enjoy the delicious food, which was served buffet style. Outside in the street, ladies ate the famous ices, brought to them in their carriages (it was not yet respectable for women to be seen in restaurants). Ices which were better and creamier than any served in Paris before. This particular recipe was invented by Tortoni's son in honour of his father – a 'biscuit' is an oblong ice cream, which is cut down into slices for serving.

> ½ pint each double and single cream
> 2 oz. icing sugar
> ¼ pint hard macaroon crumbs
> 1 glass brown sherry
> pinch of salt
> extra icing sugar and macaroon crumbs

Whip the creams with the 2 oz. of icing sugar and the salt, and freeze until just firm. Transfer to a basin and fold in the macaroon crumbs and sherry. Add more sugar if necessary. Freeze in an oblong plastic box or metal loaf tin. Turn out and decorate with a sprinkling of macaroon crumbs.

The best way of turning out the ice cream is to invert the whole thing on to a serving dish, and then to put a cloth wrung out in very hot water round the metal mould. This should free the ice cream. Dipping the mould into a bowl of hot water, or running it under the hot tap, can soften the ice cream too much.

Cream and custard ices

This recipe makes the best textured and best flavoured ice cream. It takes longer to make than the pure cream ices above, and it's more expensive, but there's no better recipe. Milk can be substituted for the single cream, but it brings a watery granular element into the mixture which is out of place.

> ½ pint each double and single cream
> 4–6 egg yolks
> 5–6 oz. vanilla sugar

Bring the single cream just up to the boil, then pour it on to the egg yolks beating vigorously. Stir in about 4 oz. of sugar. Set the pan over a basin of simmering water, and whisk or stir until the mixture thickens to a custard. Strain and leave to cool. Whip the double cream, fold it into the custard and add more sugar (or the flavouring you have chosen, see below). Freeze at the lowest possible temperature in a metal mould. Turn the sides to middle when they begin to harden. Serve with thin almond or vanilla biscuits.

VARIATIONS

Chocolate: flavour the custard with coffee essence or instant coffee. Tia Maria may be added when the mixture is cold. Fold in 3 oz. of chocolate chips, or grated chocolate, after adding the whipped cream.

Prune: soak, stew and purée 8 oz. dried prunes. Sweeten slightly and flavour with rum when cool. Mix in with the cooled custard, before adding cream. Taste and add more rum if necessary. Serve with walnut (page 320) or almond biscuits (page 353).

Walnut and rum: add 4 oz. shelled and grated walnuts to the single cream before heating it. When the custard has cooled, liquidize then sieve it (this extracts the maximum flavour from the nuts, and removes the gritty bits that always seem to remain). Or put the custard through the finest plate of the *mouli-légumes.* Beat in the whipped cream, and flavour discreetly with rum – just enough to enrich the flavour without being really recognizable.

Other nuts can be substituted for walnuts. With almonds, kirsch is a better flavouring than rum.

Honey and orange: add a tablespoon of honey to the hot custard. When the mixture is cool, add the juice of a large orange, some orange liqueur and the whipped cream. Do not overdo the honey.

Nesselrode: said to have been invented by M. Mony, chef to the great Russian diplomat and foreign minister, Count Nesselrode. He was a friend of Talleyrand, the French foreign minister – both men were devotees of good food. No doubt it drew them together. This is an ice for a special occasion.

To the ingredients for the cream and custard ice, you must add.

> 4 oz. unsweetened chestnut purée
> 1 oz. each seedless raisins and sultanas
> 1 oz. each glacé cherries and orange
>   peel, chopped
> 4 oz. Málaga wine (or sweet sherry)
> whipped cream and marrons glacés
>   to garnish

Add the chestnut purée to the custard when hot, and mix to a smooth paste. Soak raisins and sultanas in hot water for 1 hour, then put with the chopped cherries and orange peel into the Málaga for a further hour (drain off the surplus water first). Add the whipped cream to the custard and fold in the fruit and peel and wine. Freeze in the usual way, stirring up from time to time. Serve decorated with whipped cream and marrons glacés.

Mulberry: flavour to taste with mulberry syrup, p. 263.

Praline: flavour with the praline powder on p. 329. The best ice cream of all.

Cooked fruit ice cream

When one thinks of fruit being used to flavour ice cream, one thinks of strawberry, raspberry, peach or blackcurrant ice cream. In these the uncooked fruit is sieved to a purée and blended with cream or cream and custard (see the recipe following). One does not think of the hard fruits, or the dried fruits and fruits which need cooking as being suitable for ice cream. But they are. They give unusual and delicious flavours which sometimes puzzle people.

Apple (or pear) and quince ice cream

Water ice and whipped cream are the best ingredients for most soft fruit ice creams. For hard fruits such as apples and pears and quinces, or for dried fruits such as apricots and peaches, this is a good method:

> 8 oz. eating apples or pears ⎫ or 12 oz.
> 4 oz. quinces ⎬ apples or pears
> 2 oz. unsalted butter
> 2 tablespoons water
> sugar to taste
> 2 eggs
> ¼ pint each single and double cream
> toasted almonds

Wash and cut up the fruit. Stew it slowly in a covered pan with the butter and water. Sieve to remove peel and cores. Flavour with sugar (if you are using apples alone add some apricot jam as well, or some cinnamon; with pears, lemon juice and a piece of cinnamon stick may be added as they stew). There should be about ½ pint of purée. Stir in the 2 egg yolks, beat well and reheat gently, keeping below the boil, for 5–10 minutes until the mixture thickens. Cool. Fold in the 2 creams, which should first be beaten together until thick, then freeze. When the mixture is almost solid, beat the egg whites and add spoonfuls of the frozen mixture until you have a thick frothy mass. Refreeze. Serve garnished with toasted almonds.

The beaten whites are an optional addition, but they lighten the ice cream in a very agreeable way. It's worth making an effort to find a supply of quinces (see page 256); they are a wonderful flavouring for apples and pears.

VARIATION

Iced Gooseberry Fool: substitute gooseberries for apples and quinces. Flavour with a muscatel dessert wine such as Frontignan. Or put a head of elderflower in with the gooseberries as they stew (page 273). Serve almond biscuits, and omit the garnish of toasted almonds.

Strawberry ice cream

This is a simple way of turning soft fruit which doesn't need cooking into ice cream. It can be adapted to raspberries, peaches (weigh the fruit after skinning and stoning), or mulberries. The quantities of sugar and citrus juices need to be adapted to the sharpness or sweetness of the fruit.

> ½ lb. strawberries
> 4 oz. icing sugar
> juice of ½ lemon
> juice of ½ orange
> ½ pint whipping cream,
>   or ¼ pint each double and single
>   cream

Liquidize the fruit, or put it through a *mouli-lègumes*, then put it through a fine sieve to catch the seeds. Sweeten with sugar and sharpen with lemon and orange juice to emphasize the flavour. Whip the cream until it's stiff. Fold in the fruit purée, and freeze, at the lowest possible temperature, as usual. Garnish with fine strawberries.

Camembert ice cream

This unusual recipe from the thirties makes a good ending to the meal. The ice and the hot biscuits are an important part of the recipe:

> 1 Camembert, soft and mature, not
>   over-ripe
> ¼ pint each double and single cream
> Cayenne pepper or tabasco
> cracked ice
> hot water biscuits

Mash up (or liquidize) the cheese with the two creams. Season well with Cayenne or tabasco, and salt to taste. Freeze until just firm, but not hard. No need to stir. Serve sliced on a bed of cracked ice cubes, with the heated water biscuits in a separate dish.

Biscuit flowers

I am not one for fiddly cooking (particularly when the results are fattening), but I make an exception for these biscuit flowers to hold ice cream. The first ones you try may come to disaster. Don't despair; the quantities are enough for twelve flowers, which leaves plenty of chance for improvement.

3 oz. butter
3½ oz. vanilla sugar
1 egg
2 egg whites
4 oz. plain flour

Cream butter and sugar, add eggs and flour until the mixture turns to a smooth, thick batter. Cut vegetable parchment to fit a baking tray: on it, draw three circles with a 5-inch saucer. Turn the paper over and brush lightly with oil. Spread a generous teaspoon of batter over each circle. Bake at Mark 2, 300°F, for 10–20 minutes, watching the biscuits to see that they turn brown, not black, at the edges. Meanwhile oil the exterior of a Thermos mug (or the base of a ginger jar), and invert it on the table to act as a mould for the biscuits. When they are cooked, remove one of them and quickly slap it right side down on the oiled mould. Press gently, with a cloth, concentrating on the centre, and you will find that the edges cool into a wavy-edged flower. Transfer to an inverted cup and start on the second biscuit (keep the waiting biscuits warm in the oven, with the door ajar so that they don't over-cook).

Store in an airtight tin.

Almond biscuits

Unwanted egg whites are a problem in the mayonnaise and ice cream season. Here's a delicious solution. These biscuits go so well with mousses and creams and all kinds of ices that no one could accuse them of being made from leftovers.

4 egg whites
4 oz. ground almonds
4 oz. caster sugar
2 heaped teaspoons plain flour
rice paper (about 4 sheets)

Beat the egg whites until they are firm. Mix the other dry in-gredients, the almonds, sugar and flour, together and fold into the whites lightly but firmly.

Lay the rice paper on a baking tray (with the brand I buy, it takes two sheets to line the tray). Pipe the mixture on top in cat's tongue shapes. Bake at Mark 2, 300°F, for 10–20 minutes. Cool on a wire tray, then tear off the surplus rice paper.

The mixture can also be baked on greased trays, and then rolled into 'cigarettes' keeping the top side outside.

Store in an airtight tin.

Fruit Liqueurs and Ratafias

Fruit ratafias – fruit liqueurs made with brandy, not *eau de vie* distilled from the fruit itself – came to this country from France, like the word itself, in the seventeenth century. Brandy then was infinitely cheaper.

In France they are still abundantly made, particularly in the wine-growing areas. But the old habit may soon be on the way out. Little by little the right to have *eau de vie* distilled from *marc*, except commercially, is being phased out to reduce alcoholism, the extent of which is pretty terrifying in some French villages. Nowadays the licences die with their present owners. They can only be inherited by a widow or widower, not by the children or other relatives. Nor can a licence be sold with a vineyard: the previous owner must retain it, and cannot dispose of it to anyone else. One sees the point. But it will mean an impoverishment of the hospitality which has always been so marked in poor households in the wine districts of France. (It will also mean an end of the travelling *marc*-maker with his antique-looking still.)

One sits at an oilcloth-covered table, eating asparagus, *omelette aux fines herbes*, chicken cooked with morel mushrooms, salad, strawberries, fresh goat cheese, and drinking wine and liqueurs of quality. Hens walk in and out, dogs snore at one's feet with an eye half-open for chicken bones. Apart from bread, oil, coffee, sugar, everything has come from garden, vineyard, farmyard or commune woods. There will be no book, bathroom, television set or easy chair in the house. The normally divisive effect of poverty is not felt, because the host is well aware that few people in France can be offering their guests better food, and – more important – better drink.

Here are fruit liqueurs to make at home if you are prepared (1) to spend the money on brandy or *eau de vie de marc*, and (2) to wait for at least two months.

But then consider, you are turning one bottle of brandy into two or three bottles of liqueur, and you are storing up summer and autumn for mid-winter and Christmas. And the basis is not 3-star cognac, but the cheapest brandy you can find. Or gin, or better still vodka, which has no taste.

I shall be heretical and say that these fruit drinks (though admittedly you don't have the fun of creating the alcohol) are finer flavoured and more rewarding than the vast number of home-made 'wines' (which aren't wines, because *ipso facto* a wine is something made from the fruit of the vine). As with wines, though, you must not try to sell them, or you'll be in trouble with the Excise.

I find myself making bottles of one kind or another, and then putting them at the back of the cupboard and forgetting about them. The discovery months later is wonderful, promising a cordial end to meals and one which can be relied upon to delight other people.

There is little skill involved. Nothing can go wrong, unless you leave the bottles in too warm or too sunny a place.

These liqueurs are very good tempered. One friend tops up his sorb liqueur with brandy and syrup from time to time, particularly in a year when the sorbs have been very good. In another bottle he has finely pared orange peel submerged in brandy and syrup: every time he eats an orange, he adds to his bottle, putting in more brandy and syrup as the peel-level rises. I have a bottle of prunes in Armagnac; when I take out a few to serve with cream to an unexpected visitor, I replace them with unsoaked prunes and leave the bottle for at least another ten days before raiding it again.

It's worth making your own experiments. There are few fruits that can't produce a good liqueur; and some of the most unpromising – I'm thinking particularly of the fruits, the clustered berries, of the wild service tree – make the best of all. The guiding principle is that dry texture fruits and peel need preserving in syrup and brandy, soft fruits need only sugar and brandy (their juice supplies the place of water in syrup).

Sloe (and mulberry) gin

It may seem difficult to be enthusiastic about anything made with sloes. They set the mouth on edge. They nestle into a fakir's bed of thorns. One wonders how the welcomed blackthorn flowers of March and April could produce finally such bitter fruits. But don't be discouraged: sloes are easy to find (blackthorn grows all over northern Europe, but it's in this country that it flourishes most), and sloe gin is easy to drink.

Pick sloes on a dry day when they have been mellowed by an early frost. Remove the stalks and prick them all over with a darning needle.

To each ½ lb. fruit, allow ¾ pint gin, 2 oz. sugar and 6–10 blanched, bruised almonds. Bottle and leave for 3 months before straining and rebottling (large wide-mouthed bottling jars are the best to use for fruit liqueurs, though small fruit such as sloes and cherries can be put into ordinary wine bottles and corked firmly).

Mulberries make a finer drink, but they are more difficult to come by. Lucky the owner of an old garden with an ancient mulberry tree. Pick them when ripe and sweet and follow the above proportions. They will not need pricking.

Apricot or peach ratafia

Choose fruit which is ripe and has a good flavour. Avoid woolly
apricots or watery peaches. The kernels add a delicate almond
flavour, which is very good; it can be increased by adding some
blanched and bruised almonds.

> 12 large apricots, or generous lb.
>   peaches
> 1 pint brandy
> ½ lb. sugar
> ½ inch piece cinnamon stick
> 4 cloves
> ¼ teaspoon mace

Quarter the fruit (only the peaches need be peeled). Remove the
stones and extract and bruise the kernels. If peaches are used, cut
the pieces in half again. Add the kernels and the rest of the ingredients to the fruit, mixing well. Keep in tightly closed bottling
jars for at least a month before using; three months is better
still.

As with cherry brandy, there is no need to strain off and rebottle the liqueur. Many people like eating a piece of brandy-
soaked fruit with the drink; it can also be used in fruit salads,
mincemeat, or water ices.

Cherry brandy

Sweet dessert cherries are not used for this favourite English liqueur, but more acid-flavoured kinds like the morellos. There is, if
you can find it, a very suitable variety called ratafia. In France
where they are more popular than in Britain, varieties of sharp,
tangy-tasting guignes are used for liqueur making. These small
crimson-to-black cherries grow in many cottage gardens – sometimes a deserted site will have a tree of guignes still surviving,
although the cottage is in ruins or has long disappeared.

Cut the cherry stalks down to a quarter or half inch. Prick each cherry five or six times with a darning needle as you put it into the bottling jar, which should be filled. Pour granulated sugar into the jar until it comes just under halfway up the fruit. Add brandy to cover it. Fasten the lid and leave for at least 3 months – or 20 years. The fruit will be almost as delicious as the liqueur, which acquires the desirable almond flavour from the cherry stones.

This recipe can be followed using grapes, but the entire stalk should be removed.

Ratafia

To the small wine-growers of the Loire, who boast no *appellations contrôlées*, there is only one fruit brandy deserving the name of ratafia. Inevitably it is made from that fruit of fruits the grape; when it's cold, sweet juice pours from the *pressoirs* in an opaque purple stream. Four litres are taken from the barrel, and a litre of *eau de vie de marc* is added. This stops the juice fermenting. Sugar is not required with the high proportion of fruit juice to brandy. Of all the ratafias it tastes the freshest and most invigorating.

The best home *pressoir* is the *mouli-légumes* (or the liquidizer for 3 or 4 seconds only). Mouli the grapes until they are mangled, pips and all, but not reduced to a purée. Strain debris and juice through a double muslin, squeezing until the residue, the *marc*, is dry. Measure the juice and add a quarter or more of its volume in brandy. Bottle and leave to clear.

In his great cooking dictionary Alexandre Dumas gave a slightly different recipe for a ratafia of muscat grapes. Mangle, squeeze and measure the fruit as above, but add an equal quantity of brandy, plus sugar to taste. Leave to clear. The liqueur can then be poured off into clean bottles or jars.

Orange liqueur

6 very large oranges
1¾ pints brandy
1 lb. sugar
½ teaspoon coriander
1 inch cinnamon stick

Peel the oranges thinly – there must be no white pith adhering – and cut the peel into strips. Squeeze the oranges, and add the strained juice to the peel with the other ingredients. Put into bottling jars and cover tightly.

As I mentioned above, extra peel can be added to the liqueur when you eat an orange.

Quince ratafia

Anything made with quinces is bound to be delicious, and this ratafia is no exception. If the only ones you can buy are still green, let them ripen to yellow in the house. A word of warning – handle them carefully, as they are easily bruised.

Take 2 large quinces. Rub the grey down off them with a cloth, rinse and grate them, peel and core included. Put into a 2-pint bottling jar. Pour in granulated sugar to come about a third of the way up the bottle, add ¾ teaspoon each cinnamon, ginger and mace, then fill the bottling jar with brandy or vodka.

The reader who sent me this recipe remarks that the flavour of the quinces begins to predominate after only a week, that all fruit expel their flavours surprisingly soon. This is true, but I think that if these ratafias are left for a month or two or three, their taste seems to mellow and become more subtle.

Ratafia of red fruits

Assemble a medley of summer fruits – cherries, redcurrants, raspberries and mulberries. Bruise them and leave in a cool place for
3 days. Strain and add to the juice an equal quantity of brandy. To
each pint of this mixture add 4 oz. sugar, and a piece of cinnamon
stick about 1 inch long. Leave for two months.

Sorb, medlar and wild service liqueurs

'Chestnuts in their spiky cases, squashy medlars, and tart-tasting
sorb apples – the autumn drives before it a profusion of modest
fruits which one does not pick, but which fall into one's hands,
which wait patiently at the foot of the tree until man deigns to
collect them.'* I like these lines of Colette's (and recommend you
to search out the medlar and wild service or sorb trees of your
neighbourhood) because small tawny gold sorb apples and
medlars and the clusters of wild service berries make the best of
fruit liqueurs. One important point – make sure that the fruit is
bletted before it goes into the bottling jars, i.e. that it is darken-
ing and bruised in appearance, almost rotten, one might think,
with perhaps the beginnings of a white mould. Should the fruit be
hard when it's gathered, it should be laid on flat dishes in a warm
room until it reaches the desired state.

Make a syrup for these liqueurs, by simmering together $\frac{3}{4}$ lb.
sugar and $\frac{1}{2}$ pint water for five minutes. Leave to cool.

Fill bottling jars with the fruit. Add syrup, according to the
sweetness of the sorbs, medlars, or berries, either up to one third
of the height of the fruit, or to just under half. Top up – make sure
the fruit is covered – with brandy. Keep tightly covered for at
least 2 months. Better still for a year and 2 months.

*Translated by Derek Coltman for *Colette: Earthly Paradise* by Robert
Phelps, Secker & Warburg, 1966.

Eau de vie de poire

We have one friend, a resourceful Gaul of the Asterix breed, who is always busy with some new project connected, ultimately, with the pleasures of the belly. He may be smoking a ham from the family pig, or showing the children how to bottle the cider.

One day our daughter watched him tying wine bottles over several barely-formed pears on the espalier pear tree. What was he doing? Well, the pears would grow and ripen in their individual greenhouses. Then he would break the stems and fill the bottles up with a mixture of syrup (see recipe above) and *marc*. At Christmas and New Year, his pear liqueur would cause a sensation – like a ship in a bottle, but much better, because the contents of these bottles would be drinkable.

Even if you have no pear tree, there is no reason to go short of pear liqueur. Buy fruit of a good-flavoured variety such as Williams, and let them ripen in a warm kitchen. Cut in quarters, fill a bottling jar and add a mixture of ⅓ syrup and ⅔ brandy. Fasten tightly, and leave until Christmas, or for two months.

Pineapple liqueur

Choose a fine ripe pineapple, pare it and slice it thinly. In a wide-mouthed bottling jar arrange one slice on top of the other, following the shape of the pineapple. Pour in any juice that came out while preparing the pineapple, and then sugar to come up to half the height of the fruit. Then cover with brandy (the jar need not be full, but there should be more brandy than sugar, and the fruit must be covered as in all these recipes).

Leave for at least two months.

Eau de vie de noix, or Brou

Among the pleasures of the Corrèze, next door to the Dordogne, are the walnut orchards. Brilliant green grass – it rains in those parts – and small groups of elegant trees with grey trunks. The nuts go mainly to oil factories (see page 322) or to the markets, but some are turned into an excellent black liqueur known as *Brou*, *brou de noix* being the French for a green walnut.

The home-made liqueur is not so sweet or smooth. I think, though, that it's worth making as a flavouring, and to add to red wine in the Poitou style:

Quarter 6 fine green walnuts (at that summer stage of development when they are used for pickling). Put them in a bottling jar with ¾ pint brandy, cover tightly and leave for 2 months. Add 6 oz. sugar and ½ inch piece of cinnamon, and leave for another month. Pour off and rebottle.

A wineglass and a half (about 7 oz.) of this liqueur is often added to 1¼ pints red wine, to make *vin de noix*. Bottle and leave for 1 month. The balance of liqueur to wine may be altered according to taste: the liqueur itself can be made stronger or sweeter by adding more brandy or more sugar.

Prunes in brandy

This is a delicious preserve for the store cupboard. The prunes can be served in small glasses with the liqueur, or they can be presented as a dessert on their own and served with whipped cream and almond biscuits (page 353). Use giant prunes, which can be bought at health food stores.

Fill wide-mouthed bottling jars three-quarters full of prunes, unsoaked prunes, pushing a few curls of orange peel and a small stick of cinnamon, about 1 inch long, well down among the fruit. Make up a syrup by boiling sugar and water together, in the proportion of 3:2, i.e. 6 oz. sugar and ¼ pint water, for five minutes. Cool and pour into the jar so that it is between a third and a half full. Top up with Armagnac if possible, or with *marc* or grape brandy. I think vodka is too neutral.

Crème de cassis

Although Canon Felix Kir, who died in 1968 at the age of 92, was a hero of the French resistance, the immortality of his name is assured not by his courage but by an aperitif. He is said to have invented it with the idea of helping blackcurrant growers around Dijon, where he lived, to find a wider market for their fruit, or rather the liqueur made from it. (French children are not brought up on cordials of the Ribena type.) Kir consists simply of a glass of chilled, dry white wine – preferably from Burgundy – spiced with a teaspoonful of blackcurrant liqueur. For this alone it is worth trying a home-made *crème de cassis*: it's also a wonderful improver of blackcurrant sorbets (page 341), summer pudding, or properly made blackcurrant jellies.

> 1 lb. blackcurrants
> 1 pint brandy or gin
> ¾ lb. sugar
> ½ inch piece of cinnamon stick
> clove
> 5 young green blackcurrant leaves
>   (optional)

Break up the blackcurrants with your hands, or a fork, or with a *mouli-légumes*. Mix juice, debris and all the other ingredients in a large bowl. Put in an ordinary bottling jar, fasten and leave in a warm place (ideally the sun) for a month. Strain through a double muslin cloth, squeezing out the juice. Rebottle. It's now ready for use.

Tarragon liqueur

The important thing about this recipe is to get the right tarragon in the first place. You need the true French variety, *Artemisia dracunculus*, and not the coarse hardy Russian variety which has little flavour. It will flourish in a sunny window or balcony, and the more warmth it gets the better it will taste.

> 2 good handfuls of tarragon
> 1 pint brandy or *marc*
> ¾ lb. sugar
> ½ pint water

Put the tarragon, picked on a hot dry day, into a bottling jar. Pour on the brandy, fasten the jar tightly, and leave in a cool place for at least a month. At the end of this time make a syrup by boiling sugar and water together for 5 minutes. Let the syrup cool. Strain off the tarragon brandy into a bowl, and add the syrup to it gradually, tasting from time to time – no hardship. When the flavour appeals to you, stop adding syrup. If both tarragon flavour and sweetness seem too strong, add a little water. Throw away the tarragon, and pour the liqueur back into the bottling jar. One fresh tarragon branch may be added for appearance. Fasten up the jar, and use as required.

This liqueur is a pale green colour, not as bright as true Chartreuse, but the flavour is not dissimilar.

Note: blackcurrant and other soft fruit liqueurs can also be made by this method.

Weights and Measures and Oven Temperatures

Liquid Measures

British

1 quart	=	2 pints	=	40 fluid oz.
1 pint	=	4 gills	=	20 fl. oz.
½ pint	=	2 gills or one cup	=	10 fl. oz.
¼ pint	=	8 tablespoons	=	5 fl. oz.
		1 tablespoon	=	just over ½ fl. oz.
		1 dessertspoon	=	⅓ fl. oz.
		1 teaspoon	=	⅛ fl. oz.

Metric

I litre = 10 decilitres (dl.) = 100 centilitres (cl.) = 1000 millilitres (ml.)

Approx. equivalents

BRITISH	METRIC
1 quart	1·1 litre
1 pint	6 dl.
½ pint	3 dl.
¼ pint (1 gill)	1·5 dl.
1 tablespoon	15 ml.
1 dessertspoon	10 ml.
1 teaspoon	5 ml.

BRITISH	METRIC
35 fl. oz.	1 litre
18 fl. oz.	½ litre (5 dl.)
9 fl. oz.	¼ litre (2·5 dl.)
3½ fl. oz.	1 dl.

American

1 quart	=	2 pints	=	32 fl. oz.
1 pint	=	2 cups	=	16 fl. oz.
		1 cup	=	8 fl. oz.
		1 tablespoon	=	½ fl. oz.
		1 teaspoon	=	⅛ fl. oz.

Approx. equivalents

BRITISH	AMERICAN
1 quart	2½ pints
1 pint	1¼ pints
½ pint	10 fl. oz. (1¼ cups)
¼ pint (1 gill)	5 fl. oz.
1 tablespoon	1½ tablespoons
1 dessertspoon	1 tablespoon
1 teaspoon	⅓ fl. oz.

BRITISH	AMERICAN
1½ pints + 3 tbs (32 fl. oz.)	1 quart
¾ pint + 2 tbs (16 fl. oz.)	1 pint
½ pint − 3 tbs (8 fl. oz.)	1 cup

Solid Measures

British

16 oz. = 1 lb.

Metric

1000 grammes = 1 kilogramme

Approx. equivalents

BRITISH	METRIC
1 lb. (16 oz.)	450 grammes
½ lb. (8 oz.)	225 g.
¼ lb. (4 oz.)	110 g.
1 oz.	25 g.

BRITISH	METRIC
2 lb. 3 oz.	1 kilo (1000 g.)
1 lb. 2 oz.	½ kilo (500 g.)
9 oz.	¼ kilo (250 g.)
3½ oz.	100 g.

Temperature Equivalents for Oven Thermostat Markings

Fahrenheit	Gas Mark	Centigrade	Heat of Oven
225°F	¼	110°C	Very cool
250°F	½	130°C	Very cool
275°F	1	140°C	Cool
300°F	2	150°C	Cool
325°F	3	170°C	Moderate
350°F	4	180°C	Moderate
375°F	5	190°C	Fairly hot
400°F	6	200°C	Fairly hot
425°F	7	220°C	Hot
450°F	8	230°C	Very hot
475°F	9	240°C	Very hot

Index of Recipes

FOR THE BEST IN PAPERBACKS, LOOK FOR THE

In every corner of the world, on every subject under the sun, Penguin represents quality and variety – the very best in publishing today.

For complete information about books available from Penguin – including Puffins, Penguin Classics and Arkana – and how to order them, write to us at the appropriate address below. Please note that for copyright reasons the selection of books varies from country to country.

In the United Kingdom: Please write to *Dept E.P., Penguin Books Ltd, Harmondsworth, Middlesex, UB7 0DA.*

If you have any difficulty in obtaining a title, please send your order with the correct money, plus ten per cent for postage and packaging, to *PO Box No 11, West Drayton, Middlesex*

In the United States: Please write to *Dept BA, Penguin, 299 Murray Hill Parkway, East Rutherford, New Jersey 07073*

In Canada: Please write to *Penguin Books Canada Ltd, 2801 John Street, Markham, Ontario L3R 1B4*

In Australia: Please write to the *Marketing Department, Penguin Books Australia Ltd, P.O. Box 257, Ringwood, Victoria 3134*

In New Zealand: Please write to the *Marketing Department, Penguin Books (NZ) Ltd, Private Bag, Takapuna, Auckland 9*

In India: Please write to *Penguin Overseas Ltd, 706 Eros Apartments, 56 Nehru Place, New Delhi, 110019*

In the Netherlands: Please write to *Penguin Books Netherlands B.V., Postbus 195, NL–1380AD Weesp*

In West Germany: Please write to *Penguin Books Ltd, Friedrichstrasse 10–12, D–6000 Frankfurt/Main 1*

In Spain: Please write to *Alhambra Longman S.A., Fernandez de la Hoz 9, E–28010 Madrid*

In Italy: Please write to *Penguin Italia s.r.l., Via Como 4, I-20096 Pioltello (Milano)*

In France: Please write to *Penguin Books Ltd, 39 Rue de Montmorency, F-75003 Paris*

In Japan: Please write to *Longman Penguin Japan Co Ltd, Yamaguchi Building, 2–12–9 Kanda Jimbocho, Chiyoda-Ku, Tokyo 101*

PENGUIN HEALTH

Positive Smear Susan Quilliam

A 'positive' cervical smear result is not only a medical event but an emotional event too: one which means facing up to issues surrounding your sexuality, fertility and mortality. Based on personal experiences, Susan Quilliam's practical guide will help every woman meet that challenge.

Medicine The Self-Help Guide
Professor Michael Orme and Dr Susanna Grahame-Jones

A new kind of home doctor – with an entirely new approach. With a unique emphasis on self-management, *Medicine* takes an *active* approach to drugs, showing how to maximize their benefits, speed up recovery and minimize dosages through self-help and non-drug alternatives.

Defeating Depression Tony Lake

Counselling, medication and the support of friends can all provide invaluable help in relieving depression. But if we are to combat it once and for all we must face up to perhaps painful truths about our past and take the first steps forward that can eventually transform our lives. This lucid and sensitive book shows us how.

Freedom and Choice in Childbirth Sheila Kitzinger

Undogmatic, honest and compassionate, Sheila Kitzinger's book raises searching questions about the kind of care offered to the pregnant woman – and will help her make decisions and communicate effectively about the kind of birth experience she desires.

Care of the Dying Richard Lamerton

It is never true that 'nothing more can be done' for the dying. This book shows us how to face death without pain, with humanity, with dignity and in peace.

PENGUIN HEALTH

Healing Nutrients Patrick Quillin

A guide to using the vitamins and minerals contained in everyday foods to fight off disease and promote well-being: to prevent common ailments, cure some of the more destructive diseases, reduce the intensity of others, augment conventional treatment and speed up healing.

Total Relaxation in Five Steps Louis Proto

With Louis Proto's Alpha Plan you can counteract stress, completely relaxing both mind and body, in just 30 minutes a day. By reaching the Alpha state – letting the feelings, senses and imagination predominate – even the most harassed can feel totally rejuvenated.

Aromatherapy for Everyone Robert Tisserand

The use of aromatic oils in massage can relieve many ailments and alleviate stress and related symptoms.

Spiritual and Lay Healing Philippa Pullar

An invaluable new survey of the history of healing that sets out to separate the myths from the realities.

Hypnotherapy for Everyone Dr Ruth Lever

This book demonstrates that hypnotherapy is a real alternative to conventional healing methods in many ailments.

GARDENING IN PENGUIN

The Adventurous Gardener Christopher Lloyd

Prejudiced, delightful and always stimulating, Christopher Lloyd's book is essential reading for everyone who loves gardening. 'Get it and enjoy it' – *Financial Times*

Gardens of a Golden Afternoon Jane Brown

'A Lutyens house with a Jekyll garden' was an Edwardian catch-phrase denoting excellence, something fabulous in both scale and detail. Together they created over 100 gardens, and in this magnificent book Jane Brown tells the story of their unusual and abundantly creative partnership.

The Startling Jungle Stephen Lacey

'A work that ought to remind the most jaundiced of readers how exciting plants can be and what a joy it is to have a garden' – Mary Keen in *The Garden*. 'A jam-packed book on colour and informal planting which ought to be read' – Robin Lane Fox

English Cottage Gardens
Edward Hyams with photographs by Edwin Smith

With the aid of Edwin Smith's evocative photographs, Edward Hyams, the distinguished garden writer, places the cottage garden in its historical perspective and provides invaluable information òn plant species and garden design.

GARDENING IN PENGUIN

The Cottage Garden   Anne Scott-James

'Her history is neatly and simply laid out; well-stocked with attractive illustration' – *The Times*. 'The garden book I have most enjoyed reading in the last few years' – *Observer*

The Pip Book   Keith Mossman

All you need is a pip and patience ... 'The perfect present for the young enthusiast, *The Pip Book* should ensure that even the most reluctant avocado puts down roots and sends up shoots' – *The Times*

The Illustrated Garden Planter   Diana Saville

How to choose plants for your garden – to cover a wall, creep between paving, provide colour in summer – and to plan for collective effect or to overcome a difficult site. 650 plants are illustrated, in all over 900 described.

Organic Gardening   Lawrence D. Hills

The classic manual on growing fruit and vegetables without using artificial or harmful fertilizers. 'Enormous value ... enthusiastic writing and off-beat tips' – *Daily Mail*

FOR THE BEST IN PAPERBACKS, LOOK FOR THE

FOOD AND COOKING IN PENGUIN

The Philosopher in the Kitchen   Jean-Anthelme Brillat-Savarin

In this utterly unprecedented collection of recipes, experiences, reflections, history and philosophy, gastronomy is raised to the level of an art. Witty, shrewd and anecdotal, it contains both some superb recipes for food and some highly satisfying observations on life.

The Food and Cooking of Russia   Lesley Chamberlain

'The first really good book on this fascinating subject. I read it from cover to cover as one would a novel' – Paul Levy. 'A fine book ... recipes to suit all tastes and moods – from the refined traditions of the nineteenth-century nobility to Ukrainian peasant dishes and spicy creations from Central Asia' – Alan Davidson

Scottish Regional Recipes   Catherine Brown

Bridal cake from Orkney, chicken stovies from the Highlands, Morayshire apples from the north-east ... Born out of local conditions and shaped by ingenuity and care throughout the centuries, these robust and satisfying recipes have stood the test of time.

English Bread and Yeast Cookery   Elizabeth David

'Here is a real book, written with authority and enthusiasm – a collection of history, investigation, comment, recipes' – Jane Grigson. 'Quite outstanding ... erudite without losing the common touch – or the interest of the reader' – *Spectator*

Josceline Dimbleby's Book of Puddings, Desserts and Savouries

'Full of the most delicious and novel ideas for every type of pudding' – *The Lady*

The Cookery of England   Elisabeth Ayrton

Her fascinating and beautifully compiled history and recipe book of English cooking from the fifteenth century to the present day is 'a lovely book, which could restore pride to our English kitchens' – *The Times Literary Supplement*

FOOD AND COOKING IN PENGUIN

Traditional Jamaican Cookery Norma Benghiat

Reflecting Arawak, Spanish, African, Jewish, English, French, East Indian and Chinese influences, the exciting recipes in this definitive book range from the lavish eating of the old plantocracy to imaginative and ingenious slave and peasant dishes.

Cooking in a Bedsit Katharine Whitehorn

Practical and light-hearted, the perfect book for those cooking in limited space, with little time and less money – problems that can easily be surmounted with imagination, common sense and a great deal of newspaper. 'All parents with bedsitter children should send them a copy' – *Observer*

The Beginner's Cookery Book Betty Falk

Revised and updated, this book is for aspiring cooks of all ages who want to make appetizing and interesting meals without too much fuss. With an emphasis on healthy eating, this is the ideal starting point for would-be cooks.

Jane Grigson's Fruit Book

Fruit is colourful, refreshing and life-enhancing; this book shows how it can also be absolutely delicious in meringues or compotes, soups or pies.

Fast Food for Vegetarians Janette Marshall

Packed with ideas for healthy, delicious dishes from Caribbean vegetables to rose-water baklava, this stimulating book proves that fast food does not have to mean junk food.

Malaysian Cookery Rafi Fernandez

A step-by-step guide to the intoxicating, fragrant, colourful cuisine of Malaysia: the origins of its three distinct culinary strands, traditional cooking techniques and customs, where to buy the more exotic ingredients – and a mouthwatering selection of recipes.

FOOD AND COOKING IN PENGUIN

The Fratelli Camisa Cookery Book   Elizabeth Camisa

From antipasti to zabaglione, from the origins of gorgonzola to the storage of salami, an indispensable guide to real Italian home cooking from Elizabeth Camisa of the famous Fratelli Camisa delicatessen in Soho's Berwick Street.

A Table in Tuscany   Leslie Forbes

With authentic recipes and beautiful illustrations, artist and cook Leslie Forbes evokes the rich flavour of Tuscany, from its Renaissance palaces to its robust red Chianti. More than a cookery book and more than mere travel writing, *A Table in Tuscany* is a culinary odyssey.

The Food and Cooking of Eastern Europe   Lesley Chamberlain

Diverse, appetizing and often surprisingly sophisticated, the cuisine of Eastern Europe goes far beyond the goulash and beetroot soup familiar to the West. From the refreshing fruit soups of Hungary to the fish dishes of Dalmatia, this is a fascinating tour of Eastern gastronomy.

Cuisine Niçoise   Jacques Médicin

The *niçoise* cook believes in simplicity, not disguise, nourishes a penchant for fish, fruit and vegetables and appreciates the importance of subtle seasoning. This infectiously enthusiastic guide to the cookery of Nice lures the reader into the enticing world of stockfish, *tians*, and *panisses* – and shows how to make a genuine *salade niçoise*.

Simple French Food   Richard Olney

'There is no other book about food that is anything like it ... essential and exciting reading for cooks, of course, but it is also a book for eaters ... its pages brim over with invention' – Paul Levy in the *Observer*

More Easy Cooking for One or Two   Louise Davies

This charming book, full of ideas and easy recipes, offers even the novice cook good wholesome food with the minimum of effort.

FOR THE BEST IN PAPERBACKS, LOOK FOR THE 🐧

FROM THE PENGUIN COOKERY LIBRARY

North Atlantic Seafood Alan Davidson

'A classic work of reference and a cook's delight' (*The Times Educational Supplement*) from the world's greatest expert on fish cookery. 'Mr Davidson has a gift for conveying memorable information in a way so effortless that his book makes lively reading for its own sake' – Elizabeth David

The Foods and Wines of Spain Penelope Casas

'I have not come across a book before that captures so well the unlikely medieval mix of Eastern and Northern, earthy and fine, rare and deeply familiar ingredients that make up the Spanish kitchen' – *Harpers and Queen*. 'The definitive book on Spanish cooking ... a jewel in the crown of culinary literature' – Craig Claiborne

An Omelette and a Glass of Wine Elizabeth David

'She has the intelligence, subtlety, sensuality, courage and creative force of the true artist' – *Wine and Food*. 'Her pieces are so entertaining, so original, often witty, critical yet lavish with their praise, that they succeed in enthusing even the most jaded palate' – Arabella Boxer in *Vogue*

English Food Jane Grigson

'Jane Grigson is perhaps the most serious and discriminating of her generation of cookery writers, and *English Food* is an anthology all who follow her recipes will want to buy for themselves as well as for friends who may wish to know about *real* English food ... enticing from page to page' – Pamela Vandyke Price in the *Spectator*

Classic Cheese Cookery Peter Graham

Delicious, mouth-watering soups, starters, main meals and desserts using cheeses from throughout Europe make this tempting cookery book a must for everyone with an interest in the subject. Clear, informative and comprehensive, it is a book to return to again and again.

FOR THE BEST IN PAPERBACKS, LOOK FOR THE 🐧

FROM THE PENGUIN COOKERY LIBRARY

The Best of Eliza Acton   Selected and Edited by Elizabeth Ray
With an Introduction by Elizabeth David

First published in 1845, Eliza Acton's *Modern Cookery for Private Families*, of which this is a selection, is a true classic which everyone interested in cookery will treasure.

Easy to Entertain   Patricia Lousada

Easy to Entertain hands you the magic key to entertaining without days of panic or last minute butterflies. The magic lies in cooking each course ahead, so that you can enjoy yourself along with your guests.

French Provincial Cooking   Elizabeth David

'It is difficult to think of any home that can do without Elizabeth David's *French Provincial Cooking* ... One could cook for a lifetime on the book alone' – *Observer*

The National Trust Book of Traditional Puddings   Sara Paston-Williams

'My favourite cookbook of the year. Engagingly written ... this manages to be both scholarly and practical, elegant without pretension' – *Sunday Times*

The New Book of Middle Eastern Food   Claudia Roden

'This is one of those rare cookery books that is a work of cultural anthropology and Mrs Roden's standards of scholarship are so high as to ensure that it has permanent value' – Paul Levy in the *Observer*

Charcuterie and French Pork Cookery   Jane Grigson

'Fully comprehensive ... a detailed and enlightening insight into the preparation and cooking of pork. Altogether a unique book' – *Wine and Food*. 'The research is detailed, the recounting lively, the information fascinating' – *The Times*